Postcolonial Wales

Postcolonial Wales

edited by
Jane Aaron
and
Chris Williams

UNIVERSITY OF WALES PRESS
CARDIFF
2005

British Library Cataloguing-in-Publication Data
A catalogue record for this book is available from the British Library.

ISBN 0-7083-1856-8

The publishers wish to acknowledge the financial support of the Higher Education Funding Council for Wales in the publication of this book.

Printed in Wales by Gwasg Dinefwr, Llandybïe

Contents

Figures

10. Tim Davies, *Postcard Series 2*. Cut postcards (1 in series of 12), 2002.

11. Iwan Bala, *Gwalia ar y Gorwel II/Horizon Wales II*. Mixed media on canvas, 51 × 61cm, 2000. Photograph: Pat Aithie.

Notes on Contributors

Jane Aaron teaches Welsh writing in English at the University of Glamorgan. She is the author of a Welsh-language book on nineteenth-century women's writing in Wales, *Pur fel y Dur: Y Gymraes yn Llên y Bedwaredd Ganrif ar Bymtheg* (University of Wales Press, 1998), which won the Board of Celtic Studies prize in 1999, and co-editor of *Our Sisters' Land: The Changing Identities of Women in Wales* (University of Wales Press, 1994). Editor of the Honno Classics series of reprints of Welsh women's writing in English, she has prepared for that series an anthology of Welsh women's short stories, *A View across the Valley: Short Stories from Women in Wales 1850–1950* (Honno Press, 1999), and other volumes.

Iwan Bala, a practising artist since 1984, is currently employed as site-artist for Galeri, the new Arts building in Caernarfon, and as part-time projects manager with Cywaith Cymru/Artworks Wales. Artist in residence at the National Gallery of Zimbabwe in 1990, and winner of the Gold Medal for Fine Art at the National Eisteddfod of Wales in 1997, he has exhibited widely, both in the UK and abroad. His art work is held in many public collections, including the National Museum and Gallery of Wales. He is also an author whose publications include the essay collection *Certain Welsh Artists* (Seren, 1999), *Offerings and Reinventions* (Seren/Oriel 31, 2000), *Darllen Delweddau* (Reading Images) (Gwasg Carreg Gwalch, 2000), and the recently launched *Here + Now* (Seren), as well as numerous journal articles.

David M. Barlow teaches and researches in the field of media and cultural studies at the University of Glamorgan. With a particular interest in local radio and community media, his publications include book chapters and refereed articles in Australian and European journals. He is the recipient of an ESRC award to examine the role of local (commercial) radio in post-devolutionary Wales, and is working on a jointly authored book on the media in Wales commissioned by the University of Wales Press.

Steve Blandford is a professor and head of the Department of Arts and Media at the University of Glamorgan. He has published widely on film, television drama and theatre in the UK and is currently working on a volume about the impact of a changed, post-devolutionary Britain on works of fiction produced for cinema, TV and theatre. He continues to write and direct occasionally for theatre, radio and TV.

Paul Chaney is lecturer in public sector management in the School of Social Sciences at Cardiff University. His research interests include public policy and administration, governance, and equality issues. He is co-editor of the academic journal *Contemporary Wales: An Annual Review of Economic and Social Research* (University of Wales Press, Cardiff, ISSN 0951-4937 – see *www.contemporary-wales.com*).

Dai Griffiths is principal lecturer in music at Oxford Brookes University. A founder member of the Critical Musicology group in Britain, his research interests include aspects of music analysis and critical musicology, historical and theoretical topics in popular music, and studies of single songwriters and songs. He has published articles on Welsh pop music in the journals *Golwg* and *Tu Chwith*, and the essay collections *Welsh Music History* (ed. Sally Harper) and *Hymns and Arias* (ed. Trevor Herbert and Peter Stead). His recent publications include chapters on the history of pop music since punk, on words in pop songs, on cover versions and on Radiohead.

Sarah Hill is a lecturer in music at the University of Southampton. She earned her doctorate from Cardiff University in 2002 for her research on issues of Welsh popular music and cultural identity. Recent work has included articles on Mary Hopkin, Peter Gabriel and Otis Redding, and she is currently working on a cultural history of popular music in the San Francisco Bay Area from 1965 to 1969.

Glenn Jordan is reader in cultural studies at the University of Glamorgan and director of Butetown History & Arts Centre in Cardiff. An ethnographer, cultural theorist and curator, his publications include *Cultural Politics: Class, Gender, Race and the Postmodern World* (with Chris Weedon, 1995); *'Down the Bay': Picture Post, Humanist Photography and Images of 1950s Cardiff* (2001); *Tramp Steamers, Seamen and Sailor Town: Jack Sullivan's Paintings of Old Cardiff Docklands* (2002); *Fractured Horizon: A Landscape of Memory/Gorwel Briwedig: Tirlun Atgof* (with Mathew Manning and Patti Flynn, 2003); *Somali Elders: Portraits from Wales* (with Akli Ahmed and Abdi Arwo, 2004); and *Race* (forthcoming in Routledge's The New Critical Idiom series). Originally from California, Glenn has lived in Wales since 1987.

Stephen Knight is professor in English literature at Cardiff University. He has wide-ranging research interests in Welsh writing in English, industrial fiction, crime fiction, Chaucer and Robin Hood, and his publications in these fields include *Form and Ideology in Crime Fiction* (1980), *Arthurian Literature and Society* (1983), *Geoffrey Chaucer* (1986), *Robin Hood: A Complete Study of the English Outlaw* (1994), *Robin Hood: A Mythic Biography* (2003), and *Crime Fiction 1800–2000: Detection, Death, Diversity* (2004). With H. Gustav Klaus, he also co-edited the volume *British Industrial Fictions* (1999), and his monograph *A Hundred Years of Fiction: Writing Wales in English* was published by the University of Wales Press in 2004.

Dylan Phillips is senior lecturer at the School of Welsh, Trinity College, Carmarthen, where he is responsible for heading various research projects on the current situation of Welsh and undertaking language-policy-related consultancy work, as well as teaching on BA and MA programmes. His main field of research is the recent political history of the Welsh language, and he is the author of *Trwy Ddulliau Chwyldro . . . ?* (Gomer Press, 1998), a book on the history of the Welsh Language Society. From 1996 to 2001 he served as a research fellow at the University of Wales Centre for Advanced Welsh and Celtic Studies and was a member of the Social History of the Welsh Language project, heading a detailed study on the impact of tourism on the Welsh language.

Robert Phillips, who died in December 2003 while this book was in preparation, was a professor in the Centre for Border Studies at the University of Glamorgan. The editors would like to take this opportunity to acknowledge his rich contribution to the field of history education and British nation studies. Previously he had been professor of education at the Institute of Education, Manchester Metropolitan University, and had served for many years as a senior lecturer in history education at the University of Wales Swansea. He was a fellow of the Royal Historical Society and a director of the project British Island Stories: History, Identity and Nationhood (BRISHIN) funded by the ESRC. He published extensively on history teaching, national identity and education policy, and was probably best known for his volume *History Teaching, Nationhood and the State: A Study in Educational Politics* (Cassell, 1998), which won the Standing Conference for Studies in Education prize for the most outstanding scholarly work on education in 1998. Edited essay collections of his include *Issues in History Teaching* (edited with J. Arthur, Routledge, 2000), *Education Policy Making in Wales: Explorations in Devolved Governance* (edited with R. Daugherty and G. Rees, University of Wales Press, 2000), and *Education, Reform and the State: Twenty-Five Years of Politics, Policy and Practice* (edited with J. Furlong, Routledge, 2001). Amongst his last publications were the volume *Reflective Teaching of History: Meeting Standards and Applying Research* (Continuum, 2002), a book on the First World War entitled *Wales in the World: The Battle of Mametz Wood* (CAA/ACCAC, 2003), and the essay collection he co-edited with Helen Brocklehurst, *History, Nationhood and the Question of Britain* (Palgrave, 2003).

Alys Thomas currently holds a post as researcher with the National Assembly of Wales Parliamentary Service; previously she was a senior lecturer in politics at the University of Glamorgan, where she was involved with the Joseph Rowntree Foundation research project on the impact of devolution on local government in Wales. She has published widely on politics and government in Wales, particularly on devolution and intergovernmental relations.

Chris Williams is professor of Welsh history at the University of Wales Swansea. Until 2004 he was Professor and Director at the Centre for Modern and Contemporary Wales and co-director of the Centre for Border Studies at the University of Glamorgan. His publications include *Democratic Rhondda: Politics and Society, 1885–1951* (1996) and *Capitalism, Community and Conflict: The South Wales Coalfield, 1898–1947* (1998). With Bill Jones he has published *B. L. Coombes* (1999), *With Dust Still in His Throat: A B. L. Coombes Anthology* (1999) and an edition of B. L. Coombes's *These Poor Hands: The Autobiography of a Miner Working in South Wales* (2002). He has edited *The Labour Party in Wales, 1900–2000* (2000) (with Duncan Tanner and Deian Hopkin) and *A Companion to Nineteenth-Century Britain* (2004). He is a series editor of Studies in Welsh History for the Board of Celtic Studies, general editor of the South Wales Record Society, and is co-editing two volumes of the forthcoming Gwent County History. He is currently working on a history of Victorian and Edwardian mountaineering, and on collective identities in nineteenth-century Newport, Monmouthshire.

Preface

JANE AARON AND CHRIS WILLIAMS

Is it feasible to think of Wales as postcolonial? In what ways, if any, does the concept of postcolonialism aid our understanding of Welsh cultural and political life? Such questions as these pre-occupy the contributors to this volume, in which aspects of historical and contemporary Wales are viewed from perspectives coloured to a greater or lesser extent by the concept of postcolo-nialism. Its editors were alerted to the need for such a book by the often contradictory but always thought-provoking responses (from the general public, the media, politicians and academics) to the culture and politics of post-devolution Wales. The referendum vote on devolution in September 1997 was, of course, very close, and subsequent opinion polls, while recording popular acceptance of the existence of the National Assembly for Wales, have not suggested that the public views its activities to date with unquali-fied enthusiasm. Nationalist politics have waxed (1999 Assembly elections) and waned (2001 general election, 2003 local and European elections), and internal struggles over the place of the Welsh language in Plaid Cymru's and the Labour Party's strategies have recently resurfaced. The Assembly's arguably inadequate responses to crises in the steel industry and in agriculture has raised the question of whether it needs more powers to function effectively, and its reputation has not been unaffected by scandal ('Rongate', 'Germangate').

At the same time its creation has, seemingly, boosted Welsh self-confidence, particularly in cultural matters. The official transmission of authority to the Assembly in May 1999 was popularly celebrated as if it marked the coming into being of a liberated nation. Images associated with that evening's concert – of the red dragon in flames over Cardiff Bay, for example, or

draped over Shirley Bassey as she sang in her birthplace –
appeared to many as symbols of a regenerated Wales, embarked
on a new mode of existence promising greater national self-determination in spheres not restricted to the political. The same spirit
was manifest in subsequent gala occasions, such as the opening of
the Rugby World Cup later that year, and the Manic Street
Preachers' millennium eve concert, both held in a Millennium
Stadium which itself appeared to function as an emblem of a
newly energized nation. The strength of public protest against the
absence of a Welsh ethnicity tick-box on the 2001 Census forms
also suggested a change in Welsh consciousness towards a more
assertive sense of national identity.

We believe that the application of questions, hypotheses and
concepts drawn from postcolonial thinking to such issues of
Welsh culture and politics has the potential to be extremely
fruitful. This position does not presuppose that the relationship
between Wales and England (or the British state) should be
conceptualized as equivalent to that between a (former) colony
and an imperial power, although there may be areas in which
precisely that view is appropriate. Nor is this necessarily an 'old
Wales bad, new Wales good' volume. Postcoloniality embraces
concepts such as ambivalence (the mix of attraction and repulsion
that may characterize relationships between imperial power and
colony) and hybridity (the creation of 'transcultural' forms in the
contact zone between the two) that raise many awkward questions for Wales and the people of Wales. Then again if, for
instance, the Welsh are to be thought of as a 'subaltern', or infer-
iorized, people, how might that subalternity be ended? Given the
continuing globalization of the world economy and the location
of effective economic policy-making outside Wales, is it feasible to
expect the National Assembly to take greater control over the
material well-being of Wales? Is the current form of devolution
superficial rather than meaningful? Is the new political climate
conducive to Welsh cultural regeneration, and, if so, is there a
danger that such regeneration will seek to impose a hegemonic
and uniform understanding of 'authentic' Welshness on what
appears to be a plural society capable of exercising situational
identities? To what degree is Welsh identity being reshaped to
involve explicit recognition of, for example, the black Welsh, or
the English-born?

Structured into three parts, the first political and socio-historical, the second more concerned with contemporary Wales and the impact of devolution, and the third dealing with Welsh culture, this book addresses such questions in thirteen chapters, exemplifying very diverse responses to the issue of postcoloniality and its relation to Wales. As editors we have not attempted to impose any false homogeneity or 'party line' on the contributors. Given the degree of disagreement between the two of us on some of these issues it would in any case have been impossible for us to have arrived at any one agreed view – apart, that is, from the view that these are questions that contemporary Wales needs to debate. The variety of interpretations of Welsh history, politics and culture provided by the contributors to this book will serve all the better, we trust, to promote further discussion precisely because their viewpoints do at times conflict.

The four opening chapters of the first part are each concerned, from differing perspectives, with the relation between ways in which Wales has historically been understood and the concept of postcoloniality. In the first chapter Chris Williams introduces the central question of whether Wales is, in any meaningful sense, 'postcolonial', and suggests that, for all its problematic connotations in the Welsh context, postcolonial theory can be utilized to unlock rigidities in the ways in which Wales has previously been historicized. In the second Richard Wyn Jones examines the colonial legacy in Welsh politics, revisiting the concept of 'internal colonization' and suggesting that postcolonial thinking is vital to the understanding of the political life of Wales. Focusing on recent changes in the Welsh school curriculum, Rob Phillips's chapter considers the impact of postcolonialism on the teaching of Welsh history, with its important role in the 'imagining' of the nation. Lastly in this historical section Glenn Jordan asks to what extent Wales can be said to be postcolonial in the sense of having accepted that it consists of plural cultures and identities? Has Welshness successfully rethought itself as heterogeneous, as inclusive of difference?

A greater democratic inclusiveness of all its inhabitants' points of view in its political, as well as cultural, life was one of the promises made for post-devolutionary Wales, a promise which can be seen as in part motivated by an understanding of the divisive but also potentially culturally enriching consequences of the country's previous participations in colonial processes, both as colonized and colonizer. The second part of this book focuses on the moment of Welsh devolution, and its hopes for the political resolution of Welsh internal differences. Alys Thomas in the first chapter of this section compares and contrasts the system of governance in post-devolution Wales to those in other former British dominions, asking to what degree it is pertinent to think of Welsh policy-makers as previously affected by 'mental colonization' but now in the process of quietly revolutionizing the political environment. The status and survival, post-devolution, of the indigenous language of Wales – that most potent marker of difference – is the subject of the next chapter, by Dylan Phillips. Contrasting current Welsh-language policies with those of the 'colonized' past, and comparing them with the policies of other areas similarly threatened by language erosion, he assesses the likelihood of the fulfilment of the National Assembly's stated aim of creating a bilingual Wales. Finally in this section, Paul Chaney assesses the degree to which women, in a post-devolutionary Wales pledged to promote equality of opportunity, have succeeded in correcting their former marginalized position in previous 'colonial' styles of Welsh governance, and asks to what extent devolutionary processes in Wales have engaged women as citizens, as well as elected representatives.

That enhanced sense of belonging to a more fluid and many-faceted Welshness, towards which Welsh devolution may be said to aspire, also needs embodiment in cultural as well as political forms, of course, if it is to engage the populace at large. The third and final section of this book consists of a series of chapters in which commentators on, and participants in, various art forms reflect upon the usefulness or otherwise of postcolonial thinking to an understanding of Welsh culture. Jane Aaron, in the first chapter of this section, suggests that Welsh poetry, as a genre, has a long historic tradition of operating as an anti-colonialist influence, and that it continues to do so today, in both of Wales's languages. In the second chapter, Stephen Knight explores the degree to which the Anglophone fiction of Wales has been affected by colonization, and traces resemblances between its characteristic themes and styles and the literatures of other former British dominions. To what extent a postcolonial ethos is currently animating contemporary, post-devolution Welsh drama

– in film and television as well as on the stage – is the primary question preoccupying Steve Blandford in his chapter.

The difficulty of working free from an internalized sense of peripheral status in relation to a centre of power elsewhere, a key issue in postcolonial cultural politics, is explored in David Barlow's chapter, on the mass media in Wales as the site of a struggle for independent identity. One art form which has recently succeeded in establishing a Welsh voice on the international stage is pop music; Dai Griffiths and Sarah Hill ask, in their chapter, to what extent the Welsh bands which came to prominence in the 1990s can indeed be seen as representative of their national provenance. Finally in the last chapter of the book, Iwan Bala seeks to establish the degree to which issues related to postcoloniality have shaped the contemporary practice of visual art in Wales. Flexible in their approach and diverse in their conclusions, the chapters of this section, and indeed of the book as a whole, aim not so much to produce a blueprint for the application of postcolonial theory to Wales, but rather to stimulate ideas and suggest further avenues for investigation.

I

IS WALES POSTCOLONIAL?
NATION, 'RACE' AND HISTORY

1

Problematizing Wales:
An Exploration in Historiography
and Postcoloniality

CHRIS WILLIAMS[1]

There is nothing sacrosanct about the history of a nation.
(Glanmor Williams, 1971: 57)

There must surely be in existence somewhere a secret handbook for
aspiring postcolonial theorists, whose second rule reads: 'Begin your
essay by calling into question the whole notion of postcolonialism'.
(The first rule reads: 'Be as obscurantist as you can decently get away
with without your stuff going absolutely unread').
(Terry Eagleton, 1998a: 24)

In beginning this chapter I wish to raise two questions. The first
is whether it is reasonable to view contemporary Wales as postcolonial. The second is whether it is useful to think of a
'postcolonial Wales'. In response, I will argue 'no' to the first
question, but 'yes' to the second. Those readers unacquainted
with some of the debates that have been generated by postcolonial theory may, at this stage, feel that such answers are mutually
contradictory. It is my intention to explain, without too much
obscurantism, why I think they are actually complementary.

What is the importance of a hyphen? Does 'post-colonial' mean
something different from 'postcolonial'? There are various assessments of this issue (see Ashcroft, Griffiths and Tiffin, 1998, for a
survey and Ashcroft, 1996, for an argument) but here I follow
McLeod (2000: 5), for whom 'post-colonial' denotes a particular
historical period or epoch (literally, after colonialism, or after
empire), whereas 'postcolonial' refers to disparate forms of

'*representations, reading practices* and *values*' that may circulate '*across* the barrier between colonial rule and national independence' (italics as in original). In assessing whether contemporary Wales is 'post-colonial' one is therefore assessing whether it is 'after colonialism', but of course this raises a further set of questions, not least concerning the definition of 'colonialism', which is often inseparable from a term equally evasive: 'imperialism'. Rather than carry on with ever-receding prospects of clarity, it makes more sense to locate Wales historically, in relation to the power exercised over it (primarily politically and economically but also culturally) by England, and in relation to other societies that were unambiguously 'colonies' and part of the British Empire. It will also be helpful to note whether there is any consensus amongst historians as to Wales's colonial status at various points over the past 1,000 years.

Immediately one needs to distinguish between the history of Wales before and after the Acts of Union of the sixteenth century. Before 1536, and particularly after the death of the 'last' Prince of Wales, Llywelyn ap Gruffydd, in 1282, it is plausible to argue that Wales stood in something of a colonial relationship to England. In the late thirteenth century Edward I conquered those parts of Wales that had, until then, remained outside his full control. The English continued their work of building a network of castles with which to keep the Welsh subjugated, the Welsh had inferior status under the law and the English monopolized the higher offices of administration. English people were settled in Wales, especially in the boroughs, and in places the indigenous population was expropriated. In the early fifteenth century the Glyndŵr rebellion erupted, and took on at least some of the characteristics of a national revolt or anti-colonial rebellion. Rees Davies, the pre-eminent historian both of medieval Wales and of what he has termed the 'first English Empire', has argued that, particularly between 1282 and 1400, Wales displays 'most of the well-recognized features of a colonial society' (1974: 3; also 2002).

But it is a long chronological stretch from the Middle Ages to the twenty-first century, from the Wales of Owain Glyndŵr to the Wales of Rhodri Morgan, and the constitutional and legal relationship between England and Wales was transformed by the Acts of Union of 1536 and 1543. The English system of local government was extended to Wales, Wales sent Members of Parliament to Westminster and, with one exception, Welsh people acquired equal status with the English under English law. The remaining discrimination was that although no Welshman was to be debarred from office on the grounds of his nationality, he had to be able to speak English as well as Welsh. Whilst we might see in this the seeds of a later linguistic discrimination or cultural imperialism, it should be counterbalanced by the awareness that the Elizabethan state was prepared to allow the Welsh language to continue to be used in religious services, and sponsored the translation of both the prayer book and the Bible into Welsh, acts which gave the Welsh language a formal written status that has been vital to its longevity. The Reformation took hold, eventually, as surely in Wales as it did in England, and laid the foundations of a common Protestantism that has been seen as critical to a consciousness of 'Britain' (Colley, 1992). Furthermore, the ban on monoglot Welshmen occupying positions of power could not actually be carried into effect and, as Evans has noted, 'Welsh was to be a language of administration for a century and more' (1991: 242). For all intents and purposes the Acts of Union abolished the distinctions between Wales and England: Wales was no longer a colony, but part of an expanded England or Greater Britain. The Welsh largely welcomed the change in their status, not least because they had been able to claim, since the victory of the part-Welsh Henry Tudor at the Battle of Bosworth in 1485, to have regained the 'British' throne (G. A. Williams, 1982a).

After the Acts of Union all legislation that applied to England applied also to Wales. The border between the two countries, codified by the rearrangement of the Welsh Marches into counties, largely ceased to have any meaning. The anomalous position of the border county of Monmouthshire was created precisely by a lack of clarity in the legislation of the sixteenth century as to its national status: a lack of clarity that flowed, to a marked degree, from the irrelevance of the issue obtaining under these new conditions. Neither the Tudor state nor the Stuart state nor the Hanoverian state were particularly interested in forcing cultural assimilation on Wales and so, notwithstanding certain pejorative attitudes towards the Welsh as a poor, ill-educated, coarse, shifty, garrulous and untrustworthy people, worth mentioning but not worth overstating, Wales became a junior partner in the expanding British state. Not even the 1847 reports of the education commissioners, the Brad y Llyfrau Gleision (Treason of the Blue Books), make much of a dent in this essentially beneficent picture, for the reaction they provoked helped to assert and defend Welsh nationality and culture, and the extreme positions the commissioners took up (many of which need to be viewed in the context of mid-Victorian reforming efforts aimed at the working class, Welsh or not) were not followed through in the action of the British state. Whilst it is possible to read the 1847 texts as documents of cultural imperialism (Roberts, 1998), it is not valid to extend such perspectives to the full range of connections between Wales and England at this time, and historians should beware of the 'evident methodological absurdity' in basing 'general claims about colonial mentalities on a single text' (Howe, 2002: 109). On the contrary, any separatist sentiment in Wales in the nineteenth century was killed by kindness (Evans, 1991: 253). The passage of the Welsh Sunday Closing Act in 1881, the first modern piece of legislation to treat Wales differently from England, was a recognition of the legitimacy of Welsh cultural and religious identities, in an era which saw the creation of key Welsh civic institutions such as a university, national library and national museum. This was followed by educational provision targeted at specific Welsh needs and, in the twentieth century, by the disestablishment in Wales of the Church of England (Morgan, 1980). In 1951 a Conservative government created a minister of state for Wales and in 1964 a Labour government extended this to a secretary of state and a Welsh Office. From the late 1960s down to the 1990s a growing volume of administrative devolution transferred significant powers and funding to the Welsh Office and, in 1999, following the narrow success of the devolution referendum of 1997, the National Assembly for Wales was created.

Although the recent Richard report (2004) holds out the tantalizing prospect of further devolution for Wales, it is quite clear that contemporary Wales is far from being independent of England or of the British state more generally. The National Assembly has powers of secondary, not primary, legislation, has no means by which to vary taxes, and has a very limited budget. At least for the time being public interest (measured by turnout at elections) remains higher with regard to Westminster than to Cardiff Bay. In relation to whether Wales is 'post-colonial' this level of interconnectedness is only relevant if one believes that Wales, post-1536, has remained a colony of England/Britain. I have already given indication that I think it has not. Welsh men and more latterly women have, since the sixteenth century, held the vote on the same basis that it has been enjoyed by their English counterparts, it has been possible for Welsh politicians (such as David Lloyd George, Aneurin Bevan, James Griffiths and George Thomas) to rise to positions of high office and there has been no bar to migration and/or settlement between England and Wales. Nationalist movements have very largely taken constitutional form, whether as ginger groups within existing political parties (such as the Cymru Fydd movement inside Welsh Liberalism in the 1890s), or as political parties in their own right (such as Plaid (Genedlaethol) Cymru since 1925). Violent nationalist activity (such as that by the Free Wales Army or Mudiad Amddiffyn Cymru in the 1960s and by the Welsh Army of the Workers' Republic and Meibion Glyndŵr in the 1980s and 1990s) has been small in extent and very limited in appeal. One might say that, in terms of Wales's existence within the United Kingdom, the ratio of English or British coercion to Welsh consent has been very low. If Wales is, therefore, 'post-colonial', it has been so since the sixteenth century and in ways unlike those experienced by any other post-colonial society of more modern times.

Furthermore, one has only to lift one's eyes from the limited horizon of mainland Britain to begin to realize that the Welsh have been the active agents as well as the passive subjects of imperial expansion. An authoritative account of Welsh involvement in the British Empire has yet to be written, but such work that exists leaves us in little doubt that the Welsh were frequently willing participants in imperial adventures, as soldiers, missionaries, administrators and colonists (Aaron, 2003; A. Jones, 2003; A. Jones and B. Jones, 2003; B. Jones, 2004). Of course there were dissenting voices, as there were in England, and 'empire' was not simply a means by which indigenous peoples could be exploited and oppressed (a point which should be applied as much to Wales before 1536 as it should to later British colonies in Asia and Africa). But if the Welsh iron industry of the late eighteenth century was, in Dai Smith's phrase, the 'love child of war and empire' (1984: 18), then the coal industry of the late nineteenth century, of that 'Imperial South Wales' (G. A. Williams, 1982b), was its gloriously abandoned direct descendant. And by the end of the nineteenth century Nonconformist Wales was beginning to shed its inhibitions as it responded jingoistically to the Boer War and first with excitement and later with stoicism to the Great War (Morgan, 1995; Gaffney, 1998). If, as Jones and Jones note (2003: 58), late twentieth-century unease over a history of participation in British imperial expansion 'may have served as a powerful motive for avoiding the integration of colonial activity fully into the history of modern Wales', it is high time this issue was addressed. Contemporary ideological preferences aside, we should be able to recognize that, as Davies has argued, 'the Welsh have gone along with, contributed to, and benefited from membership of the political and cultural construct that is the British state, especially in its great imperial age' (2003: 36).

To argue that Wales is not a colony of England and has not been since 1536 is not, however, to argue that there are no inequalities in the relationship between the two societies. Various scholars have attempted to find ways of describing this relationship in terms that give some indication of its lopsided nature. Hechter (1975) famously termed Wales, along with Ireland and Scotland, an 'internal colony'. Hechter's suggestive, even provocative work had its moment in the political spotlight when its terminology was seized gleefully by the Welsh nationalist movement (see P. Williams, 1977) but it did not stand up to much scrutiny. Welsh economists, historians and sociologists have found Hechter's analysis unconvincing, his data flawed, his presuppositions misleading and his conclusions untenable (Lovering, 1978; Smith, 1980; Evans, 1991; Fevre and Thompson, 1999; Day, 2002). Beyond Wales *Internal Colonialism* received no less critical a reception (Page, 1978; Sloan, 1979; Nairn, 1981; Hind, 1984) and Hechter himself has conceded that his 'incomplete' book's central hypothesis was not adequately tested (Hechter, 1985: 19, 25). According to Evans, who has penned the most wide-ranging and thoroughgoing assessment of Hechter's ideas as they (do not) apply to Britain, 'Wales moved from being a colony to being a part of the Kingdom. At no stage was it an internal colony' (1991: 244).

More productive is a view of Wales as, generally, a 'dependent periphery' (Evans, 1991: 236). The success of the industrial Wales of the late nineteenth century has led many historians to view Glamorgan and Monmouthshire at least as part of a 'metropolitan core' at this time, but in any long-term view this pre-eminence should be considered very short-lived. The model of economic development in Wales was historically one-sided, heavily slanted towards extractive industries and the export market and with a relatively narrow development of the manufacturing sector. Much of the capital initially came from outside Wales and from the mid-1920s onwards the Welsh economy struggled to keep pace with the more prosperous areas of the south-east of England and the English Midlands, notwithstanding the expansion of the 1950s and 1960s. Welsh per capita GDP has lagged significantly behind most other British regions, and some of the former industrial areas of south Wales are today amongst the most deprived in the United Kingdom. The economic historian L. J. Williams (1995) asked the question 'Was Wales industrialised?' and, although he left the question by his own admission hanging in the air, there are some relevant parallels to be drawn between nineteenth-century Wales and some underdeveloped economies of the twentieth century. Whatever the centrality of Welsh iron, coal, steel and slate to the British Industrial Revolution, in the long run Wales has lost out in the distribution of wealth and resources: a fact that is likely to remain a major challenge for the National Assembly.

Finally in this audit of Wales's 'post-colonial' status there is the matter of what might be termed 'cultural imperialism'. One does not need to subscribe to the historically untenable view that the British state pursued a sustained and deliberate policy to exterminate the Welsh language none the less to acknowledge that the precariousness of Welsh in contemporary Wales owes much both to the huge cultural presence of England and the English language and to the demographic transformations that followed industrialization, whereby thousands of English (and Irish) migrants settled in the industrial districts of south and north-east Wales, shifting the linguistic balance in communities within a matter of years rather than decades. In broader terms one can also speculate, somewhat vaguely, as to a Welsh 'inferiority complex' or 'schizophrenia' (Gramich, 1997: 98). But attempts to link Raymond Williams's description of Welsh culture as 'a post-colonial culture, conscious all the time of its own real strengths and potentials, longing only to become its own world but with much too much on its back to be able, consistently, to face its own future' (D. Williams, 2003: xxx) to Humphreys's bizarre assertion that Wales remains in a 'post-colonial situation' in which 'colonial "occupation"' has become consolidated into 'a settled state of affairs' (Humphreys, 2002: 189) are strained and unconvincing. Raymond Williams nowhere explains his 1975 'post-colonial' observation, but an assessment he made a decade later is an appropriate reminder of the need to place everything in its context:

> It can be said that the Welsh people have been oppressed by the English for some seven centuries. Yet it can then also be said that the English people have been oppressed by the English state for even longer. In any such general statements all the real complications of history are temporarily overridden. (R. Williams, 1985: 18)

The final stage in assessing whether contemporary Wales may be viewed as 'post-colonial' is to locate Wales in a comparative framework. It should not take long for us to recognize that any parallels that might be drawn between Wales and any of the former 'non-white' colonies of the British Empire, let alone of the French, Dutch, German, Spanish or Portuguese empires, are little more than self-indulgent and potentially offensive illusions. Where, in the history of modern Wales, is the Welsh equivalent of the Amritsar Massacre? (And no, neither the Merthyr nor the Newport Risings qualify.) Welsh people made money out of slavery: they were not slaves themselves. The Welsh experience of colonization and decolonization simply does not translate into the standard language of Third World historical trajectories. It is scarcely more relevant to think in terms of the White Dominions (Australia, Canada, New Zealand and South Africa) or of the United States of America, the establishment of each of which involved a major reordering of indigenous peoples and their access to power (although, ironically, in the Dominions it often appears to be the descendants of the European settlers who bene-fited from precisely this reordering who are the keenest to articulate postcolonial views). The clearest parallels are instead with Scotland and Ireland, with the Irish debates being the most developed (though see Schoene, 1995, for Scotland).

With regards to Ireland's 'post-colonial' status there is a division of opinion between historians, some of whom qualify as 'revision-ists' in the Irish historiographical sense (for more, see Brady, 1994), and literary critics and other cultural commentators, many of whom are aligned with left-nationalist positions. There is not the space here to map the contours of what is a fascinating and highly instructive debate, but one can extract three key points from the arguments, that could be applied, with appropriate modifications, to Wales. First, even the most ardent advocates of a 'post-colonial' position concede that Ireland's history cannot be equated with that of non-white overseas colonies. Eagleton sees Ireland as a 'metropolitan colony, at once part of the imperial nation and peripheral to it . . . a kind of political monstrosity' (1998b: 127), whilst Gibbons locates Ireland at the 'intersection of both metropolis and subaltern histories' (1998). Second, those most opposed to a 'post-colonial' reading stress that it is more appropriate to locate Ireland in a British and European comparative context, whether one is assessing economic development or the growth of modern nationalism (Walker, 1990; Kennedy, 1992/3; Howe, 2002). Finally, the nature of the 'post-colonial' reading has itself become contested, with the theory being turned back on nationalist interpretations. According to Graham (1994: 35), 'contemporary post-coloniality has the potential to shatter the self-image of nationalism rather than to radicalise it'.

The first two of these points (transferred from a more obviously 'colonial' Ireland) bolster my argument thus far that it is not meaningful to view contemporary Wales as 'post-colonial' (I shall return to the third point later). Wales's colonial status ended in the sixteenth century, and from that time forward it has to be seen as part of what was, until the late nineteenth century, the most advanced imperial and commercial state in the world. In fact, given that historians sometimes write of post-1945 Britain as 'post-imperial', we might more profitably think of Wales in similar terms.

At this point it is necessary to remind ourselves of the apparent paradox with which this chapter began: if we cannot think of Wales as 'post-colonial', how can we think of a 'postcolonial Wales'? To answer this we need to start not with Wales but with postcolonial theory. It is important to begin by realizing that there is no single body of theory, no common set of assumptions, that constitutes postcolonialism. It is true that most postcolonial writing takes some inspiration from at least one of a small group of thinkers including Frantz Fanon, Edward Said, Homi Bhabha and Gayatri Spivak, but there is no 'single magic theory of postcoloniality' (Chun, 2000: 379). Indeed, Russell Jacoby (cited in Slemon, 2001: 100) argues that 'post-colonial theory is all over the map . . . the field is inchoate', and Washbrook (1999: 598) goes further still by suggesting that 'colonial discourse *critique* is inherently anti-theoretical and hence can scarcely be held to constitute a coherent body of *theory* itself' (italics as in original). The legacies of the aforementioned postcolonial gurus are contested as much within the loose community of postcolonial scholars as without, are subject to massive reinterpretation, and absorbed into wildly differing epistemologies and methodologies. Young, introducing the new postcolonial journal *Interventions*, conceded that 'strictly speaking there is no such thing as postcolonial theory as such', suggesting instead that 'there are shared political perceptions and agenda which employ an eclectic range of theories in their service' (1998: 5). But even this seems controversial. Young might argue that a postcolonial politics is 'morally committed to transforming the conditions of exploitation and poverty in which large sections of the world's population live out their daily lives' (2003: 6) but there are dissenting voices prepared to criticize postcolonial thought for its political ambivalence, neutrality or simple lack of interest in the material conditions obtaining in the post-colonial world (Dirlik, 1994; McClintock, 1994; S. Hall, 1996: 242; Eagleton, 1998a: 26; Eagleton, 1998b: 125). And, as has already been suggested by the Irish example, postcolonial thought does not automatically align itself with a nationalist position. Rather, as Slemon observes (1995: 45), postcolonialism can be attached to a 'remarkably heterogeneous set of subject positions, professional fields, and critical enterprises', ranging from critiques of Western historicism to oppositional forms of reading practice and from a subset of postmodernism and poststructuralism to the condition from which postmodernism and poststructuralism emerge. The application of postcolonial theory is evidently not confined to the histories or current conditions of those societies that, unambiguously, were themselves colonies. Rather, as Ashcroft notes (1996: 23), 'the term "postcolonialism" has come to represent an increasingly indiscriminate attention to cultural difference and marginality of all kinds, whether a consequence of the historical experience of colonialism or not.'

In bringing together postcolonialism and Wales, my approach is confessedly eclectic. It is to take (sometimes deliberately to invert or read 'against the grain' as postcolonial theorists would have it) three postcolonial concepts and approaches in order to see what light they might shed on an understanding of historical and contemporary Wales. According to Fish (1989: 579), this is precisely the approach taken by Said himself, who asks his readers to 'try on this belief; make it, rather than some other assumption, the content of your perception, and see what you see'. The concepts and approaches I have chosen – ambivalence, hybridity, and post-nationality – are indicative rather than exhaustive; they also represent the beginning, rather than the end, of a debate about contemporary Wales.

According to Ashcroft, Griffiths and Tiffin (1998: 12–13), ambivalence 'describes the complex mix of attraction and repulsion that characterizes the relationship between colonizer and colonized. The relationship is ambivalent because the colonized subject is never simply and completely opposed to the colonizer.' In the hands of Bhabha ambivalence may involve the 'mimicry' of colonial attitudes by the colonized, 'mimicry' which has the potential to disrupt and subvert colonial power. In the Welsh context (and excusing the application of anachronistic terms such as 'colonized' and 'colonizer') one may observe ambivalence working in a rather different direction. I have already outlined the degree of willing involvement by the Welsh in the British Empire, and one may add to this balance sheet the admiration of many Welsh people for England, English culture and the English language, the historic complicity of Welsh people with the structures of the British state, the endorsement of the idea of Britain and the devotion to the British royal family. Some of these things have weakened in recent decades, but historically they are important features of the Welsh past. They have been exhibited (admittedly, not in any uncomplicated fashion) in the tenacity of anti-Welsh nationalist sentiment, in the rejection of devolution in 1979 and in the stronger than expected 'No' vote in 1997. There has been an affective borderland (Moore-Gilbert, 2000: 458) between England and Wales, a deeply ambivalent attitude towards the English by the Welsh, that merits more than sideways dismissals as either a self-serving accommodation or an increasingly outmoded form of false consciousness (dismissals endorsed by Humphreys, 2002). For, as Fevre and Thompson (1999: 8) have observed, there are no 'right' or 'wrong' identities. Indeed, much postcolonial writing embraces what Bhabha (1992: 57) calls the perspective of the 'edge', celebrating the ambivalent, the fractured identity and giving voice to those positions in the interstices of nationhood, those on the margins of the 'nation-space' (Bhabha, 1997). In a Welsh context this might mean paying greater attention to the geographical borderland as well as the affective borderland, for the border may offer 'a privileged angle of observation, a place from where one can relate Wales to

England and Wales to its own history and myth, to the various
"imagined communities" which constitute the idea of "Wales" as
the nation experienced by different people at different times' (di
Michele, 1993: 30). Various commentators, from Sir Alfred
Zimmern (1921) to E. G. Bowen (1957) to Denis Balsom (1985),
have generated models of Wales's internal divisions which margin-
alize the border as 'English Wales', 'Outer Wales' or 'British
Wales'. It is time such essentializing perspectives were recognized
for the museum pieces they are.

'Hybridity' is, in this context, a close cousin of ambivalence. I
use it here to mean the way in which migration, settlement and
intermarriage have blurred Welsh frontiers of ethnic identification. Recently there has been a welcome upsurge of interest in the
histories and present-day realities of immigrant groups in Wales
(see, especially, Hughes, 1991; Henriques, 1993; O'Leary, 2000;
C. Williams, Evans and O'Leary, 2003) but there is relatively little
that deals with the numerically easily much more significant
subject of English inward migration, other than that written from
a perspective primarily concerned with the fortunes of the Welsh
language. There are various reasons for this lacuna, not least the
fact that, as already observed, English migration in parts of Wales
was so substantial that it forced wholesale changes in the culture
of those areas; that the English were only ever temporarily it
seems, in industrial south Wales at least, a visible minority; and
that the process of settlement and ethnic mixing was considerably
less violent and contested than it was for most other ethnic
groups. Yet, concerned to advance the political and cultural
claims of the Welsh nation, most Welsh intellectuals (not only
nationalists) have been reluctant to face up to the implications of
Wales's 'fuzzy borders' and its long inheritance of multicultural
experiences, if not of multiculturalism (G. E. Jones, 1999: 2). In
Wales, according to the last census, there are 582,000 people who
can speak Welsh. Quite rightly there are policies and strategies,
funding streams and initiatives, that are dedicated to shoring up
the Welsh language and helping it to revive. Also according to
the last census, there are 590,000 people in Wales who were
born in England, 'by far the biggest ethnic grouping in Wales'
(C. Williams, 2003: 222). A definition of Welshness that ignored
Welsh-speakers would generally be held to be untenable. A definition of Welshness that recognizes that only three-quarters of the
people of Wales were born in Wales has yet to be articulated.

Our preoccupation with cultural identity has gradually been relaxed from seeing identity in the singular (Welsh, English, Irish etc.), to being prepared to view identity as hybridized or hyphenated (Anglo-Welsh, English-speaking Welsh, Irish-Welsh, Black-Welsh etc.) and has moved on to embrace concepts of situational or multiple identities. But an essentialist notion of the self (even if it is hyphenated) is one in which questions of national identity are more pre-eminent than any other. Some postcolonial ideas, however, from their origin in the experience of the diaspora, advance the idea of the fragmented, performative or multiple self, whereby one's authenticity flows not from the membership of a particular collective group, but from one's existence as an individual. As Stuart Hall (1992: 277) has written: 'If we feel we have a unified identity . . . it is only because we construct a comforting story or "narrative of the self" about ourselves . . . The fully unified, completed, secure and coherent identity is a fantasy.' Rethinking what Bhabha (cited in Slemon, 2001: 101) calls 'the very language of cultural community . . . from a post-colonial perspective' involves rejecting essentializing characteristics, and instead seeking bonds that will have 'an encompassing range and universalising intent which enable them effectively to rival the appeal of national, religious, "ethnic" or "racial" claims' (Howe, 2002: 242). Denying 'monoculturalism' is one way of resisting the potentially repressive effects of cultural homogeneity (Goldberg, 2000: 73).

A more sophisticated, fluid and non-judgemental understanding of identity may lead to a *post*-national position. Postnationality is not exclusively an idea generated by postcolonial thought, as works by Habermas (2001) and Held (1998) indicate, but it has been an important theme in the more recent work of *Subaltern Studies* scholars such as Chatterjee (1999), Pandey (1990) and Amin (1995) (for an overview of *Subaltern Studies*, see Chakrabarty (2000)). Their critique of the possibility of constructing totalizing national histories and their advocacy of alternative frameworks for approaching Indian 'pasts' stems from a concern with the history of the subaltern groups – the working class, the peasantry, women, migrants, those of different racial or ethnic backgrounds – who tend to be marginalized by dominant imperialist and nationalist narratives. In extending this concern, again the work of Bhabha (1990) is useful, for he points to the fact that whilst myths of the nation may unite a people in opposition to colonial rule, they often do so by ignoring the diversity of those individuals they wish to homogenize as members of the nation, and thus risk turning a nationalism of liberation into a nationalism of domination. As George (1996: 14) writes, 'nationalism leads to the interpretation of diverse phenomena through one glossary . . . erasing specificities, setting norms and limits, lopping off tangentials.' Discourses of nationality operate by 'othering', by identifying borders between 'us' and 'them'. Such reactive and essentialist binarisms erect psychological barriers between peoples, excite unnecessary antagonisms towards others, and render marginal or invisible those whose characteristics do not fit those of the imagined nation (Ashcroft, 1996: 25). They close frontiers both internally and externally. In Wales we would do well both to avoid what Said (1994: 19) called the 'rhetoric of blame' that often exists between imperial and newly independent states, and to refrain from indulging in an anachronistic burst of nation-building, just as the nation-state finally begins to recede from its central position on the world stage. A 'post-national' Wales is a more attractive prospect.

A post-national Wales would be a partially autonomous Wales where that autonomy has a liberating effect for all citizens, and not just for those who subscribe to conventional views of what the characteristics and direction of that nation-state should be. It would be a society that has discarded the notion of a homogeneous nation-state with singular forms of belonging, in favour of inclusivity and cultural diversity (C. Hall, 1996: 67, 69). The discourse of national identity and the rhetoric of Welshness would be left behind as the idea of a national culture would be decoupled from the civic rights and responsibilities that go with being a citizen of Wales. In moving, as R. Merfyn Jones (1992: 357) puts it, 'beyond Wales', we make Wales 'a place with citizens, not a cause with adherents', embracing the prospect of a global democracy. The concept of a postnational citizenship crosses existing political borders and cultural boundaries, aiming for a consensus of universal moral values that enshrines the rights of the individual through democratic participation, that speaks in terms of respect for all human beings of all levels of wealth and status, that aims to reduce inequality within and between countries and continents and that seeks human societies that are more in tune with environmental pressures and demands. This at least approximates to Young's radical postcolonial agenda (2003: 7): 'to demand equality and well-being for all human beings on the earth.'

It will readily be admitted that there is more than an element of utopianism about such ambitions. The present (2005) global situation is hardly encouraging and it seems difficult for many people to think beyond the conceptual confines of the nation-state, to realize that it is a product of a specific period of modern history that does not have to govern our minds and allegiances for infinity. As for Wales, when civil society is (re)dressing itself more obviously in national garb than for some considerable time, and when the new democracy is so fragile, the suggestion that we should bypass the nation-state is unlikely to be popular with many. For some, taking a stronger hold of nationality is crucial to making devolved Wales a success. There is so much to be contested and fought for, the 'process' of devolution is perhaps not yet at an end, and to problematize the notion of Wales may be seen as putting that project in jeopardy. But a Wales that does not recognize fully and take proper account of the ambiguities and complexities that render the national project so problematic, that does not look at its own past with honesty in order to reject simplistic if comforting half-truths, will only generate a future embraced by or fully relevant to a minority of its citizens. As Raymond Williams once claimed (1985: 28), it is only the 'painful recognition of real dislocations, discontinuities [and] problematic identities' that can lead 'not only to division and confusion but to new and higher forms of consciousness'.

NOTES

[1] I would like particularly to thank Neil Evans and Rod Jones for their helpful observations on some of the ideas trailed in earlier versions of this essay, and to audiences who responded with varying mixtures of animation and animadversion in Edmonton, Gregynog, London, Newcastle upon Tyne, Pontypridd and Syracuse, NY.

REFERENCES

Aaron, J. (2003). 'Slaughter and salvation: Welsh missionary activity and British imperialism', in C. Williams, N. Evans and P. O'Leary (eds), *A Tolerant Nation? Exploring Ethnic Diversity in Wales*, Cardiff: University of Wales Press.

Amin, S. (1995). *Event, Metaphor, Memory: Chauri Chaura 1922–1992*, Berkeley: University of California Press.

Ashcroft, B. (1996). 'On the hyphen in "post-colonial"', *New Literatures Review*, 32, 23–31.

Ashcroft, B., Griffiths, G. and Tiffin, H. (1998). *Key Concepts in Post-Colonial Studies*, London: Routledge.

Balsom, D. (1985). 'The three-Wales model', in J. Osmond (ed.), *The National Question Again: Welsh Political Identity in the 1980s*, Llandysul: Gomer Press.

Bhabha, H. K. (1990). 'DissemiNation: time, narrative and the margins of the modern nation', in H. K. Bhabha (ed.), *Nation and Narration*, London: Routledge.

Bhabha, H. K. (1992). 'Postcolonial authority and postmodern guilt', in L. Grossberg, C. Nelson and P. Treichler (eds), *Cultural Studies*, New York and London: Routledge.

Bhabha, H. K. (1997). 'Life at the border: hybrid identities of the present', *New Perspectives Quarterly*, 14, 30–1.

Bowen, E. G. (ed.) (1957). *Wales: A Physical, Historical and Regional Geography*, London: Methuen.

Brady, C. (ed.) (1994). *Interpreting Irish History: The Debate on Historical Revisionism 1938–1994*, Blackrock: Irish Academic Press.

Chakrabarty, D. (2000). 'A small history of Subaltern Studies', in H. Schwarz and S. Ray (eds), *A Companion to Postcolonial Studies*, Oxford: Blackwell.

Chatterjee, P. (1999). *The Nation and its Fragments: Colonial and Postcolonial Histories*, in *The Partha Chatterjee Omnibus*, New Delhi: Oxford University Press.

Chun, A. (2000). 'Introduction: (post)colonialism and its discontents, or the future of practice', *Cultural Studies*, 14, 379–84.

Colley, L. (1992). *Britons: Forging the Nation 1707–1837*, New Haven: Yale University Press.

Davies, R. R. (1974). 'Colonial Wales', *Past and Present*, 65, 3–23.

Davies, R. R. (2002). *The First English Empire: Power and Identities in the British Isles 1093–1343*, Oxford: Oxford University Press.

Davies, R. R. (2003). 'On being Welsh: a historian's viewpoint', *Transactions of the Honourable Society of Cymmrodorion, 2002*, New Series, 9, 29–40.

Day, G. (2002). *Making Sense of Wales: A Sociological Perspective*, Cardiff: University of Wales Press.

di Michele, L. (1993). 'Autobiography and the "structure of feeling" in *Border Country*', in D. L. Dworkin and L. G. Roman (eds), *Views Beyond the Border Country: Raymond Williams and Cultural Politics*, New York: Routledge.

Dirlik, A. (1994). 'The postcolonial aura: Third World criticism in the age of global capitalism', *Critical Inquiry*, 20, 328–56.

Eagleton, T. (1998a). 'Postcolonialism and "postcolonialism"', *Interventions: International Journal of Postcolonial Studies*, 1, 24–6.

Eagleton, T. (1998b). 'Postcolonialism: the case of Ireland', in D. Bennett (ed.), *Multicultural States: Rethinking Difference and Identity*, London: Routledge.

Evans, N. (1991). 'Internal colonialism? Colonization, economic development and political mobilization in Wales, Scotland and Ireland', in G. Day and G. Rees (eds), *Regions, Nations and European Integration: Remaking the Celtic Periphery*, Cardiff: University of Wales Press.

Fevre, R. and Thompson, A. (1999). 'Social theory and Welsh identities', in R. Fevre and A. Thompson (eds), *Nation, Identity and Social Theory: Perspectives from Wales*, Cardiff: University of Wales Press.

Fish, S. (1989). *Doing What Comes Naturally: Change, Rhetoric, and the Practice of Theory in Literary and Legal Studies*, Oxford: Clarendon Press.

Gaffney, A. (1998). *Aftermath: Remembering the Great War in Wales*, Cardiff: University of Wales Press.

George, R. M. (1996). *The Politics of Home: Postcolonial Relations and Twentieth-Century Fiction*, Cambridge: Cambridge University Press.

Gibbons, L. (1998). 'Ireland and the colonization of theory', *Interventions: International Journal of Postcolonial Studies*, 1, 27.

Goldberg, D. T. (2000). 'Heterogeneity and hybridity: colonial legacy, postcolonial heresy', in H. Schwarz and S. Ray (eds), *A Companion to Postcolonial Studies*, Oxford: Blackwell.

Graham, C. (1994). '"Liminal spaces": Post-colonial theories and Irish culture', *Irish Review*, 16, 29–43.

Gramich, K. (1997). 'Cymru or Wales? Explorations in a divided sensibility', in S. Bassnett (ed.), *Studying British Cultures: An Introduction*, London: Routledge.

Habermas, J. (2001). *The Postnational Constellation: Political Essays*, translated, edited and with an introduction by M. Pensky, Cambridge: Polity Press.

Hall, C. (1996). 'Histories, empires and the post-colonial moment', in I. Chambers and L. Curti (eds), *The Post-Colonial Question: Common Skies, Divided Horizons*, London: Routledge.

Hall, S. (1992). 'The question of cultural identity', in S. Hall, D. Held and T. McGrew (eds), *Modernity and its Futures*, Cambridge: Polity Press.

Hall, S. (1996). 'When was "the post-colonial"? Thinking at the limit', in I. Chambers and L. Curti (eds), *The Post-Colonial Question: Common Skies, Divided Horizons*, London: Routledge.

Hechter, M. (1975). *Internal Colonialism: The Celtic Fringe in British National Development, 1536–1966*, London: Routledge and Kegan Paul.

Hechter, M. (1985). 'Internal colonialism revisited', in E. A. Tiryakian and R. Rogowski (eds), *New Nationalisms of the Developed West: Toward Explanation*, Boston: Allen and Unwin.

Held, D. (1998). 'Democracy and globalization', in D. Archibugi,

D. Held and M. Köhler (eds), *Re-imagining Political Community: Studies in Cosmopolitan Democracy*, Cambridge: Polity Press.

Henriques, U. R. Q. (ed.) (1993). *The Jews of South Wales: Historical Studies*, Cardiff: University of Wales Press.

Hind, R. J. (1984). 'The internal colonial concept', *Comparative Studies in Society and History*, 26, 543–68.

Howe, S. (2002). *Ireland and Empire: Colonial Legacies in Irish History and Culture*, Oxford: Oxford University Press.

Hughes, C. (1991). *Lime, Lemon and Sarsaparilla: The Italian Community in South Wales, 1881–1945*, Bridgend: Seren Books.

Humphreys, E. (2002). *Conversations and Reflections*, ed. M. W. Thomas, Cardiff: University of Wales Press.

Jones, A. (2003). 'The other internationalism? Missionary activity and Welsh Nonconformist perceptions of the world in the nineteenth and twentieth centuries', in C. Williams, N. Evans and P. O'Leary (eds), *A Tolerant Nation? Exploring Ethnic Diversity in Wales*, Cardiff: University of Wales Press.

Jones, A. and Jones, B. (2003). 'The Welsh world and the British Empire, c.1851–1939: an exploration', *Journal of Imperial and Commonwealth History*, 31, 57–81.

Jones, B. (2004). '"Recognition is a wonderful stimulant": desiring and maintaining a Welsh profile in Victoria c. 1930–1960', unpublished paper.

Jones, G. E. (1999). 'The people's nation', in G. E. Jones and D. Smith (eds), *The People of Wales: A Millennium History*, Llandysul: Gomer Press.

Jones, R. M. (1992). 'Beyond identity? The reconstruction of the Welsh', *Journal of British Studies*, 31, 330–57.

Kennedy, L. (1992/3). 'Modern Ireland: post-colonial society or post-colonial pretensions?', *Irish Review*, 13, 107–21.

Lovering, J. (1978). 'The theory of the "internal colony" and the political economy of Wales', *Review of Radical Political Economics*, 10, 55–67.

McClintock, A. (1994). 'The angel of progress: pitfalls of the term "post-colonialism"', in P. Williams and L. Chrisman (eds), *Colonial Discourse and Post-Colonial Theory: A Reader*, London: Harvester Wheatsheaf.

McLeod, J. (2000). *Beginning Postcolonialism*, Manchester: Manchester University Press.

Moore-Gilbert, B. (2000). 'Spivak and Bhabha', in H. Schwartz and S. Ray (eds), *A Companion to Postcolonial Studies*, Oxford: Blackwell.

Morgan, K. O. (1980). *Wales in British Politics, 1868–1922*, Cardiff: University of Wales Press.

Morgan, K. O. (1995). 'Wales and the Boer War', in K. O. Morgan, *Modern Wales: Politics and People*, Cardiff: University of Wales Press.

Nairn, T. (1981). *The Break-Up of Britain: Crisis and Neo-nationalism*, London: Verso.

O'Leary, P. (2000). *Immigration and Integration: The Irish in Wales, 1798–1922*, Cardiff: University of Wales Press.

Page, E. (1978). 'Michael Hechter's internal colonial thesis: some theoretical and methodological problems', *European Journal of Political Research*, 6, 295–317.

Pandey, G. (1990). *The Construction of Communalism in Colonial North India*, New Delhi: Oxford University Press.

Richard Commission (2004). *Report of the Richard Commission: Commission on the Powers and Electoral Arrangements of the National Assembly for Wales*, London: TSO.

Roberts, G. T. (1998). *The Language of the Blue Books: The Perfect Instrument of Empire*, Cardiff: University of Wales Press.

Said, E. (1994). *Culture and Imperialism*, London: Vintage.

Schoene, B. (1995). 'A passage to Scotland: Scottish literature and the postcolonial British condition', *Scotlands*, 2, 107–22.

Slemon, S. (1995). 'The scramble for post-colonialism', in B. Ashcroft, G. Griffiths and H. Tiffin (eds), *The Post-Colonial Studies Reader*, London: Routledge.

Slemon, S. (2001). 'Post-colonial critical theories', in G. Castle (ed.), *Postcolonial Discourses: An Anthology*, Oxford: Blackwell.

Sloan, W. N. (1979). 'Ethnicity or imperialism?', *Comparative Studies in Society and History*, 21, 113–25.

Smith, D. (1980), 'Introduction', in D. Smith (ed.), *A People and A Proletariat: Essays in the History of Wales, 1780–1980*, London: Pluto Press.

Smith, D. (1984). *Wales! Wales?*, London: Allen and Unwin.

Walker, B. (1990). 'Ireland's historical position – "colonial" or "European"?', *Irish Review*, 9, 36–40.

Washbrook, D. A. (1999). 'Orients and occidents: colonial discourse theory and the historiography of the British Empire', in R. W. Winks (ed.), *The Oxford History of the British Empire, Volume V: Historiography*, Oxford: Oxford University Press.

Williams, C. (2003). 'Claiming the national: nation, national identity and ethnic minorities', in C. Williams, N. Evans and P. O'Leary (eds), *A Tolerant Nation? Exploring Ethnic Diversity in Wales*, Cardiff: University of Wales Press.

Williams, C., Evans, N. and O'Leary, P. (eds) (2003). *A Tolerant Nation? Exploring Ethnic Diversity in Wales*, Cardiff: University of Wales Press.

Williams, D. (2003). 'Introduction: the return of the native', in R. Williams, *Who Speaks For Wales? Nation, Culture, Identity*, ed. D. Williams, Cardiff: University of Wales Press.

Williams, G. (1971). 'Local and national history in Wales', *Welsh History Review*, 5, 45–66.

Williams, G. A. (1982a). 'Welsh wizard and British Empire: Dr John Dee and a Welsh identity', in G. A. Williams, *The Welsh in Their History*, London: Croom Helm.

Williams, G. A. (1982b). 'Imperial south Wales', in G. A. Williams, *The Welsh in Their History*, London: Croom Helm.

Williams, L. J. (1995). *Was Wales Industrialised? Essays in Modern Welsh History*, Llandysul: Gomer Press.

Williams, P. (1977). 'The internal colony', *Planet*, 37/8, 60–5.

Williams, R. (1985). 'Wales and England', in J. Osmond (ed.), *The National Question Again: Welsh Political Identity in the 1980s*, Llandysul: Gomer Press.

Young, R. J. C. (1998). 'Ideologies of the postcolonial', *Interventions: International Journal of Postcolonial Studies*, 1, 4–8.

Young, R. J. C. (2003). *Postcolonialism: A Very Short Introduction*, Oxford: Oxford University Press.

Zimmern, A. (1921). *My Impressions of Wales*, London: Mills and Boon.

2

In the Shadow of the First-born: The Colonial Legacy in Welsh Politics

RICHARD WYN JONES[1]

Postcolonialism as both field and mode of enquiry depends on the validity of two presuppositions, the first of which seems to me to be almost entirely uncontroversial and the second only slightly less so. They are that:

(1) Colonialism is more than simply a set of political-constitutional relationships, but is rather a complex web of interlinked constitutional, political, economic, social and cultural ties, all of which are suffused with relations of power and domination.

(2) Even when the constitutional manifestation of a colonial relationship is brought to an end, many of those other links remain in place and can still usefully be regarded as 'colonial' in character. Moreover, these links are not merely passive legacies in the past tense. Rather the power relationships of the colonial age 'proper' – that is, colonialism as a particular political-constitutional relationship – continue to be produced and reproduced in the 'post-colonial' age.

On the whole, colonialism *qua* particular political-constitutional relationship has been brought to an end by the granting of constitutional independence to the colony, and it is the peoples of these new states, and their associated diasporas, that have tended to form the subject matter of what we might term postcolonial studies. But colonial relationships have also been resolved, if that is indeed the appropriate term, in other ways. In some cases, colonial dependencies have been annexed to the colonial power itself. Examples would include the incorporation of Algeria into the metropolitan French state between 1848 and 1962, and the current status of Martinique, New Caledonia and French Guyana as (constitutionally speaking) parts of the French state. Wales's incorporation into the English state via the Acts of Union is another case in point.

The argument of the present chapter proceeds as follows. First, it is argued that Wales was once a colony of England in the political-constitutional sense, and that it is therefore reasonable to expect that manifestations of this colonial relationship persisted (including in the political realm) even after Wales was formally incorporated into the English state. Secondly, it is argued that to understand the colonial legacy in Welsh politics, in particular, we must first recognize and grapple with the *sui generis* nature of English state development. England was 'God's first-born', to cite Liah Greenfeld's famous chapter title: the forerunner of the modern state, the first capitalist society, and the first world empire of the modern era (Greenfeld, 1992). It is the developmental priority of England, it is argued here, that has shaped the way in which particular colonial legacies have permeated – and continue to permeate – Welsh society. While the (in)famous *Encyclopaedia Britannica* entry on Wales in its 1888 edition ('For Wales see England') may indeed have fallen very wide of the mark, it remains a fact that very little in Welsh society (past or present) can be understood without reference to the close, often uneasy, and always unequal relationship that Wales has enjoyed with its dominant English neighbour. What gives Wales its distinctiveness is, in many ways, the distinctiveness of England. This argument is developed via three subsections that briefly sketch some of the possible implications of the developmental priority of the English state for our understanding of Wales with reference to state form, economy and empire respectively.

Much of what follows is controversial. Given the space available, it has not been possible to properly substantiate even those arguments of which I am confident. Moreover, I have felt free to postulate and speculate on those areas of which I am less certain. I make no apology for this inasmuch as contributions to a volume of this nature should surely seek to provoke and cajole. The splinter of glass in the eye, to recall one of Adorno's darkest aphorisms, is often the best magnifying glass. Moreover it seems to me that, in marked contrast to studies of earlier periods in Welsh history, one of the weaknesses of modern Welsh studies is an aversion to big-picture thinking, witnessed, for example, in the hysterically hostile reception afforded Michael Hechter's *Internal Colonialism*. But as Neil Evans argued in a much more measured assessment of Hechter's thesis, 'A large hypothesis which is wrong can be more fruitful that a minor one that is correct' (Evans, 1991: 258). While I would of course wish to claim that what follows is (in its broad outlines) fundamentally correct, I trust that even those who disagree will find useful an essay that clearly states bold claims.

Finally, by way of introduction, a note on method: aficionados of post-colonial studies will find little mention here of those authors and conceptual vocabularies that form the cornerstones, so to speak, of the postcolonial approach. But accretions of time and dominant (essentially unionist) ideologies and historiographies, have so served to obscure the nature of the Welsh–English relationship that it seems to me that the form of historical sociology – for want of a better term – outlined in the following also has a role to play in clarifying our understanding of this particular postcolonial relationship.

COLONIAL WALES

In the first sentences of a path-breaking essay titled 'Colonial Wales', published in 1974, that doyen of medieval historians, R. R. Davies, made the following observation:

> The term 'colonial' has been extensively used by historians to characterize a wide variety of situations and societies ranging chronologically from the ancient world to the twentieth century. Strangely enough it is a term which has rarely been applied, at least among professional historians, to the history of Wales. The omission is surprising since the history of Wales displays at various stages most of the well-recognized features of a colonial society. (R. R. Davies, 1974: 3)

The remainder of the essay goes on to sketch how some of those features manifested themselves in the Wales of 1282 to 1400. They include: the settlement of colonists in Wales as part of a deliberate state policy aimed at, *inter alia*, underpinning and upholding the post-conquest political settlement, with a proportion of the new settlers being settled on land which had been subject to what is now known as ethnic cleansing (the phrase used by Davies is 'racial resettlement'); the imposition of a legal system, based on what H. M. Cam described as 'the first colonial constitution', that discriminated systematically in favour of the settler population; the attempt to 'civilize the Welsh' by bringing them 'in to the mainstream of the moral practices of Western Christendom on such issues as marriage and legitimacy'; the granting of far-reaching commercial privileges to the settler population; and so on (R. R. Davies, 1974: 3–12, 20, 21).

In colonial Wales, the categories of settler and native – colonizer and colonized – became central to almost all aspects of social organization. In the following extended quotation Davies deftly summarizes the situation:

> Welsh society of the fourteenth century was ... divided into two major categories: Welshman and Englishmen, *Wallici* and *Anglici*. That division corresponded broadly to the division between native and settler and even overrode the other basic distinction in the social terminology of the period, that between free and unfree. This racial distinction manifested itself in a whole range of ways: in a distinction at law between those who were allowed, indeed obliged, to proceed according to Welsh or English law and to appear in Welsh or English courts; in an administrative distinction between Welshry and Englishry, each subject to separate officers; in a tenurial distinction between English and Welsh land tenures and between English rents and Welsh renders; in the differences in the incidence of taxation; in separate charters of liberties; even in a distinction between the pannage paid for the pigs of Englishmen and for those of Welshmen. (R. R. Davies, 1974: 12–13)

Whatever the accommodations and adjustments that were undoubtedly made, it remains the case that the colonial power relationships permeated all aspects of Welsh life from high politics to animal husbandry.

Davies's subsequent writing has more than made good the omission that he identified and began to address in the opening sentences of his 'Colonial Wales' essay. The nature of colonial society in Wales has been laid bare in a series of essays and books, including such landmark studies as *Lordship and Society in the March of Wales, 1282–1400* and *The Age of Conquest: Wales 1063–1415*. Colonialism and imperialism are also key themes in *The First English Empire*, his brilliant short study of political power in the medieval British Isles. *The Revolt of Owain Glyn Dŵr*, surely Davies's *magnum opus*, provided the definitive account of what he regards as 'in many respects a classic example of an anti-colonial rebellion' (1974: 23). After Davies, it is hard to imagine that anyone could seriously seek to deny that Wales was an English colony from the conquest until the Acts of Union. But what of post-colonial Wales?

GOD'S FIRST-BORN

The central claim of this essay is that any attempt to understand the nature of post-colonial Wales must involve the recognition of the particularities of the colonial power into which Wales was incorporated, and in particular its developmental priority. That England/Britain was a forerunner of modernity – socially, politically and economically – formed a central plank of the so-called 'Nairn–Anderson thesis', an analysis of the rise and putative fall of the British state named after its two central proponents Perry Anderson and Tom Nairn (Anderson, 1992, and Nairn, 1964, 1977 and 1994).[2] Their thesis encompassed a vast array of elements, all of which they regarded as ultimately interconnected. These ranged from the nature of capitalist development in Britain to the dominance of 'empiricism' in British intellectual life, and from the characteristics of 'Labourism' (their name for the dominant ideology in the labour movement and party) to the peculiar role of monarchy in contemporary Britain. Yet, at its heart, lies a deceptively simple claim, namely that the British state even today still betrays some of the characteristics of its crystallization in the 'transition from absolutism to capitalist modernity' (Nairn, 1977: 64). Tom Nairn explains why in a characteristically Nairnian idiom:

> As the road-making state into modern times, it inevitably retained much from the mediaeval territory it left behind: a cluster of deep-laid archaisms still central to English society and the British state. Yet the same developmental position encouraged the secular retention of these traits, and a constant return to them as the special mystique of the British Constitution and way of life. Once the road-system had been built up, for other peoples as well as the English, the latter were never compelled to reform themselves along the lines which the English revolutions had made possible. They had acquired such great advantages from leading the way – above all in the shape of empire – that for over two centuries it was easier to consolidate or re-exploit this primary role than to break with it. (Nairn, 1977: 64–5)

Paradoxically, leading the way to modernity allowed Britain to be less thoroughgoingly modern than those who were forced to

follow in its wake. Put in other words, if bureaucratic rationaliza-
tion is one of the characteristics of modernity then one of the
consequences of going first was that Britain could afford to be a
little irrational, if no less bureaucratic.

State Form

Until very recently at least, most student textbooks routinely characterized the United Kingdom of Great Britain and Northern
Ireland as a 'unitary state'. This was always, however, misleading.
In what sense can a state with three distinct legal systems (for
Scotland, Northern Ireland, and England and Wales, respectively)
be considered unitary in any meaningful sense? And while we may
live in distinctly secular times in which the significance of such
matters as Church–state relationships tend to be deprecated by
the majority, surely we must accept that it is a misnomer to
describe as 'unitary' a state with four territorially distinct types of
Church–state relationship with three different Churches? In recent
years, a number of Scottish academics, acutely aware of the defi-
ciencies of the unitary characterization, have adopted an
alternative terminology developed by the Norwegian scholar,
Stein Rokkan. In his terms, Britain should not be regarded as a
'unitary state' but rather as a 'union state', which is understood in
the following terms:

> The union state does not enjoy direct political control everywhere.
> Incorporation of parts of its territory has been achieved through treaty
> and agreement; consequently integration is less than perfect. While
> administrative standardization prevails over most of the territory, the
> union structure entails the survival in some areas of variations based
> on pre-union rights and infrastructures. (Rokkan and Urwin, 1983:
> 181)[3]

It is immediately apparent how this characterization captures
and makes sense of important elements of the United Kingdom
body politic, elements that appear as anomalous or eccentric from
the perspective of the unitary model. The advantages of developmental priority meant that Britain was never forced to reform and
rationalize in the thoroughgoing fashion that has characterized
the historical experience of those that came after. Rather, in terms
of state form at least, it remained suspended between absolutism
and modernity.

In the Welsh context, the main marker of this 'in-betweenness' was not, on the whole, institutional differentiation *à la* Scotland or Ireland. Rather the main Welsh difference lay in the cultural sphere. Despite being conquered during the heyday of the Edwardian imperialism of the thirteenth century, and thereafter, in the sixteenth century, being incorporated into England by a legal framework that explicitly ordained the eradication of Wales's cultural and linguistic distinctiveness, Wales remained culturally and linguistically rather distinct even until a later Edwardian era. Viewed in comparative terms this is striking. France, for example, saw deliberate efforts to forge Frenchmen (*sic*) from the mosaic of cultural and linguistic differences that existed in what became the national territory (see Weber, 1977). The United States, to recall another example, was built upon the annihilation of the native population. Moreover, efforts to integrate and create uniformity within the national territory were not exceptional – in fact this is arguably one of the basic characteristics of politics in the modern era. But in Wales, although there were certainly a declaration of intent in the Acts of Union, and various attempts at Anglicization, there was certainly no consistent, sustained effort in this direction, whatever the role of the 'Welsh Not' in nationalist mythology. Indeed, as some of our best nationalistic writers from Emrys ap Iwan to Hywel Teifi Edwards have demonstrated, much of the most sustained pressure for cultural and linguistic homogenization emanated from amongst the Welsh themselves rather than reflecting state fiat.

The explanation for this relatively enlightened approach – to adopt contemporary evaluations of the value of diversity – is not that the British state was particularly civilized and humane. After all, when cultural and linguistic differences threatened the state regime, as was the case with the 1745 Jacobite rebellion, it responded with great brutality. Rather, if the form of state power was not threatened, differences – even those as substantial as Wales's cultural differences – could be ignored. There was no a priori objection to such differences built into the DNA, so to speak, of the British state form. In this it was quite unlike post-revolutionary America and France, where constitutional and cultural irregularities and anomalies were an affront to the rational state.

To speak in very broad-brush terms, Wales between the Acts of

Union and the nineteenth century was essentially a backwater. The state's attitude – if that is not too active a noun – was essentially one of neglect. There was no great political, bureaucratic or strategic imperative to do more. This is not to claim, of course, that this was an uneventful period, nor to deny that seeds were planted in this era that were to bear important fruit in later periods (see Jenkins, 1983). But it is to claim that despite being part of a state that was the harbinger of modernity, Welsh society remained distinctly unmodernized, in large part because the state was never required to become thoroughly modern itself, isolated as it was by the benefits of primacy, not least empire. It was this, rather than any particular commitment to maintaining linguistic diversity, that allowed Welsh difference to persist. Those of us who cherish the survival of the language have cause to view some consequences of the neglect of Wales during this period as benign – but not all of them.

Economy

There is a tendency in Wales to celebrate our (allegedly central) role in the Industrial Revolution. But this widely held belief must be regarded as yet another manifestation of what the Polish historian Jerzy Jedlicki has identified as the combination of 'collective inferiority complex and national megalomania' that is so characteristic of 'the educated strata of peripheral countries' (1998: xiii).[4] Rather the evidence suggests that the influence of industrialization was still confined to relatively few parts of Wales in the period around 1830 when it had already begun to have a much more widely felt impact in England. Indeed in his provocatively titled essay 'Was Wales industrialised?', John Williams compared the overdependency of the nineteenth-century Welsh economy on primary production, and the comparative weakness of its manufacturing sector, with the position of less developed countries on the periphery of the current world economic system (J. Williams, 1995: 14–36). As is the case with the less developed countries, Wales's role in the world economy was as a provider of raw materials. It did not become a growth node – in contemporary parlance – in its own right. In this sense, Wales played a peripheral and dependent role in the Industrial Revolution, even while the development of the industrial world economy impacted upon every facet of the country's social life.[5]

But the Welsh economy was still more peripheral than even this thumbnail sketch has suggested. For one all-important factor widely ignored in the debates over the nature of economic development in Wales is the particular nature of capitalist development in Britain. Yet, as Geoffrey Ingham has demonstrated, Britain 'constitutes a unique case . . . in which international commercial capitalism has been dominant, and has had a determinant impact on its class and institutional structure' (Ingham, 1984: 6). In other words, it is that sector of the economy involved in international commerce and finance – 'the City' remains a convenient shorthand – rather than industry that has tended to have most influence on the direction of economic development in Britain. Indeed, the evidence suggests that the latter has had to pay a high price for the dominance of the former. And once again, it is Britain's imperial role that accounts for this 'unique' form of capitalist development. So many benefits flowed from Britain's dominant role in the empire and the international economy in general, and from the central role of sterling in international trade and commerce, that investing and reinvesting in the City tended to be much more attractive and profitable than industrial development. The odd coal exchange notwithstanding, Wales or the Welsh played relatively little part in the commercial and banking sector.[6] It is hardly surprising, therefore, that the detrimental impact on Wales of 'England's' imperial commitments, as well as the dominance of the City over the anthracite pits in which he had laboured, were a recurrent feature in the writing of Plaid Cymru's most perceptive economic analyst during the interwar years, D. J. Davies (see, for example, Davies, 1927). It may also be considered significant that one of the periodic (and unsuccessful) industrially based 'modernization' movements directed towards shifting the balance of power in the British economy, the 'Mondism' of the interwar era, took its name from pioneering industrialist, speculating scourge of the anthracite areas of west Wales, and sometime Liberal MP for Swansea, Sir Alfred Mond.

It is clear that in economic terms, Wales was subject to what may be termed a double process of peripheralization. The Welsh economy was primarily a supplier of raw materials rather than a growth node in its own right. But beyond that, industry itself played a secondary role in the British economy as a whole to the commercial/banking sector. Despite the relatively small number employed there, it was (and arguably is) the City that has played the dominant role in determining the overall direction of British economic development. It is a part of the British economy in which the role of Wales has been – and is – pretty much insignificant.

Whether Wales may be considered industrialized or not, *pace* John Williams, Wales was certainly part of the modern world. There was no way that a territory so closely attached, both geographically and historically, to the forerunner of modernity could avoid this. Yet, it was Wales's fate to be pitched into the flow with little by way of oars or sail. When the current and elements were set fair, there followed prosperity – and substantial prosperity at that on occasion. But when the winds turned and waters rose the Welsh social economy was left without any means of setting an alternative course. Indeed, during the raging storms of the Great Depression, Wales was totally capsized after floundering on a British economic policy designed, of course, to protect the commercial and financial sector. Wales's economic peripherality reflected her subordinate role in the first economy to develop the characteristics of a capitalist economy; an economy that, allied to the first state to take on the characteristics of a modern state, was able because of this priority to construct the first modern empire.

Empire
Naturally enough, the empire was central to the sense(s) of national identity that developed around and through this state. Perhaps the most striking feature of British identity has been its flexibility. The plasticity of national identities has been the subject of much recent comment, but, even so, the sheer variety of competing and indeed contradictory conceptualizations that have found a home under the banner of Britishness is bewildering. Contemporary observers have often noted the tendency of many in England to view Englishness and Britishness to be essentially synonymous. But while most in contemporary Wales would view Welshness and Britishness as distinct – if, for the majority, compatible – identities, Dafydd Glyn Jones has frequently reminded us that this was not the case even relatively recently. Rather, traditional Welsh historiography regarded Welshness and Britishness as synonymous, although clearly distinct from Englishness (Jones, 2001).[7] The situation is different again in Scotland, while the complexities of the situation in Ireland need hardly be stressed.

Once again, the necessary condition of this extraordinary variety was the fact that there was little by way of a sustained attempt to forge uniformity within the British state. In the same way that institutional variety could be tolerated, so could alternative versions of national identity be allowed to persist – as long as they did not pose a threat to the integrity of the state. One of the most important factors in binding the various narratives of national identity together was, of course, the empire. '[T]he triumph, profits and Otherness represented by a massive overseas empire', together with the shared experience of military conflict and militarism, were central underpinnings of Britishness (Colley, 1994: 6). It may well be true, as Linda Colley implies, that, relatively speaking, the Welsh of the mid-nineteenth century were less engaged in the imperial project than the populations of England and Scotland. But it really was only a matter of degree. So, for example, recent work has shown just how thoroughly the symbolism and ideology of British imperialism permeated Welsh language culture (see, *inter alios*, Edwards, 1989; Millward, 1998; Lloyd, 1987; Edwards and Millward, 2002). More generally, the Greatness of Britain was part of the common sense – in the Gramscian sense – of Welsh political culture. It has remained so even as the imperial edifice has crumbled.

The break-up of the British Empire *qua* process need not detain us here. It is sufficient to note that this process has raised far-reaching questions for Britain as state, economy and society. If the advantages that flowed from her international dominance played such an important role in shaping and perpetuating Britain's social, economic and cultural institutions and practices, then how are they to be maintained in an era in which that dominance has come to an end? It is no coincidence – as Marxists used to say in more confident days – that the key, recurring theme in British politics since the early 1960s has been Renewal. One need only recall the political rhetoric of that period's key political leaders, Harold Wilson, Margaret Thatcher and Tony Blair. Britain's Greatness must be maintained or even regained. Various strategies – rhetorical or actual – were suggested in order to achieve this: the white heat of technology; taking control of the country back from the unions; smashing the forces of conservativism; reforming the public services; cutting back the nanny state; the cult of the New; punching above our weight; cleaving to Europe and/or the Atlantic alliance, or rejecting both in favour of some 'alternative economic strategy'; and even – a sure sign of crisis this – constitutional reform.[8] Since 1997 there have also been conscious attempts at the highest level of government to develop an alternative narrative of Britishness. These efforts have ranged from the serious – so, for example, Linda Colley was invited to deliver a talk to assorted Downing Street policy-makers in 1999 – to the less than serious – for example, the appointment of a subsequently invisible 'patriotism envoy'.[9] Most persistently, ministers have implied that the National Health Service can somehow stand as a metaphor for those things that bind the peoples of Britain together. It is arguable that the role of empire in underpinning a previous sense of Britishness went much further than as provider of 'values' – though it was certainly that as well. But be that as it may, it is also ironic, to say the least, that the role of standard-bearer for Britishness is being allotted to an institution that has been devolved on national lines since 1999. Such are the contradictions of post-imperial Britain.

CONCLUSION

Perhaps the single most influential book published in the field of political science over the past couple of decades is, ostensibly at least, a study of devolution in Italy. In *Making Democracy Work*, Robert Putnam demonstrates the extent to which the varying historical experiences of the Italian regions have impacted on the efficacy and legitimacy of the devolved governments established there in the 1970s (Putnam, 1993). Of course, it is hardly news that history matters. But what was clearly surprising to some is the sheer intractability demonstrated by Putnam's analysis.[10] That the success of latter-day efforts at institution-building in a modern, highly developed liberal-democratic society could be so beholden to centuries-old patterns of social organization and interaction should certainly give us pause in the Wales of the National Assembly.

   One certainly need not look far across the Welsh political landscape for striking historical continuities. The most immediately apparent is surely the enduring reliance of the Conservatives on support from those long-standing 'outposts of English influence in Wales', namely the old boroughs (Pelling, 1967: 368).[11] But I would also want to argue that the defining structural feature of Welsh politics in the democratic era, namely 'one-partyism', is ultimately rooted in the nature of the English/Welsh relationship. Stateless nations tend to be characterized by what Miroslav

Hroch has felicitously termed 'incomplete class structures' (see Hroch, 1985). Social elites, be they aristocratic or bourgeois in character, have frequently tended to adopt the dominant state identity, leaving the identity of the subordinate nation in question to the subordinate orders. This has clearly held true in Wales (in the general sense meant by Hroch). Indeed, survey evidence abounds to suggest that it is still the case even today: Welsh identifiers are far more likely to identify themselves as 'working class' than people living in Wales who regard themselves as having a British identity, and this – crucially – notwithstanding their objective class position (as measured by income and position in the productive process).

This fusing of class and national identity underpinned what Gwyn A. Williams called the 'two archetypal myths' that have, successively, overshadowed so much of Welsh political and cultural life for well over a century (1985: 237). The idea of *gwerin* underpinned Liberal hegemony while that of the *working class* continues, even today, to provide very significant buttressing to Labour's continuing dominance. When focused through the prism of a first-past-the-post electoral system that, in the Welsh context, serves to produce grotesquely disproportionate outcomes, these particular 'national popular' blocs have produced a degree of one-party domination that has few parallels in ostensibly democratic societies. Unfortunately, while one-partyism is an interesting enough phenomenon for the curious political scientist, it leaves a great deal to be desired as a form of political life (see Pempel, 1990). Rather one-partyism tends to be associated with conformist, stagnant and even corrupt political cultures. In the Welsh case, the fact that the dominant party at the national level has regularly failed to win power at the state level has, of course, tended to mitigate some of the negative effects. But it is a case of mitigation rather than full-scale remission. Morbid symptoms of the debilitating effect of one-partyism on Welsh political life still abound.

In view of the persistence of these and many other continuities, and in view also of the evidence presented by Putnam concerning the Italian experience, is it right to ask whether devolved government in Wales is destined simply to replicate the rather dismal pattern of pre-devolutionary politics? Not necessarily. There is one dimension of Welsh devolution that makes it fundamentally different from Italian devolution; it is also a dimension that – intentionally or not – signals the opening up of a fault line between the pre- and post-Assembly eras. Welsh devolution is *national* devolution. And despite regular pronouncements that the era of nationalism is at an end – claims that have proved as premature as premonitions of the death of the nation-state – it indubitably remains the case that the nation remains at the core of claims to political legitimacy, even in integrating Europe. It is the animating potential of a Welsh national discourse that gives devolved Wales the potential to be different. Wales may be walking backwards, *pace* Walter Benjamin, towards a much more conventional post-colonial future – a national future. There are, of course, risks inherent in such a journey, but it is also a journey pregnant with more positive possibilities.

NOTES

[1] I would to thank Roger Scully, Jerry Hunter, Gwenan Creunant and Jane Aaron for their assistance, helpful comments and forbearance. None should bear responsibility for the infelicities that remain. Some of the following draws on my forthcoming book *Rhoi Cymru'n Gyntaf: Syniadaeth Wleidyddol Plaid Cymru*, Cardiff: University of Wales Press.

[2] Perry Anderson's original and seminal *New Left Review* essays were republished, with amendments and helpful further reflections, in his *English Questions*. See in particular the Introduction, Chapter 1 and Chapter 4. Tom Nairn's most muscular statement of the thesis may be found in Chapter 1 ('The twilight of the British state') of his *Break-up of Britain*. Also of enduring value are Nairn's analysis of Labourism in 'The nature of the Labour Party (Part I)', *New Left Review*, 27 (September/October 1964), 38–65 and 'The nature of the Labour Party (Part II)', *New Left Review*, 28 (November/December 1964), 38–62, as well as his reflections on monarchy in *Enchanted Glass: Britain and Its Monarchy*, London: Verso, 1998. The best of his recent books on Britain is *Pariah: Misfortunes of the British Kingdom*, London: Verso, 2002.

[3] The same terminology has also been applied in the Welsh context by Jonathan Bradbury; see, for example, his contributions to Bradbury and Mawson, 1997.

[4] I am grateful to Iver Neumann for drawing my attention to Jedlicki's work.

[5] See, for example, the remarkable statistical evidence presented by Brinley Thomas in his justly famous essay 'Wales and the Atlantic economy', in Thomas, 1962, pp. 1–29.

[6] For details of the relative importance of various sectors of the Welsh economy in the nineteenth and twentieth centuries, see Trystan, 2000.

[7] For a particularly valuable mediation on identities in early modern Wales, see Hunter, 2000.

[8] Tom Nairn remains the most perceptive and caustic observer. See, for example, Nairn, 1998.

[9] See Wyn Jones, 2001, for a detailed analysis of these attempts.

[10] Unsurprisingly, a major scholarly debate has developed around these findings. See Tarrow, 1996, for an excellent entry point.

[11] On the Conservatives in Wales more generally, see Wyn Jones et al., 2002.

REFERENCES

Anderson, P. (1992). *English Questions*, London: Verso.

Bradbury, J. and J. J. Mawson (eds) (1997). *British Regionalism and Devolution*, London: Jessica Kingsley.

Colley, L. (1994). *Britons: Forging the Nation 1707–1837*, London: Pimlico.

Davies, D. J. (1927). 'The economic aspects of Welsh self-government', reprinted in *Towards Welsh Freedom*, ed. C. Thomas, Cardiff: Plaid Cymru, 1958, pp. 30–9.

Davies, R. R. (1974). 'Colonial Wales', *Past and Present*, 65, 3–23.

Davies, R. R. (1978). *Lordship and Society in the March of Wales 1282–1400*, Oxford: Clarendon Press.

Davies, R. R. (1991). *The Age of Conquest: Wales 1063–1415*, Oxford: Oxford University Press.

Davies, R. R. (1995). *The Revolt of Owain Glyn Dŵr*, Oxford: Oxford University Press.

Davies, R. R. (2000). *The First English Empire: Power and Identities in the British Isles 1093–1343*, Oxford: Oxford University Press.

Edwards, H. T. (1989). *Codi'r Hen Wlad yn ei Hôl 1850–1914*, Llandysul: Gomer.

Edwards, H. T. and Millward, E. G. (2002). *Jiwbilî y Fam Wen Fawr*, Llandysul: Gomer.

Evans, N. (1991). 'Internal colonialism? Colonization, economic development and political mobilization', in G. Day and G. Rees (eds), *Regions, Nations and European Integration: Remaking the Celtic Periphery*, Cardiff: University of Wales Press.

Greenfeld, L. (1992). 'God's first-born', in *Nationalism: Five Roads to Modernity*, Cambridge, Mass.: Harvard University Press, pp. 27–87.

Hroch, M. (1985). *The Social Preconditions of National Revival in Europe: A Comparative Analysis of the Social Composition of Patriotic Groups among the Smaller European Nations*, trans. B. Fowkes, Cambridge: Cambridge University Press.

Hunter, J. (2000). *Soffestri'r Saeson: Hanesyddiaeth a Hunaniaeth yn Oes y Tuduriaid*, Cardiff: University of Wales Press.

Ingham, G. (1984). *Capitalism Divided? The City and Industry in British Social Development*, London: Macmillan.

Jedlicki, J. (1998). *A Suburb of Europe: Nineteenth-Century Polish Approaches to Western Civilization*, Budapest: CEU Press.

Jenkins, G. H. (1983). *Hanes Cymru yn y Cyfnod Modern Cynnar 1530–1760*, Caerdydd: Gwasg Prifysgol Cymru.

Jones, D. G. (2001). *Agoriad yr Oes*, Talybont: Y Lolfa.

Lloyd, D. T. (1987). *Drych o Genedl*, Abertawe: Tŷ John Penry.

Millward, E. G. (1998). *Yr Arwrgerdd Gymraeg: Ei Thwf a'i Thranc*, Caerdydd: Gwasg Prifysgol Cymru.

Nairn, T. (1964). 'The nature of the Labour Party (Part I)', *New Left Review*, 27, 38–65; 'The nature of the Labour Party (Part II)', *New Left Review*, 28, 38–62.

Nairn, T. (1977). *The Break-up of Britain: Crisis and Neo-nationalism*, London: Verso.

Nairn, T. (1994). *Enchanted Glass: Britain and Its Monarchy*, London: Vintage.

Nairn, T. (1998). 'Virtual liberation: or, British sovereignty since the election', *Scottish Affairs*, special issue: 'Understanding constitutional change', 13–37.

Pelling, H. M. (1967). *Social Geography of British Elections 1885–1910*, London: Macmillan.

Pempel, T. J. (ed.) (1990). *Uncommon Democracies: The One-Party Dominant Regimes*, Ithaca: Cornell University Press.

Putnam, R. (with Leonardi, R. and Nanetti, R. Y.) (1993). *Making Democracy Work: Civic Traditions in Modern Italy*, Princeton: Princeton University Press.

Rokkan, S. and Urwin, D. (1983). *Economy, Territory, Identity: Politics of Western European Peripheries*, London: Sage.

Tarrow, S. (1996). 'Making social science work across space and time: a critical reflection on Robert Putnam's *Making Democracy Work*', *American Political Science Review*, 90, 2, 389–97.

Thomas, B. (ed.) (1962). *The Welsh Economy: Studies in Expansion*, Cardiff: University of Wales Press.

Trystan, D. (2000). 'The Welsh political economy: globalisation in question', unpublished Ph.D. thesis, University of Wales, Aberystwyth.

Weber, E. (1977). *Peasants into Frenchmen: The Modernization of Rural France, 1870–1914*, London: Chatto and Windus.

Williams, G. A. (1985). *When Was Wales? A History of the Welsh*, Harmondsworth: Penguin.

Williams, J. (1995). *Was Wales Industrialised? Essays in Modern Welsh History*, Llandysul: Gomer.

Wyn Jones, R. (2001). 'On process, events and unintended consequences: national identity and the politics of Welsh devolution', *Scottish Affairs*, 37, 34–57.

Wyn Jones, R., Scully, R. and Trystan, D. (2002). 'Why the Conservatives do (even) worse in Wales', in Lynn Bennie, Colin Rallings, Jonathan Tonge and Paul Webb (eds), *British Parties and Elections Review*, 12 , 229–45.

3

Island Stories and Border Crossings: School History and the Discursive Creation of National Identity in Wales

ROBERT PHILLIPS

INTRODUCTION: BRITISH ISLAND STORIES

The peoples of Ireland, Scotland and Wales have much in common. They are Celtic peoples related by blood, culture and history. They speak the Celtic languages of Welsh and Gaelic. They also shared a hatred for the English.

(Turvey, 1995: 76)

This chapter considers an important aspect of 'post'-Wales, namely education in a post-devolutionary context. As I have suggested with other colleagues (Daugherty, Phillips and Rees, 2000; Phillips and Daugherty, 2001), education in Wales provided a vital cultural/political arena within which debates over nationhood took place and encouraged an opportunity for the articulation of a distinctively Welsh education system and curricular culture. In the 1980s, one area of education, in particular, provided a catalyst for important debates about nationhood, culture, citizenship and identity, namely the teaching of school history within the National Curriculum.

This chapter draws upon work carried out for the ESRC-funded project British Island Stories: History, Identity and Nationhood (BRISHIN), which is part of the ESRC's Devolution and Constitutional Change Programme (*www.devolution.ac.uk*). The reference within the project to 'island stories' is appropriated from the late Raphael Samuel who dedicated much of his life to articulating ways in which historiography had overemphasized the centrality of English history and had marginalized the so-called 'peripheral' historical narratives – including Welsh narratives – associated with the rest of the British Isles. One of Samuel's contributions was to emphasize the ways in which these alternative 'island stories' make 'Englishness problematical and invite[s] us to see it as one amongst a number of competing ethnicities' (Samuel, 1998: 28). This type of historiography looks at the nation not in terms of one dominant culture but as a 'Union of Multiple Identities' (Brockliss and Eastwood, 1997).

As the ESRC's Devolution and Constitutional Change Programme recognizes, British reconfiguration will depend partly upon the influence of 'past loyalties', but much of this 'reimagining' of the nation will also ultimately depend upon the perceptions and attitudes of young people. This is why school history became such a focus of attention in the late twentieth century (Phillips, 1998). For most of the century, history teaching in Britain was dominated by the English/British conflation (Phillips, 1999). Yet by the turn of the century, school history began to reflect British reconfiguration, as each of the constituent parts of Britain developed '*devolved* history syllabuses which . . . are distinctive and reflective of particular cultural characteristics, political imperatives and historical legacies' (Phillips et al., 1999: 154, original emphasis).

The enormous public and political interest in what became known as the 'great history debate' showed that the controversy 'was not about the past but the present; its dynamism stemmed from the tension between contrasting discourses on the nature, aims and purposes of history, linked to correspondingly different conceptions of nationhood, culture and identity' (Phillips, 1998: 129). Discussions in the House of Lords (Hansard: 27 March 2000), for example, on the portrayal of national identity within contemporary school history textbooks show that the debate is vibrant. Lamentations about the demise of the first person plural 'we' in school history textbooks have symbolized the imagined 'death' of English national identity.

But crucially for the discussion here is that they have also marked the reconfiguration of 'other' British identities, illustrated, for example, by the rather extraordinary claims made in one of the core history textbooks for the National Curriculum in Wales, cited above (Turvey, 1995). Thus, in this alternative 'island story', a discursive reinvention of ancient ties has taken place where 'we', the Celts, are joined by 'blood, culture and history' in a 'new' Britain against 'them', the 'hated' English. This chapter therefore focuses upon the discursive role of history in the creation and re-creation of national identity, by concentrating upon the teaching of history in Wales. First, I want to place this debate in the context of the wider theoretical literature exploring history, discourse and nationhood.

DISCURSIVE SITES OF HISTORICAL REPRESENTATION

Given the resonance of such discursive imageries as the one mentioned above, it is not surprising that many theorists of nationhood place history and particularly the role of the historian as central in the construction of the 'imagination' of the nation (Anderson, 1983). As Reicher and Hopkins (2001: 17) illustrate, history's importance has now become a leitmotif in the study of the nation. For Cubitt (1998: 8) 'nations are imagined as things enduring – endowed with origin, tradition, memory, heritage, history, destiny'. Calhoun (1997: 5) emphasizes the importance to the nation of what he calls 'temporal depth – a notion of the nation as such existing through time, including past and future generations, and having a history'. Johnston et al. (1988) stress that 'the nation is historically derived' and also alert us to the relationship between history and geography, for in the construction of nationhood 'both are at stake.'

But Reicher and Hopkins (2001: 17) are also right to point out that this is where the consensus ends, for there is debate and disagreement on precisely what role history plays: 'the argument is not so much as to whether nations have history or not, but rather about the ways in which nations use historical themes as part of their national imagination.' This should not surprise us when we consider that 'repertoires of national symbols do not arise painlessly from consensual reflection on a naturally homogeneous national experience; they are forged in conditions of contest between different political and social as well as cultural interests' (Cubitt, 1998: 6). Thus, as Allan and Thompson (1999: 40) make clear,

> scholarly treatments of 'the nation' as a cultural construction have often sought to centre for debate the historical factors which gave rise

to its emergence. Once we consider how the dynamics of collective memory inform the configuration of 'the nation', however, it becomes apparent that pivotal to this debate is a temporal and spatial engagement much more complex than that implied by historicism.

A major aim of BRISHIN is to theorize about the relationship between the past, history and the present. Like Tonkin et al. (1989) we are interested in two interrelated questions: 'How did the past lead to the present?' and 'How does the present create the past?' Our central argument is that the traditional conceptualization of the interrelationship between history and national identity has overestimated the primacy of academic historiography. The emphasis here is not on the linear, formulaic relationship between history and national identity formation but the complex, *ad hoc*, often contradictory interface between a range of 'pasts' and the present. This draws attention, too, to the interrelationship between the past and the future via the present (Furedi, 1992).

Central to the process of national imagination, then, is the important part played by discourse, what Wodak et al. (1999) and other social scientists refer to as the discursive construction of national identity. They recognize that history is vital to the discursive production and reproduction of 'the narrative of the nation', which is 'presented in national narratives, in literature, in the media, and in everyday culture and it creates connections between stories, landscapes, scenarios, historical events, national symbols and national rituals which represent shared experiences' (p. 24). Wodak et al. argue that the complex collective schema that underpins national identity here is similar to Bourdieu's concept of 'habitus', which includes a belief in a common culture (in the past, present and future), a distinctive national territory and certain notions of and attitudes towards other national communities, culture and history, that is, a 'disposition towards solidarity with one's own group as well as towards excluding the "others" from this constructed collective' (p. 4).

Therefore, following Hall (1996), Wodak et al. stress that discursive constructs of nations and national identities

> primarily emphasise national uniqueness and intra-national uniformity but largely ignore intra-national differences. In imagining national singularity and homogeneity, members of a national community simultaneously construct the distinctions between themselves and other nations, most notably when the other nationality is believed to exhibit traits similar to those of one's own national community.

Wodak et al. reject the essentialist view that there is only 'one' national identity. Because nationhood is produced and reproduced discursively, it is notoriously fragile and ambivalent. The stress on discursive practice means that Anderson's (1983) notion of the 'imagined community' can be taken further. Therefore, drawing again upon the work of Hall (1996) but also A. D. Smith (1999) and Hobsbawm and Ranger (1983), Wodak et al. argue that national identity construction involves five discursive features:

(1) national narratives expressed in literature, in the media and, crucially in everyday culture (included here are historical events);
(2) an emphasis on origins, continuity, tradition and timelessness;
(3) the invention of tradition;
(4) a foundational myth or myth of origin;
(5) a fictitious idea of a pure, original people or folk.

Like other theorists, they therefore stress the importance of history in nation formation but, unlike others, Wodak and her colleagues emphasize *history in the sense of discursive practice.* Because it is constructed around narratives, rooted in the past, national identity thus proceeds from 'the series of corrections that new historians bring to their predecessors' descriptions and explanations, and step by step, to the legends that preceded this genuinely historiographical work ... history always proceeds from history' (p. 15). This leads Wodak et al. to use a matrix to analyse the discursive practices that create national identity. They are particularly interested in the ways the national 'we' or 'us' is constructed through binary oppositionalism ('them'); and the construction of the national 'we' is, of course, vital. They recognize that the construction of the 'historical we – where the connection between the past and the present via history is made to justify the nation – is particularly important'.

Similarly, Duara (1996: 165) refers to what he coins the

master narrative of *descent* – a discursive meaning – seeking to define and mobilize a community ... by privileging a particular symbolic meaning (or set of cultural practices) as the constitutive principle of the community – such as language, religion, or common historical experience – thereby heightening the self-consciousness of this community in relation to those around it.

All this has profound implications for power and notions of inclusion/exclusion because it is fraught with danger. Narratives are necessarily selective processes which repress various historical and contemporary materials as they seek to define a community; these materials are fair game for the spokesmen of those on the outs or on the margins of this definition who will seek to organize them into a counternarrative of mobilization. (p. 168)

Duara's distinction between 'hard' and 'soft' boundaries is important here. As every cultural practice is essentially symbolic, symbolic practices (for example, rituals, language, dialect) are 'soft' if they allow 'others' of 'difference' in. On the other hand,

when a master narrative of discent – a discursive meaning – seeks to define and mobilize a community, it usually does so by privileging a particular symbolic meaning (or set of cultural practices) as the constitutive principle of the community – such as language, religion, or common historical experience – thereby heightening the self-consciousness of this community in relation to those around it. When this occurs, there is a hardening of boundaries. (pp. 168–9)

A key consideration for BRISHIN is to explore, using some of the theoretical work mentioned above, the ways in which British national identity is being discursively reconfigured through history, or, put another way, how is history used as a resource in pursuit of national identities? Thus, three 'sites' of historical representation have been selected for the focus of the research within the constituent parts of the UK: historiography, school history and 'history debates' in the media. In this chapter I would like to consider some of the ways in which the 'historical we' is being constructed in Wales today.

THEORIZING HISTORY AND NATIONAL IDENTITY IN A WELSH CONTEXT

That a new order of things for Wales lies in the design of Providence is clear: the sun of her Midsummer Day is on the horizon; what her future is going to be, depends not only upon her administrative capacity, but upon her discretion and her patience to bide her time. (J. V. Morgan, 1914: ix)

This quotation is taken from the Revd J. V. Morgan's *The Philosophy of Welsh History*, completed on St David's Day, 1914, just over a week before E. T. John's unsuccessful attempt to introduce a bill for Home Rule for Wales in the Commons on 11

March 1914. It could so easily be applicable to the circumstances surrounding us today, ninety years later. As a number of scholars have recently pointed out, the ending of the millennium 'coincided with the establishment of the most far-reaching degree of institutional independence in Wales since the thirteenth century' (Jones, 1999: 2). If the subsequent record of the Welsh Assembly in its first few years of office makes this kind of claim seem unjustified, there can be no doubting the symbolic importance of the creation of the Assembly for initiating fundamental debates about the nature of nation, identity and culture in contemporary Wales. It is also a time, as Dai Smith (1999: 243) has rightly pointed out, that at the beginning of the new millennium 'almost all of the living touchstones of identity – material and cultural, antique and modern – which have given the Welsh whatever distinctive singularity they have possessed are now in doubt . . . Or, to put it another way, Wales itself is now a *Question for History*.'

The emphasis here upon contingency and malleability is surely central to any discussion of Welsh history, nationhood and identity. It was recognized many years ago by probably one of our greatest (and most colourful) historians, Gwyn Alf Williams (1979: 192), when he stated (four years before Benedict Anderson's seminal work in 1983) that 'Nations have not existed from Time Immemorial as the warp and woof of human experience. Nations are not born; they are made. Nations do not grow like a tree, they are manufactured.' To quote Dai Smith (1999: 243) again, 'if a nation is a box, a people are not to be boxed. They overflow the constraints of the imperious container.' The question here, then, is what are some of the factors associated with history – broadly defined – that are influencing this box?

An attempt was made to answer this question by the BRISHIN Project through a colloquium held at Gregynog in May 2002.[1] Academics from a range of disciplines wrestled with the complex ways in which Wales is being reimagined, discursively, through 'history' in the sense of the broad definition discussed earlier. Thus, there were papers which analysed:

(1) the main developments in academic historiography, including the relationship between Welsh and wider British historiography;
(2) the ways in which a more eclectic range of historical representations offer differing perspectives of Welsh nationhood,

revealing some of the contradictory tensions between these sites;

(3) the role of school history, thus shedding some light on the ways in which young people are being socialized into nation-hood via schools.

Thus, a paper by C. Williams (2002) shed light upon both the collective and nationalist traditions over the past four decades or so which have given Welsh historiography its dynamism. Like K. O. Morgan (1999) Williams rightly pointed to the relative demise of the collective tradition from the mid-1980s to the present day, the inevitable consequence of the effect of Thatcherism and the decline of the collective tradition associated with industrial communities. A concomitant trend, as Williams suggested, has been the parallel decline of the narrative of 'Britishness' upon which this collective tradition was based and its partial replacement by a more focused form of identity politics centred on Welsh nationhood.

In this sense, it is important to stress that Wales is experiencing a degree of post-colonialism but also post-collectivism. Other papers read at the colloquium reflected the complex and often contradictory ways in which Welshness and Welsh nationhood are being represented in the early twenty-first century. For the purposes of this chapter, I will concentrate upon the third category identified above, namely school history.

THE TEACHING OF HISTORY IN SCHOOLS IN WALES: A CASE OF NATION-BUILDING?

Education, and history-teaching in particular, provides an interesting arena of research for those social scientists interested in nationhood and citizenship but also devolved governance. For at the beginning of the twenty-first century school history began to reflect British reconfiguration, as each of the constituent parts of Britain developed '*devolved* history syllabuses which . . . are distinctive and reflective of particular cultural characteristics, political imperatives and historical legacies' (Phillips et al., 1999: 154, original emphasis).

But it was not always so. When describing the typical history syllabus in England for most of the twentieth century, a former school inspector commented that historical content was 'largely

British, or rather Southern English; Celts looked in to starve, emigrate or rebel; the North to invent looms or work in mills; abroad was of interest once it was part of the Empire; foreigners were either, sensibly allies, or, rightly, defeated' (Slater, 1989: 1). Yet interestingly, if we take it as axiomatic that one of the fundamental features of national identity is a perception of a shared past ('the historical we'), then it could be argued that prior to 1989, Wales did not exist at all!

Thus, one of the most significant events in the 'history of history' in Wales was the establishment of the National Curriculum History Committee for Wales (HCW) in 1989. The government had no obligation to create a separate history curriculum for Wales but, by doing so, it offered official recognition of the distinctive nature of Welsh culture, heritage and history. Prior to this, curiously, history in schools in Wales consisted of 'mostly a jumble of Acts of Parliament, of kings and battles largely in English history, leavened in the latter decades by forays in local history and modern social history' (Jeremy, 1989: 11).

If historians working in the future are searching for a good starting-point to understand and appreciate the complexity of politics and cultural life in late twentieth-century Wales, they need look no further than the final report of the HCW (Welsh Office, 1990). It had to work within the broad framework laid down for both history working groups and was expected to 'give weight to the essential core of British history which should be common to all children in England and Wales, as well as covering the history of Wales' (Parliamentary Debates (Hansard), vol. 144, 746, 13 January 1989). The HCW had to face two other specific challenges (see Phillips, 1999, for a more detailed discussion). Firstly, it had to convince politicians and the teaching profession in Wales that a distinctively Welsh history syllabus was required. Secondly, and far more difficult, it had to convince readers that it was not producing a quasi-nationalist document. It therefore provides an interesting example of the discursive articulation of the nation via reference to history.

Early in the report, the HCW went to great pains to endorse the notion of a broad and balanced approach to the selection of historical content. This not only included the need to introduce pupils to 'different interpretations of the past' and a range of 'historical inheritances' (Welsh Office, 1990: 10, note the emphasis upon the plural *inheritances*) but also to varying 'perspectives and standpoints', including the 'history of the rich, the poor, of men and women, of different ethnic groups, of particular ideologies' (ibid.: p. 11). These notions of breadth, and different interpretations and perspectives needed to be applied, said the HCW, in particular to British history, which should not simply be 'the history of England writ large' (ibid.: p. 12). Historical examples would therefore have to be drawn from the 'broad spectrum' of British history. But interestingly, the committee emphasized that this breadth also had to be applied to the history of Wales, thus emphasizing the 'different parts and peoples of Wales'. Yet, according to the HCW, Welsh history was 'far more than a regional exemplification of British history', for in the most important paragraph of the report, the committee went to the heart of debates over Welsh identity and nationhood:

> The history of Wales is the history of a distinct people and nation. That is how it has been and is perceived by Welsh men and women. It is true that since the thirteenth century Wales has not had a separate machinery of government, or the organs of statehood. She has, however, retained her own language and culture and a strong awareness of a separate identity. (ibid.: pp. 12–13)

This is an excellent illustrative example of Wodak's notion of 'the historical we', a 'distinct people and nation' united around a common history. On the other hand, as if to placate those wary of the nationalistic implications of such sentiments, the same page of the report stressed that

> To insist on the separate identity of Wales is not to claim that this history of Wales should be taught in isolation. To do so would be both to impoverish the rest of the history curriculum and to distort the history of Wales . . . Pupils in Wales will need to understand the separate identity in Wales, the close relationship between Wales and England, and the place of Wales within the history of the British Isles as a whole. (ibid.: p. 13)

Now, despite major reforms to the National Curriculum in 1993–4 and 2000, the basic framework suggested by the committee remains broadly in place. The programme of study (ACCAC, 2000) is organized around knowledge, skills and understanding. The main difference between England and Wales is that in Wales, pupils are taught about the history of 'Wales *and* Britain' (my emphasis) and are encouraged to consider the history of Wales within national, European and world contexts (for a more detailed discussion of the history curriculum in Wales see Phillips, 1999). Younger pupils study mainly early history, while medieval and early modern history is confined predominantly to the first two years of the secondary school. Modern history consists of the study of social and economic history in the nineteenth century, as well as the history of the twentieth century.

One of the most pertinent aspects of the nature of history-teaching in Wales is the cross-curricular context in which it operates. For here, there is real evidence of nation-building occurring via the history curriculum, not only via the materials mentioned above but through cross-curricular themes. Two are particularly important in this context, namely *Curriculum Cymreig* (CCW, 1993) and *Community Understanding* (CCW, 1991) in the early 1990s. *Curriculum Cymreig* stresses that pupils should be given opportunities to explore their Welshness through 'place and heritage' and a 'sense of belonging', interpreted according to the 'different settings' of schools. History plays a very important role in this respect; thus, using an example from the modern period, pupils are encouraged to study how important figures, such as Lloyd George or Aneurin Bevan, have shaped the modern world. *Community Understanding* places emphasis upon the need to show how communities in Wales have developed and operate today. This can be promoted, for example, by introducing pupils to the industrial, social and economic development of Wales in the late nineteenth/early twentieth centuries, which has a profound legacy for the distinctive nature of Welsh society and economy today.

CONCLUSION: BORDER CROSSINGS

Educationalists face an interesting situation in the post-devolutionary world as far as education and the teaching of history in particular are concerned. A constant question that history teachers have to ask themselves now and in the future is: 'What kinds of people do we want to help produce via the history curriculum?' In a previous publication (Phillips, 2000: 156), I argued that I would like to see a history curriculum and an education system that seeks to:

- produce citizens who have a properly informed perception of their own identity, as well as those of others;

- actively promote an inclusive, as opposed to an exclusive, view of community, society and nation;
- cultivate a depth of vision amongst pupils which addresses some universal values such as tolerance, social justice and honesty;
- cultivate a view of the world which looks outwards, not inwards;
- develop an attitude of mind which has confidence to celebrate the familiar and the less familiar;
- encourage pupils to recognize and celebrate a multiplicity of potential identities.

I have argued elsewhere that *Curriculum Cymreig* is an 'unashamed attempt to promote the distinctive culture and heritage of Wales' (Phillips, 1996a). It has potential, at least, to be inward-looking and nationalistic. This is why it is important to place distinctive Welsh experiences within the wider British, European and world contexts, and all the evidence suggests that this is what schools are attempting to achieve. For the record, in my view *Community Understanding*, with its emphasis upon community rather than nation provides a more universal definition of citizenship and has great potential to encourage cultural diversity by showing, for example, how various groupings in Wales created communities in the nineteenth and twentieth centuries (Phillips, 1996b).

An essential element feature of history-teaching in the 'post'-devolutionary context is the need for reflexivity amongst history teachers. This is particularly important for history teachers, given the loaded ideological, cultural and social dimensions of their subject. Reflexivity would help them counteract some of the least inclusive elements of the discursive national/historical 'we' as exemplified by the quotation cited at the very beginning of this chapter.

In this context, drawing upon the work of Henry Giroux, I have argued strongly for a 'border pedagogy' (Phillips, 2002: Chapter 12). Giroux himself argues that border pedagogy

> extends the meaning and importance of demystification as a central pedagogical task . . . students must be offered opportunities to read texts that affirm and interrogate the complexity of their own histories . . . to engage and develop a counter discourse to the established boundaries of knowledge . . . In this perspective, culture is not viewed as monolithic or unchanging, but as a shifting sphere of multiple and

heterogeneous borders where different histories . . . intermingle . . . There are no unified subjects here, only students whose multi-layered and often contradictory voices and experiences intermingle with the weight of particular histories that will not fit easily into the master narrative of a monolithic culture. (Giroux, 1992: 50)

I want to suggest that border pedagogy provides a means through which pupils growing up in Wales can appreciate their own complex, contingent and often contradictory identities in ways that may encourage some of the traits and characteristics articulated above (Phillips, 2000; see Phillips, 2002 for a lengthier discussion of 'border pedagogy'). This may therefore help counteract negative discursive representations that relate our 'own' identity ('us') to that of others ('them'). However, more empirical research is urgently required in this area in order to evaluate, more precisely, the ways in which young people internalize the discursive historical images presented to them and the impact this has upon their sense of national identity.

In a post-devolutionary context we need to reject claims that history is somehow at an end (Fukuyama, 1992) or the equally complacent belief that school history does not matter and should not be taught. It is precisely because there is so much at stake here with regard to nationhood, culture and identity that we need to continue to debate it. This chapter has therefore sought to draw attention to

the central role of historians and history educationalists in enabling the citizens of these islands to be better prepared to think critically about important issues relating to national identity and come to their own informed, historically valid judgements . . . these, in turn, will invariably translate into political, social and cultural responses and whatever these turn out to mean for British identity and nationhood it is surely better that they are arrived at on the basis of historical perception, combined with informed contemporary reflection, rather than on prejudice and misunderstanding based on historical distortion, polemic and misrepresented imagery. (Phillips and Morgan, 2003)

NOTES

[1] The Gregynog colloquium was entitled *Past/Now: Theorising History and National Identity in Wales* (17–18 May 2002).

REFERENCES

ACCAC (2000). *History in the National Curriculum at Key Stage 3: Wales*, Cardiff: ACCAC.

Allan, S. and Thompson, A. (1999). 'The time-space of national memory', in K. Brehony and N. Rassool (eds), *Nationalisms Old and New*, London: Macmillan.

Anderson, B. (1983). *Imagined Communities: Reflections on the Origin and Spread of Nationalism*, London: Verso.

Brockliss, L. and Eastwood, D. (1997). *A Union of Multiple Identities: The British Isles 1750–1850*, Manchester: Manchester University Press.

Calhoun, C. (1997). *Nationalism*, Buckingham: Open University Press.

CCW (1991). *Community Understanding: A Framework for the Development of a Cross-Curricular Theme in Wales*, Cardiff: CCW.

CCW (1993). *Advisory Paper 18 – Developing a Curriculum Cymreig*, Cardiff: CCW.

Cubitt, G. (ed.) (1998). *Imagining Nations*, Manchester: Manchester University Press.

Daugherty, R., Phillips, R. and Rees, G. (eds) (2000). *Education Policy in Wales: Explorations in Devolved Governance*, Cardiff: University of Wales Press.

Duara, P. (1996). 'Historicizing national identity, or who imagines what and when', in G. Eley and R. G. Suny (eds), *Becoming National*, Oxford: Oxford University Press.

Fukuyama, F. (1992). *The End of History and the Last Man*, London: Hamish Hamilton.

Furedi, F. (1992). *Mythical Past, Elusive Future*, London: Pluto.

Giroux, H. (1992). *Border Crossings: Cultural Workers and the Politics of Education*, London: Routledge.

Hall, S. (1996). 'The question of cultural identity', in S. Hall, D. Held, D. Hubert and K. Thompson (eds), *Modernity: An Introduction to Modern Societies*, Oxford: Oxford University Press.

Hobsbawm, E. and Ranger, T. (eds) (1983). *The Invention of Tradition*, Cambridge: Cambridge University Press.

Jeremy, P. (1989). 'History in the secondary schools of Wales: a centenary review', *Welsh Journal of Education*, 1.

Johnston, R. J., Knight, D. B. and Kofman, E. (eds) (1988). *Nationalism, Self-Determination and Political Geography*, London: Croom Helm.

Jones, G. E. (1999). 'Introduction', in G. E. Jones and D. Smith (eds), *The People of Wales: A History*, Cardiff: University of Wales Press.

Morgan, J. V. (1914). *The Philosophy of Welsh History*, London: John Lane.

Morgan, K. O. (1999). 'Consensus and conflict in modern Welsh history', in D. Howell and K. O. Morgan (eds), *Crime, Protest and Police in Modern British Society*, Cardiff: University of Wales Press.

Phillips, R. (1996a). 'History teaching, cultural restorationism and national identity in England and Wales', *Curriculum Studies*, 4, 3, 385–99.

Phillips, R. (1996b). 'Informed citizens: who am I and why are we here? Some Welsh reflections on culture, curriculum and society', speech given at the SCAA International Invitation Conference on Culture, Curriculum and Society, 8 February, *Multicultural Teaching*, 14, 3 (1997), 41–4.

Phillips, R. (1998). *History Teaching, Nationhood and the State: A Study in Educational Politics*, London: Cassell.

Phillips, R. (1999). 'History teaching, nationhood and politics in England and Wales in the late 20th century', *History of Education*, 28, 3, 351–63.

Phillips, R. (2000). 'Culture, community and curriculum in Wales: citizenship education for the new democracy?', in D. Lawton, J. Cairns and R. Gardner (eds), *Education for Citizenship*, London: Continuum.

Phillips, R. (2002). *Reflective Teaching of History, 11–18: Meeting Standards and Applying Research*, London: Continuum.

Phillips, R. and Daugherty, R. (2001). 'Educational devolution and nation building in Wales: a different "Great Debate"?', in R. Phillips and J. Furlong (eds), *Education, Reform and the State: Twenty-Five Years of Politics, Policy and Practice*, London: Routledge.

Phillips, R., Goalen, P., McCully, A. and Wood, S. (1999). 'Four histories, one nation? History teaching, nationhood and a British identity', *Compare*, 29, 2, 153–69.

Phillips, R. and Morgan, A. (2003). 'Wales! Wales? Britain! Britain? Teaching and learning about the history of the British Isles in secondary schools in Wales', *International Journal of History Education Teaching and Research*, 6 (Autumn).

Reicher, S. and Hopkins, N. (2001). *Self and Nation: Categorization, Contestation and Mobilization*, London: Sage.

Samuel, R. (1998). *Island Stories: Theatres of Memory*, vol. II, London: Verso.

Slater, J. (1989). *The Politics of History Teaching: A Humanity Dehumanized?*, Institute of Education, Special Professorial Lecture, London: Institute of Education.

Smith, A. D. (1999). *Myths and Memories of the Nation*, Oxford: Oxford University Press.

Smith, D. (1999). *Wales: A Question of History*, Bridgend: Seren.

Tonkin, E., McDonald, M. and Chapman, M. (eds) (1989). *History and Ethnicity: ASA Monographs 27*, London: Routledge.

Turvey, R. (1995). *Wales and Britain in the Early Modern World, c.1500–c.1760*, London: Hodder & Stoughton.

Welsh Office (1990). *National Curriculum History Committee for Wales: Final Report*, Cardiff: Welsh Office.

Williams, C. (2002). 'Problematizing Wales: an exploration of post-colonialism in Welsh historiography', paper given at the BRISHIN Colloquium, Past/Now: Theorising History and National Identity in Wales, Gregynog, 17–18 May 2002.

Williams, G. A. (1979). 'When Was Wales?', in S. Woolf (ed.), *Nationalism in Europe, 1815 to the Present Day*, London: Routledge, 1996.

Wodak, R., de Cillia, R., Reisgl, M. and Liebhart, K. (trans. A. Hirsch and R. Mitten) (1999). *The Discursive Construction of National Identity*, London: Routledge.

4

'We Never Really Noticed You Were Coloured': Postcolonialist Reflections on Immigrants and Minorities in Wales

GLENN JORDAN

As the Red Dragon pulled out of Chester station and crossed the border on its journey towards Holyhead, I might as well have shed my skin. Colour didn't exist in Wales. It dawned on me that there were literal geographic spaces in Britain where it was legitimate to be black and where it was legitimate to speak about race and there were great white spaces where it was outlawed. Race was just an ugly rumour spreading into Wales from across the border. That's what I began to notice more than ever on my return. That the idea of black Welsh wasn't really lodged in the cultural consciousness or in fact in the cultural memory. It was one of those sickening pieces of cultural amnesia that had conveniently managed to disassociate the Welsh from any implication in the facts of black history and in doing so rendered us with an invisible present.

   The idea of a pure Welsh race was becoming difficult to challenge
. . .

(Williams, 2002: 177–8)

Is Wales a homogeneous nation? Can it claim a singular mode of belonging? This chapter is an intervention, a rewriting of past and present, raising issues about Welsh history, culture and identity – in the light of two factors: (1) the long presence of immigrant, ethnic minority and mixed-race people in Wales; and (2) developments in postcolonial theory.

Is Wales a postcolonial nation in the sense in which India or Jamaica or Nigeria are? That is a contentious matter, which I will avoid. For my purposes, all I need are a few claims related to ideas of the 'postcolonial'. The first is that Wales, like many other countries in Europe, has become increasingly ethnically diversified as a result of the presence of substantial numbers of immigrants and minorities, many of whom have arrived as a result of empire and its postcolonial aftermath. The second is that, in order to assist our reflections on multicultural, multiracial Wales today, we can make good use of certain concepts and ideas from postcolonial theory. Thus this chapter weaves between two related themes: empire and its aftermath and postcolonial theory.

What will be my method here? At the risk of displeasing positivists and grand theorists, I will proceed through engagement with fragments, with bits of lives revealed via photographic images and personal narratives. I will present a collage on the theme of *Sameness* and *Otherness*, *identity* and *difference*, *exile* and *belonging*.

NAMELESS

I begin with photographs of two men (see figures 1, 2a and 2b). One of them is identified as 'Thomas Nepal', the other as 'John Doe Wesley'.[1] Who are they? What are they doing with such names? What have these images, and the names ascribed to them, to do with Wales and Welshness?

Our first observation: 'They are from Elsewhere. They are immigrants.'

Immigrants? Before we proceed further, 'I'd like you to think about this word "immigrant", because it seems to me to demonstrate the extent to which racist concepts have been allowed to seize the central ground. And to shape the whole nature of the debate' (Rushdie, 1991a: 132). We must remember to tread carefully, to be vigilant in our use of concepts and language – for as we freely exercise our God-given right to speak, we may effortlessly, inadvertently, reproduce prevailing discourses.

Workers? The uniforms and documents of the men in figures 1 and 2 signify that they were workers, specifically, that they were seamen – one of them a cook from Liberia who worked on steamships and died in the 1990s, the other a steward from Nepal who originally worked on sailing ships and died in the 1930s. They were not political refugees or asylum seekers but part of that huge pool of cheap labour which moved over the past century from the periphery to the centre, from the colonies (and former colonies) to the heart of the empire. Like scores of their countrymen, both worked for years on tramp steamers out of Cardiff. (Interestingly, the steward's daughter married a bosun, Camdon bin-Brahim, an immigrant from Malaysia, and their son, John Osmond 'Bumpy' Brahim, was also a bosun. Why did they not move further in three generations? Because non-white seamen could not become officers: being a supervisor in the engine room or kitchen was as high as they could possibly go.)

Nameless? Since they are both deceased and the records of their births are not to hand, we cannot be certain about where and how Thomas Nepal and John Doe Wesley obtained such names, but there are reasons to be suspicious. It was too often the case that colonial officials, who spoke and wrote the language of power, literally renamed subjects (thus avoiding the hassle of having properly to understand their names); and 'John Doe' is the name given by the police to unidentified dead bodies. One doubts that the steward's family in Nepal[2] called him 'Thomas Nepal' or that the Liberian was called 'John Doe Wesley' by his kindred, although he may well have been Methodist, as many of the West African seamen in south Wales were. Whatever names these seamen were given by their families, it was the tamper-proof identities inscribed by colonial power on official documents that came to matter. The power to name the Other is, as Edward Said reminds us, a crucial element in the exercise of Western power (Said, 1978; see also Jordan and Weedon, 1995: 11–13).

> Echoes: When I come across the mention of the fact that early sea captains brought indentured Indians to the United States in the eighteenth century, and when I see the names of these first Indian immigrants to North America – James Dunn, John Ballay, Joseph Green, George Jimor, Thomas Robinson – I . . . reflect on the massive, institutional rewriting of peoples and their identities in history. (Kumar, 2000: 62–3)

These men were not uprooted and stateless. They had their papers. But what did these documents say? Mr Wesley died a few years ago. I knew him reasonably well but I never got to ask him whether, during his life in Wales (Land of No Racism), he heard:

> An innocent sounding voice: 'Are you from Africa? I bet it's hot in your country. Are you feeling the cold? Do you eat this sort of food where you come from? Are you that colour all over? Can you speak

English? You people are so good at dancing . . . Can't tell when you're
dirty can we? You don't need to wash so often I suppose? That's some
suntan you've got there. Have they all got little ears like you? Let me
feel your hair. People like you don't blush do they? I mean, there's no
point.' (Williams, 2002: 49)

I suspect that he did.

MARGINALIZED

Question: What does it mean to reduce someone's visage, his or her
history, to a mug shot? (Kumar, 2000: 43)

Some histories are dominant, others are marginalized. Where, for
example, are West African and Far Eastern seamen in the received
histories of Britain and Wales? From what position(s) can they
speak? Where are their memories inscribed? Knowing about lives
such as theirs contributes, if only in a small way, to a rewriting of
hegemonic notions of modern Western, British and Welsh history,
and of British and Welsh identities. In particular, we are reminded
that Wales did not remain outside projects of Western imperialism
and colonial domination: on the contrary, Wales, and Welsh coal,
were often integral to them.[3]

A voice: The decolonised peoples of Jamaica, Trinidad, Barbados,
Guyana, India, Pakistan, Bangladesh and other once colonies of the
Empire who have made their home in Britain, together with their children and their children's children, act as a perpetual reminder of the
ways in which the once metropolis is intimately connected to its
'peripheries'. Both colonists and colonised are linked through their
histories, histories which are forgotten in the desire to throw off the
embarrassing reminders of Empire . . . (C. Hall, 1996: 67)

Engaging with traces of such lives – with their photographs, documents and stories – helps us to challenge hegemonic narratives
and to open up spaces for the articulation of alternative voices,
histories and meanings.

Consider figure 3. This is Mr Wesley's own photograph. It
contrasts strongly with those official documents in which he is
photographed, written and stamped as Other; in which he is
objectified and categorized in terms such as birthplace, height,
complexion, colour of eyes and shape of head and nose. Here, he
reframes himself – in a world of his own choosing. In this digni-
fied, humanist portrait, which he claimed as his own, he is shown

content and proud. Look at him there with his shipmate, in his cook's uniform, in a place (the deck of a tramp steamer) where he belonged. He proudly donated a copy of this image, along with copies of various certificates he earned, to the Butetown History & Arts Centre. Perhaps he felt a need to rewrite himself, to construct his own identity, to inscribe traces of his existence otherwise.

PLACE, HOME

In an important article, entitled 'When was the "post-colonial"?', Stuart Hall writes:

> [T]he most serious criticism which the post-colonial critics and theorists have urgently now to face . . . is succinctly put by Dirlik: 'What is remarkable . . . is that a consideration of the relationship between postcolonialism and global capitalism should be absent from the writings of postcolonial intellectuals.' Let us not quibble and say of *some* post-colonial intellectuals. It *is* remarkable. And it has become seriously damaging and disabling for everything positive which the post-colonial paradigm can, and has the ambition to, accomplish. These two halves of the current debate about 'late modernity' – the post-colonial and the analysis of the new developments in global capitalism – have indeed largely proceeded in relative isolation from one another, and to their mutual cost. (Hall, 1996: 257–8)

The postcolonial theorist who would explore histories of immigrants and minorities in Wales is immediately confronted by factors having to do with global capitalism and the legacy of empire. From the mid-1800s to the Second World War, people from more than fifty nations settled in south Wales, especially in Cardiff docklands. First came people from Ireland, England and Scotland. They were soon joined by immigrants from – it seemed – all over the world: Norwegians, Finns and Danes; Russians, Poles, Ukrainians and Eastern European Jews; Estonians, Latvians and Lithuanians; Germans; Spanish and Portuguese; Italians and Maltese; Greeks, Turks and Cypriots; Indians, i.e., people from what is now India, Pakistan and Bangladesh; Chinese and Malays; Japanese; French, Mauritians, Colonial French; Colonial Portuguese (mainly Cape Verdeans); Yemeni, Egyptians; Somalis; West Africans – i.e., people from nations that would unite to form Nigeria, Sierra Leone, Ghana, the Cameroons and Liberia; Jamaicans, Barbadians, Trinidadians, St Lucians, St

Kittsians and other West Indians; British Hondurans, Panamanians and Guyanese; Latin Americans (Brazilians, Chileans, Argentinians and others); North Americans; and a few more (e.g. at least several South Africans, a Nepalese and an artist from Mozambique). Drawn to Wales by forces of global capitalism and British imperialism, they came for generations as workers. Most of them became part of a local pool of labour ever available for work on the tramp steamers of the coal trade (see Evans, 1985). On the ships these men worked within a structured hierarchy of difference, where only white seamen could be officers, and non-white seamen were most likely to find themselves in the engine room, as donkeymen, firemen and greasers, or perhaps, like Mr Wesley, in the kitchen. But this does not mean that they experienced their lives as oppression or lack: a recurrent theme in their oral history accounts is their love of seafaring.

> Marcia: Can you remember how long your father went to sea for?
>
> Nora: Well, my father went to sea in 1914. He was in the Navy . . . He was a prisoner of war during the war, and still came back and went to sea [until about 1955]. You see, it was all they knew: the seamen considered their life very honourable . . . At first they didn't make good wages: they were working horrible ships for menial money. But after the war, wages got higher and most seamen's families had reasonably nice homes because they worked and gave their wives their money to make their children have nice homes and take care of them. And seamen were proud of being seamen.[4]

Many of them, like today's idealized postmodernist, postcolonialist subjects, became eternal wanderers, homeless always and everywhere. Others came to regard south Wales as their home. The Butetown district – an area approximately a mile long and a quarter of a mile wide located on the southern end of Cardiff, an area which locals referred to as 'Tiger Bay' and 'the Docks' – was particularly favoured as a home away from home for new immigrants and minorities. From that base, despite periods of hardship and victimization, they formed complex identities, made substantial contributions to the economic life of Wales, and bequeathed a unique, cosmopolitan heritage.

'One last point about the "immigrants". It's a pretty obvious point, but it keeps getting forgotten. It's this: they came because they were invited' (Rushdie, 1991b: 133). Note that many of the immigrants who have moved into Wales since the nineteenth-century industrial revolution have been 'white' (i.e. Irish, Greeks,

Italians, Spaniards and many others), but those I will be discussing in this chapter wear the badge of colour. They are the so-called *visible minorities*: those whose physiognomy – facial features, skin colour, hair texture, etc. – reveals them to be Other; those whose difference matters, even among a people – the (white) Welsh – who pride themselves on being a non-racist nation.

Between the two world wars, many of Wales's immigrant seamen suffered long periods of unemployment and deprivation. For example, by 1921, 'About 3,000 seamen of all nationalities were ashore because of the laying-up of shipping, and many of these were financially distressed or absolutely destitute.' Most were without insurance and most 'were being kept by the boarding-house masters without any payment' (Evans, 1985: 75). Their movement was regulated by a series of Aliens Orders, issued by the Home Office after white British seamen lobbied against a further influx of immigrant and 'coloured' seamen. They constituted what Marx called a *reserve army of labour*, a local pool of unemployed and underemployed labour that was available to work for low wages, under controlled conditions, if and when the economy picked up and their labour was deemed to be needed.

But domination is not necessarily lived as a negative experience. What are we to make of the fact that those who made up this labour force, which was underpaid and exploited, seem to have rather enjoyed their experiences? What are we to make of the fact that, in most of their oral testimonies, we hear the voices of men who really liked going to sea? Does it mean that these men were/are complicit in their own oppression? Or does it mean that we need to avoid binary, moralistic categories – like dominant and subordinate, like positive experience versus negative experience – when speaking and writing of such matters?

(Another example: In a videotaped interview recorded in 1987, Glenn Jordan asks a seaman who immigrated here from British Honduras (now Belize) during the Second World War whether he experienced racism in Britain. He answers that he had not. The scholar-activist repeats the question. The informant repeats his answer. The scholar-activist believes he is practising a form of self-delusion. But perhaps it is simply the case that race is lived differently by different individuals; that the black subject is not singular, but plural.)

What are we to make of all of this?

STRUGGLE FOR RECOGNITION

> I hope I have shown that here the master differs basically from the master described by Hegel. For Hegel there is reciprocity; here the master laughs at the consciousness of the slave. What he wants from the slave is not recognition but work. (Fanon, 1967: 220)

For generations, before the redevelopment of the 1960s, immaculately dressed colonial seamen could be seen strolling up and down Bute Street in suits and hats and, sometimes, with spats and walking sticks as well. Indeed, one of the most interesting insights revealed by old photographs and oral histories is that, whenever possible, Wales's colonial seamen, presumably like their brothers elsewhere, sought to look smart – not by wearing 'their native costumes' but by mimicking the colonizer at his best. In Bute Street, the gentleman dandy wore a brown face: the colonized, through great effort, came to resemble the well-presented colonizer, but not quite.

Their efforts, it seems, sometimes had unexpected consequences: certainly, they did not necessarily lead to acceptance, to recognition.

> A voice: And there is always the danger – I've learned that Fanon is right – of the Master laughing in my face.

Look at figure 4. This is a Bert Hardy photograph, taken in January 1950, inside a Somali milk bar in Tiger Bay. (The name of the milk bar comes from the nickname of its Somali owner: locals called him 'Berlin' because he had previously lived in Germany.) In the *Picture Post* archives, the description of this photograph reads: 'Smart Young Somalis Lounge around in Light Suits and Polished Shoes.' Third from the left, immaculately groomed and dressed, is Mahmood Mattan. A few years later, in September 1952, he would be hanged in Cardiff for a heinous crime that he did not commit – the murder of the Jewish shopkeeper Lily Volpert, whose throat was cut in her pawnbroker's shop in Bute Street.

Mattan was described in court and in the local press as a 'semi-civilized savage'.[5] Not *un*civilized, but '*semi*-civilized' – the term, on reflection, is an extraordinary one. The discourse constructs this black subject as occupying a kind of indeterminate status, between an imagined Africa and an imagined Europe. Having acquired aspects of our civilization, he resembles us. But only partially, for he remains, in his essence, a black savage.

Fanon: The colonized is elevated above his jungle status in proportion to his adoption of the mother country's cultural standards. He becomes whiter as he renounces his blackness, his jungle. (Fanon, 1967: 14)

In fact, there are no guarantees. When one is pre-defined as Other, strategies for achieving respectability and acceptance may be doomed to failure. The struggle for recognition may not lead to mutual transformation of Colonizer and Colonized (as optimistic Hegelians and Sartreans would have it) but to the 'Thought-He-Was-Civilized' Savage's death.[6]

Mahmood Mattan did not die because of his apparent prosperity, as signified by his smart, Western dress. But Others sometimes have. Reports of the 1919 riots in Cardiff indicate that one thing that especially upset the white attackers, besides the fact that black men had 'their women', was the fact that they were dressed so well.

A shout: Kill that darky! His clothes are better than mine!

This concern about fine clothes worn by black men had a history. For example, during the 1910s, Mr David Williams, then chief constable of Cardiff (his job was literally *surveillance*), stated his opposition to a coloured men's cricket club because he disapproved 'of black men wearing flannels' – which would make them more attractive than when they were wearing corduroys – 'and young girls being allowed to admire such beasts' (quoted in Evans, 1980: 10).

An analytical voice: The same old stories of the Negro's animality, the Coolie's inscrutability or the stupidity of the Irish *must* be told (compulsively) again and afresh. (Bhabha, 1993: 77)

Here, a fantasy regarding black masculinity and a fear of miscegenation is stated in a rather unexpected form: the threat to white womanhood comes not only because the black male is oversexed (with his big penis and reputed skills in how to use it), but also because he is stylishly dressed in a way that accentuates his (superior?) body. The colonizer reveals himself as *ambivalent* towards the Other – as both fearful and envious of him, as both derisive of the Other and, apparently, desiring to be in his place. This phenomenon is one postcolonialist theorists, especially Homi Bhabha, see as a defining feature of the relation between colonizers and their Others:[7] the stereotype is 'a complex, ambivalent,

contradictory mode of representation, as anxious as it is assertive'
(Bhabha, 1993: 70). Such stereotypes and fantasies played a key
role in triggering the 1919 race riots in Cardiff:

> The Chief Constable's report on the [1919] riots pinpointed their
> origins to an incident near Custom House Street on the evening of
> Wednesday, 11th June. The incident symbolized the discontents of the
> discharged soldiers. A brake containing coloured men and their white
> wives was returning from an excursion and attracted a crowd. Within
> one small vehicle the whites saw a seductive explanation of their prob-
> lems: they were experiencing difficulties because of the affluence
> (affluent enough to afford excursions in a brake) of the blacks who
> were simultaneously overturning what was seen as the natural racial
> order in their sexual relations with white women.
>
> A matter of words turned into a matter of violence; whites and
> blacks lined up on the North and South sides of Canal Parade Bridge
> respectively. A police constable tried to maintain order but there was
> a rush in which the white men threw stones and coloured men fired
> revolvers, some containing blanks. The white crowd then tried to
> reach Butetown but were hindered by the police. Some got into Bute
> Street and windows and doors were smashed with sticks. Some of the
> blacks had taken cover in Hope Street and Homfray Street; the police
> kept the crowds moving hoping to avoid serious trouble. In Homfray
> Street a house was set on fire. The disturbances covered a wide area
> and were simultaneous in several districts . . . (Evans, 1980: 15)

This incident tends to be forgotten in official representations of
Cardiff and Wales, but not in the collective consciousness of
people from Tiger Bay.

EXILED, THROWN AWAY, SILENCED

Consider figure 5. This is a picture of two young girls taken in
1954 by Bert Hardy, while he was on assignment for a photo-
essay entitled 'Cardiff: a divided city', which was subsequently
published in *Picture Post* magazine. The location is a children's
home in the Ely area of Cardiff. Who are they? I do not know.
Perhaps they are sisters, perhaps not. Certainly, the girl on the left
is mixed-race. Her image points to a forgotten, marginalized
history – that of generations of mixed-race children who were
disowned and ostracized because their mothers, white Welsh
women from Cardiff and the south Wales Valleys, dared form
relationships with men of 'the darker races'. They are those who
the Welsh writer Howard Spring referred to as 'children of the

strangest colours, fruit of frightful misalliances' (Spring, 1939: 33).[8] Perhaps if the two girls could speak, they would speak of rejection and betrayal, as Charlotte Williams has done:

> They say that in crisis you see truths. I was angry, angry with Wales for rejecting me. It was Wales that had betrayed me, let me down, cut me off . . . I'd been displaced, involuntarily exiled. I felt homeless, rootless, dislocated, effectively a refugee from an untenable set of circumstances . . . It's difficult to feel belonging when nothing tells you that you belong. (Williams, 2002: 168)

But must the muted voice only speak of pain? Is sorrow the only story the marginalized and abandoned have to tell?

> An other: Silenced. We fear those who speak about us who do not speak to us and with us. We know what it is like to be silenced. We know that the forces that silence us because they never want us to speak, differ from the forces that say speak, tell me your story. Only do not speak in the voice of resistance. Only speak from that space in the margin that is a sign of deprivation, a wound, and unfulfilled longing. Only speak your pain. (hooks, 1990: 343)

RITA'S STORY

> '[A]nd from the slaves of old to the British-born black children of the present, there have been many who could testify to the pain of being subjected to white society's view of them. (Rushdie, 1991b: 143)

One of the first audiotaped interviews I did in the Butetown ('Tiger Bay') community in Cardiff was with Rita Hinds Delpeche (b. 1931). Below is an extract from that interview, in which she recounts an incident that occurred when she was in primary school:

> I can remember I was very good at Welsh at school . . . Really good. I loved it. We had this Welsh teacher Mr —. He was going around the class this day asking everybody where they were from. Well, we were all from here.
> So . . . I said, 'I'm Welsh'. I mean, as an eight year old, I wasn't thinking about anything. He asked me what I was: I was Welsh. And he said to me, 'How can you be Welsh? You're black! Black people can't be Welsh!'[9]

When asked to state her identity, the light-brown-skinned child of a Cardiff-born, mixed-race mother and a West Indian father

says, without thinking otherwise, that she is Welsh. The teacher –
who has not learned that modern identities are plural and
complex, who cannot imagine that ethnicity is not reducible to
skin colour and phenotype – asserts that this is absolutely impossible: one cannot be both Other and Welsh. Here, white power, in
a nationalist form, patrols the boundaries of Welsh identity.[10] The
border guard, through stereotyping, judges who does and does
not belong. There is no dialogue, no recognition. The task is *to fix
difference* through an exercise of discursive power: the priority is
not simply to exclude but to disown and expel.

> A voice: And then it dawned on me that I was different from the
> others; or like, mayhap, in heart and life and longing, but shut out
> from their world by a vast veil. (DuBois, 1989: 4)[11]

One is reminded of Mary Douglas's argument, in *Purity and
Danger*, that cultures tend to create meaning through binary
oppositions – such as good and evil, clean and unclean, normal
and deviant, living and dead, man and woman, black and white,
us and them – and that what they find most dangerous and threatening is not the absolute Other but the *in-between* (Douglas,
1966). Thus, in a xenophobic and racist culture, those whose
features and/or behaviour mark them as simultaneously the Same
as the dominant group *and* Different from it – like Rita, Nora,
Charlotte and the abandoned child in this paper – may find themselves subjected to special rituals of purification and expulsion.

> A theoretical point: [S]tereotyping deploys a strategy of 'splitting'. It
> divides the normal and the acceptable from the abnormal and the
> unacceptable. It then excludes and expels everything which does not
> fit, which is different . . . (S. Hall, 1997: 258)

> A second theoretical point: We often think of power in terms of direct
> physical coercion or constraint. However, we have also spoken. . . of
> power in *representation*: power to mark, assign and classify; of
> *symbolic* power; of *ritualised* exclusion. Power, it seems, has to be
> understood here, not only in terms of economic exploitation and phys-
> ical coercion, but also in broader cultural or symbolic terms, including
> the power to represent someone or something in a certain way –
> within a certain 'regime of representation'. (S. Hall, 1997: 259)

Many years after her encounter with white Welsh power in the
classroom, Rita won a prize at the Eisteddfod. She remembered
that teacher, that incident, and wished he could have been there.

> A dominant voice: Racism is not a problem in Wales! Because we too
> are an oppressed people, we understand the plight of the Other.

A definition: Racism is the generalized and final assigning of values to real or imaginary differences, to the accuser's benefit and at his victim's expense, in order to justify the former's own privileges or aggression. (Memmi, 1968: 185)

Recently, a young person told Rita that he had been called a 'Welsh nigger' at school. Rita, laughing as she told me the story, said that he shouldn't have been so upset, because this was an improvement – a recognition that black people can indeed be Welsh.

A question: What are the existential consequences of non-acceptance and part-acceptance? Anger? Ambivalence? Pain? Displacement?

It has become fashionable among many post-structuralist and postmodernist theorists to speak of identity as choice: most black subjects in the West know that they cannot choose to be otherwise, certainly not when they encounter dominant discourses and structures of (white) power.

NORA'S STORY

That word 'why', you know, that's a terrible word. You could say, 'Why be born?' but people are born every day. And we shouldn't say, 'Why be born?' because we have a right to be born. And we have a right to be treated as human beings – all over the world, not just in the Bay . . . But the world says 'Why?' when it points to us. I don't like that word 'why'. (Nora Glasgow Richer, interview in Butetown, 8 June 1987)

Not quite the Same, not quite the Other, she stands in that undetermined threshold place where she constantly drifts in and out. (Trinh, 1991: 74)

Nora Glasgow Richer was the daughter of Blodwyn, who came to Tiger Bay from the south Welsh Valleys, and Tapakay, who came from the West African country of Liberia. Her narrative, recorded on videotape in 1987, is about identity, nation, culture and race. In the following extract, in which the questions are being posed by Thomas Nepal's granddaughter, Nora talks about her family, childhood and her community.

Marcia: Nora, would you like to start off with something about your parents?

Nora: Well, my mother is Welsh, from the Valleys of south Wales, and my father is an African from Monrovia. They met many long years ago when my mother was fifteen and they married in St Mary's

Church [in the 'Tiger Bay' area of Cardiff] and had me when she was sixteen. I come from a very Welsh, very African family. My father was very African, and my mother was very Welsh. So hence the combination.

It was a nice family – hard-working father went to sea. He was in the Royal Navy in the 1914 war and in the Merchant Navy in the Second War. He worked very hard, was never home very much. My mother was an average mother, you know, with one child – me. She worked, [doing] some of the little jobs they had around here for mothers in those days – cleaning somebody else's house or something menial.

I grew up as an average child in the Bay of a mixed family. Played in the Canal for a playground. Caught polio from the Canal [i.e. the Glamorganshire Canal, that central artery which directly linked the south Wales Valleys to global capitalism], and then went along from there living in this Bay in a wheelchair for several years. Then I went to South Church Street School, which was a very good school with all races and nationalities, and they taught us quite well . . .

We ate Welsh and African food: fufu and gari and jollof rice, and then . . . potatoes and peas and gravy like the English or the Welsh.

The example of food is very revealing. Here, the global lives within the local: 'Tiger Bay' was home to multicultural cuisine – and to cosmopolitan subjects, with complex identities – long before this became fashionable. Nora tells us that her early life was that of 'an average child' in 'Tiger Bay'; that her household, with its multicultural, 'mixed-race' environment, was typical of a kind of collective experience.

A voice: But there are marriages and there are mixed marriages and the latter inevitably signal a whole lot more to their public than the mere fact of two people promising to live their days together.

Early in the last century, Cardiff, like Liverpool, had been identified as an area of Britain where there was a need to tackle the fast growing 'colour problem'.[12] And so in 1929 the Chief Constable of Cardiff proposed a legal ban on miscegenation, the fancy word for racial intermixing. The ban was modelled on the South African apartheid system and put forward something like their Immorality Act of 1927. The fear and the threat of intermarriage follows even the smallest concentrations of black people . . . (Williams, 2002: 56)

Nora further tells us that she is from a long-established community, which includes black immigrants from before the First World War. Given their deep roots in Wales (many mixed-race families have now been here for four generations), these are people who are deeply offended by refusal of recognition.

Nora grew up in what was the most multicultural street in Wales: 'I lived in Loudoun Square, which had sixty-two houses with forty-two nations in it. We all got along with each other very well . . .' But this experience of tolerance did not extend outside the immediate community (Butetown) in which she lived. Indeed, the world in which she grew up was one of dangers, boundaries and border crossings that were prohibited:

> Nora: I told you before, there were places we couldn't go to, places they didn't like us. And mothers and fathers didn't go over the bridge very often, 'cause sometimes they were abused. Some people never went out of the estate for thirty years. Your father never walked to town with your mother – not because he didn't want to walk up town with your mother, but because he thought that somebody was gonna say, 'Look at that black man with that white woman' or something to that effect, and then there would be an argument . . .
> They never called us the very nasty names: they said 'black' . . .

The central theme in this story is racism and exclusion. Cardiff is depicted as a divided city, a terrain of power, consisting of spaces where one was or was not welcomed, depending on the colour of one's skin and that of one's partner and children.

> A voice: And so some of us were exiled within the land of our birth
> . . .

But note the final line in Nora's version of the story. Although she is talking about racial division, intolerance and violence, she rejoices in the memory that men like her father were not called 'nigger'. (Others remember otherwise, but that is not the point.[13]) She works hard to avoid saying anything negative about Wales, because of her relation to it. But that relationship is always one characterized by longing, by lack, by ultimate unfulfilment – because what she feels herself to be, and what the dominant discourses say that she is/must be, are necessarily at odds. Her identification and desires are in conflict with power. Her subjectivity is complex, contradictory – but the case does not invite postmodernist rejoicing in the pleasure of plurality and difference.

The image/experience of Cardiff as a racially divided city is deeply embedded in the collective consciousness of present and former members of the Tiger Bay community, especially those who lived during the inter-war period, i.e. after the 1919 south Wales race riots in Barry, Cardiff and Newport.

> A reminder: The trigger of the [1919] riots in Cardiff was an attack on a brake containing black men and their white wives: it was not a

dispute over singing on a ship or some direct economic cause, though such an incident had triggered the similar riots in South Shields earlier in the year. Religious pressure groups, such as the Cardiff and District Citizens' Union, and the police contributed to the situation . . . (Evans, 2003: 99)[14]

The effects of the riots were to reinforce already existing lines of difference between *'us'* and *'them'*.[15]

Glenn: Do you remember any stories about the 1919 riots?

Nora: Yes, some of our aunties and grans used to tell tales about how they used to rush in their houses and lock the doors . . . I remember my auntie telling me that she had some guns in a pinny [i.e. a pinafore] and ran up the street (laughs) to hand them out. (laughs) Because people were actually petrified! . . . The black men that were in those days were very strong men, very strong-willed. Even though we might think he was illiterate and didn't do what he was supposed to do, in order to protect himself and his children he was very strong. And that's what he thought he was doing. I mean, when they ran down here with guns and sticks and whatever, the black population just had to retaliate. If you're gonna knock my head, I'm not gonna stand there and look at you! If you're gonna come and talk to me, then I've gotta stand and talk with you. But if you're gonna kill me, and I know you're gonna kill me, I'm not gonna like you killing me.

Listen to Nora, daughter of Wales and the African diaspora, discussing relations between Butetown and the south Wales Valleys in the days before the 1960s redevelopment, which razed old Tiger Bay to the ground and replaced it with concrete tower blocks and maisonettes:

Nora: And on a Saturday night, sometimes the miners would come from the Valleys and they would call the brothers or the fathers 'Sam' or 'Joe', but they never called them anything worse than that. It was, well, Saturday Night Fight almost every Saturday night for years and years. But a 'friendly' fight because the miner would boast that he'd come down and beat up a big black man, and he'd go back feeling big; and the boys would come in and say, 'Look, we had a fight with Taffy or Dai'. And everybody would be happy. That was the miners relieving their feelings, and the seamen . . . relieving their feelings, which was a nice time.

South Wales miners, and mining communities, are famous for their socialist traditions of internationalism, including their virtual hero worship of Paul Robeson. But there is another, long-established tradition in the south Wales Valleys: the working-class community as breeding ground for racism. In the above statement, Nora decentres the myth of Wales as a Mecca of racial harmony. Or, rather, she almost does.

In fact, she provides an extraordinary statement. It begins by calling attention to serious conflict between people of the south Wales Valleys and people of Butetown, a situation that routinely gave rise to episodes of racially structured violence. Just when the listener/reader might expect the narrator to condemn this violence, she seeks to assure us that it was all perfectly all right, as a 'nice time' was had by all. As in an earlier statement where she says black people in Butetown were called racially insulting names by people from the Valleys but never very nasty ones, we have here an example of *hybridity* – not so much in the sense used by Homi Bhabha as in the sense used by Mikhail Bakhtin. Consider Bahktin's definition of hybrid discourse: 'A hybrid construction is an utterance that belongs, by its grammatical (syntactic) and compositional markers, to a single speaker, but that actually contains mixed within it two utterances, two speech manners, two styles, two "languages", two semantic and axiological belief systems' (Bakhtin, 1981: 304). Although Bakhtin is speaking more of the structure than the content of the utterances, one can ague that much of what he says applies to the preceding statement by Nora.

Who has the right to say, 'I'm Welsh'? With a background in Welsh-speaking Wales, and a mother called Blodwyn, Nora felt she had an inalienable right to claim Welsh identity. Her problem was that not everyone else agreed: indeed, ironically, those Welsh with whom she felt the closest ties seem to have felt the least affinity with her. Consider the following story.

> Nora: I'll tell you something, I was gonna join Plaid Cymru once. I filled in the form in Welsh! (laughs) They sent a man to me. I was proud of being Welsh. I am still proud, very proud of being Welsh. But, it's true, I filled in a form in Welsh and they sent a man round to my house in Ely. And he said, 'I'd like to speak to the Welsh-speaking person in here.' I said, 'Well, it's me!' 'Mind you,' I said, 'although my mother's family are Welsh-speaking, my Welsh isn't fluent.' But I'm proud of being Welsh because I'm born here. And I read the brochure, and the things that were on it at the time I thought was very good for Wales. So since I thought I was Welsh, and I lived in Wales, I wanted to do something for Wales.
>
> The man come and spoke to me, asked me why I thought I was Welsh. I said, 'Well my mother is Welsh, my grandfather is Welsh, and

my grandmother is Welsh, and her grandmother is Welsh, and my great-grandmother is Welsh. So that's why I think I'm Welsh.' So he went away from me and he came back. And he said, 'Dr Davis' – who Dr Davis is I don't know – and he said, 'Dr Davis says that you create confusion.' And I said, 'Well, why do I create confusion? Dr Davis is looking for votes. He's got lots of Welsh like me.' I said, 'I'm so loved in the community that I can go and get him a lot of Welsh people who would vote for him,' but, I said, 'It looks like Dr Davis is not willing to accept me as being Welsh.'

 I'm still confused about Dr Davis, why he thinks I'm not Welsh . . . I very much wanted to be Welsh, because that's what I thought I was. But, Siarad Cymraeg is not for us!! Apparently!

A voice: [B]eing a problem is a strange experience – peculiar even for one who has never been anything else . . . (DuBois, 1989: 4)

Here, the Welsh subject, who is both Same and Different, confronts a nationalist discourse of Welshness that is exclusive, backward-looking and racist. Her experience is painful.

Nora: I'm the oldest child in my mother's family, the oldest grand-child. And my grandmother, because I was black, always loved me to death because she thought the world would slap me in the face. That was her expression anyway; [that was] what she said. So she always gave me extra loving because she thought the world would hurt me.
 She was right, but why should Wales hurt me?

Nora says, 'Tiger Bay belongs to Wales and so do we' (but much of Wales does not agree). She wants to make herself recognized. Perhaps listening to Fanon, as he draws on Hegel's master–slave dialectic, will help us understand:

Man is only human to the extent to which he tries to impose his exist-ence on another man in order to be recognized by him. As long as he has not been effectively recognized by the other, that other will remain the theme of his actions. It is on that other being, on recognition by that other being, that his own human worth and reality depend. It is that other being in whom the meaning of his life is condensed. (Fanon, 1967: 216–17)

Change the pronouns from 'he' to 'she' in this statement and then ask yourself: Does this not help us to better understand Nora?

 Her own view of her identity was – and is? – radically at odds with prevailing notions of Welshness. Her most cherished wish is doomed to remain unfilled. Nora has since died. Perhaps the generations of her grandchildren and great-grandchildren are experiencing a better Wales. Perhaps not.

Nora: I think that's all I can say to you now. I love the Bay. I love Wales. But does Wales love me?

'COMMON SKIES, DIVIDED HORIZONS': CHARLOTTE'S STORY[16]

> I grew up in a small Welsh town amongst people with pale faces, feeling that somehow to be half Welsh and half Afro-Caribbean was always to be half of something but never quite anything whole at all. I grew up in a world of mixed messages about belonging, about home and about identity. (Williams, 2002: viii)

Echoes of Julia Kristeva: I am a stranger to myself.

Listen as Charlotte Williams, the mixed-race subject from north Wales (and the black diaspora), insightfully and sympathetically describes the Wales she knows and loves:

> Poor old mixed-up Wales, somehow as mixed up as I was; confused about where it had been, what it was and where it was going, rapidly re-writing history to make sense of itself as some kind of monolithic whole and it just wasn't working. I love its contours and its contradictions. There is the north, '*Welsh Wales*' they call it, and a very different south, connected only in name . . . The Welsh and the English, the Welsh-speaking and the English-speaking, the proper Welsh and the not so proper Welsh, the insiders and the outsiders, the Italians, the Poles, the Irish, the Asians and the Africans and the likes of us, all fighting amongst ourselves for the right to call ourselves Welsh and most of us losing out to some very particular idea about who belongs and who doesn't. How would we ever make sense of it? (Williams, 2002: 169)

How indeed? This image of Wales is postmodernist and post-colonial: divided and fragmented, characterized by diversity and struggle, this Wales bears little resemblance to dominant, romantic conceptions. Moreover, the Wales Charlotte knows and loves is a Wales of small towns and countryside – which is perhaps unfortunate, since 'Black people and countryside don't go together in white people's thinking' (Williams, 2002: 53).

Charlotte informs the reader that the trauma of her experience of racism did not derive from social exclusion and geographical boundaries but from everyday interaction and processes of *subject-ification*. This racism did not manifest itself in the form of systematic exclusion, threats or violence. On the contrary, it was, apparently, occasional and polite:

> Charlotte: Only in retrospect can I add up my experience in this way
> [i.e. as having to do with racism]. I guess back then a lot of it seemed
> inadvertent and innocuous, sporadic and disconnected. I accepted it as
> my personal battle, not anything particularly collective. We were all
> busy suppressing the reality of it, both them and us. Take the words
> 'blackie, darkie, rubber lips, gollywog, wog, nigger, coon'; shocking
> and upsetting as these words were, they rarely came our way . . . in
> our town we colluded in the wonderful deceit of what I suppose you
> could call 'polite racism'. (Williams, 2002: 49)

The problem, Charlotte suggests, is not that people in her north
Wales hometown were deliberately malicious but that they were
provincial. This world, where she has lived much of her life,
manages racial difference through ambivalence.

> Charlotte: Small town thinking has its own way of managing differ-
> ence. It both embraces it and rejects it. In its ambivalence you become
> at one and the same time highly invisible and punishingly visible. 'We
> never really noticed you were coloured', they would say in condes-
> cending tones, or 'You're not really black, you're just brown', and we
> would all be relieved of the onerous impoliteness of being black.
> (Williams, 2002: 49)

Here, aside from parochialism, we find an example of the peren-
nial problem facing the black subject: s/he is both invisible and
hyper-visible at the same time.

Nonetheless, the effects were profound. As Fanon (1968)
observes, the internalization of racism has particularly painful
consequences. Speaking of herself and her sister, Charlotte says:

> We would trade bits of ourselves for their white acceptance, denying
> ourselves to provide reassurance against the intrusion of difference.
> But it was the background assumptions embodied in the questions
> that caught me so unawares. The everyday assumptions of inferiority
> that eventually ground me down until I didn't know who or what I
> was. (Williams, 2002: 49–50)

The effects were long-lasting, not easily outgrown. Thus,
Charlotte's identity, perhaps in particular, has been *in process*, a
matter of *becoming* rather than *being*.

> Charlotte: I was born into a long journey . . . It has taken me a long
> time to puzzle the half-half alternative that was offered; to understand
> that to be mixed race is not to be half of anything; mixed but not
> mixed up. (Williams, 2002: 191)

The experience of mixed-race people in Tiger Bay/Cardiff was (and is) profoundly different. Within the immediate community where they lived, their physiognomy did not signify Otherness. They were not ground down by the everyday experience of racism – until they went outside that community. For Nora, unlike Charlotte, racial identity is not problematic and traumatic: ethnic/national identity is.

Charlotte is aware that her experience of race in small-town north Wales is very different from that in urban south Wales, especially in Cardiff. Thus she says to her Cardiffian friend: 'You're lucky, Suzanne. There are lots of people just like you in Cardiff. You've grown up with them. You're Welsh all right. I envy you that.' But her friend does not quite recognize this description as an accurate portrayal of her situation. Suzanne replies: 'You've got that one wrong for a start. I belong to a lil' bit of Cardiff, not Wales at all. Wales, what's that?' she asked looking out the window of the train at the north Wales coast as if she was in a foreign country . . . (Williams, 2002: 169).

Interestingly, although separated by geography (and generation), Charlotte Williams and Nora Glasgow Richer seem to have had some similar experiences. Among these is the *pain of identity*, which subjects of racism endure without the dominant society even bothering to notice.

> Charlotte: You mean I spent all of those years with my cheeks burning and nobody knew any different? (Williams, 2002: 49)

But note that in Nora's Tiger Bay/Cardiff experience, the pain is not over being mixed-race; it is over being both Welsh (in one's own eyes) and not Welsh (from the perspective of the dominant society) at the same time.

Both Charlotte and Nora experience the existential consequences of non-acceptance/part acceptance and displacement. Charlotte's pain, like Nora's, is particularly acute because she has a deep love for Wales and expects to be accepted: their subjectivities are, as the post-structuralists say, *plural* and *contradictory*. Listen as Charlotte speaks, in words that could have been appropriated by Nora (and so many others): 'I love Wales but there's a twist in the dragon's tail . . . Wales seemed to be speaking with a forked tongue. The choirs might have been singing of a welcome in the hillsides, but I didn't feel that welcomed' (Williams, 2002: 167).

CONCLUDING REFLECTIONS

What is the point of an intervention such as this one? My response echoes that of Michel Foucault, who once said: 'I do not conduct my analyses in order to say: this is how things are, look how trapped you are. I say certain things only to the extent to which I see them as capable of permitting the transformation of reality' (Foucault, 1991: 174).

In this chapter, through engagement with fragments of lives revealed through recontextualized images and personal narratives, I have sought to interrupt authoritative discourse, to enable historically marginalized Others to speak to power.[17] (I hope I have not distorted their voices.) Along the way, in order to make sense of lives and voices, I have made use of a number of concepts, such as *empire, exile, borders, Others, marginalized voices, polyvocality, fractured identity, in-betweeness, hybridity, ambivalence, diaspora, whiteness* and *struggle for recognition*, which are current in postcolonialist (and much post-structuralist and postmodernist) theory.

Foucault was not an optimist. Nor, arguably, are many ethnic minorities in Wales, although we readily accept that the situation could be much worse. We concede that, unlike the Union of South Africa and the United States of America, race relations in Wales have never been governed by a system of apartheid. Indeed, the black subject from the USA, confronted with Wales, may not believe his/her eyes: I myself was amazed when I first saw a group of young women, of varying shades of white, beige and brown, doing each other's hair in Nora's kitchen. Black people from Elsewhere tend to find Wales a relatively non-racist place, a comparatively easy place in which to live. It is the Others who are also the Same – i.e. the black and mixed-race people who are born here, especially those whose mothers or fathers are 'native Welsh' – who tend to experience it otherwise. Much of this essay has privileged their voices, their experiences, which differ from my own.

Fact: Truth is a matter of experience and perspective.

In 1948, Jean-Paul Sartre began his introduction to a volume of black poetry in French by asking:

> What did you expect to find, when the muzzle that has silenced the voices of black men [and women] is removed? That they would thunder your praise? When these heads that our fathers have forced to the very ground are risen, do you expect to read adoration in their eyes? (Sartre, n.d.: 7)[18]

Of the voices and writings of black and mixed-race people from Wales, we might ask: Do they speak of Wales with words of *condemnation* or *praise*? And, if we are reflexive, we might also ask: Do such binary categories, characteristic of simplistic dialectical thinking, really help us hear what they are saying?

Richard Dyer, in his book *White*, says:

> We are often told that we are living now in a world of multiple identities, of hybridity, of decentredness and fragmentation. The old illusory identities of class, gender, race, sexuality are breaking up; someone may be black and gay and middle class and female; we may be bi-, poly- or non-sexual, of mixed-race, indeterminate gender and heaven knows what class. Yet we have not yet reached a situation in which white people and white cultural agendas are no longer in the ascendant. (Dyer, 1997: 3)

This does not mean that whiteness is equally pernicious everywhere. 'Britain', Salman Rushdie tells us, 'is now two entirely different worlds, and the one you inhabit is determined by the colour of your skin' (Rushdie, 1991a: 134). In Wales, we say that this may be true in England but here it is different: whatever your colour, there is a welcome in the hillside. This chapter – or rather this fragmented text of testimony, images and reflections – suggests that the time has come to dismantle this prevailing assumption.

Both Nora Glasgow Richer and Charlotte Williams suggest that Wales has deluded itself into thinking that it is a non-racist land. Nora, who also lived in the USA, suggests this results from the fact that there is not a system of overt, systematic racial discrimination:

> Glenn: Why do you think people think that there is no problem being coloured here?

> Nora: Well, they think there's no problem for the simple reason that we don't get pushed off the sidewalk (unless there is somebody horrible that wants to push you off the sidewalk). We're allowed to go to the average place. We go to the hospitals, we go to church, we go dancing. We go to a lot of things that a lot of people can't go to . . .

An alternative (but not incompatible) view suggests the delusion is a matter of ideology:

> Charlotte: So are we all comrades under the skin? It's a curious thought. Perhaps we are in many ways. Paul Robeson in the film *The Proud Valley* isn't a Welsh folk hero for nothing. When he is refused

a job in the mines because of his colour the coal miners protest, 'But aren't we all the same colour underground?' It's a sort of civil rights film for Wales, even if the common enemy has become English and not British imperialism. Yet maybe we have woven the connection rather too deep into the mythology of Wales . . .

There may be a feeling that the nigger man and the Welsh man are one, or that the Welshman is a black man at heart but there still isn't any recognition of the black man who is Welsh or the Welshman who is black. Is it all just imagining? (Williams, 2002: 176)

The main challenge raised by the lives and voices in this 'essay' are these: Can we reimagine Wales as consisting of a plurality of experiences, cultures and identities? Can we rethink Welshness as heterogeneous, as inclusive of difference?

A voice: What is required therefore is an awareness of positions, representations, histories and exclusions . . . (Childs and Williams, 1997: 89)

NOTES

Thanks to Butetown History & Arts Centre, especially Nina Snell for her help with interview transcriptions and Paul O'Brien for his assistance with the photographic images. Thanks also to Marcia Brahim Barry, Rita Hinds Delpeche, Nora Glasgow Richer (deceased), John Doe Wesley (deceased), Charlotte Williams and Chris Weedon.

[1] These three images are from the archives of Butetown History & Arts Centre. The first was donated by Marcia Brahim Barry, granddaughter of Thomas Nepal. The other two were donated by Mr Wesley himself, who, until his death a few years ago, was a member of the seamen's group at the Centre.

[2] While preparing this discussion, I talked to a member of Thomas Nepal's family. As it turns out, the family are not absolutely certain that he came from Nepal: there are different stories about his origins. Thus, not only his name but even his country of birth remains a mystery. From the perspective of this chapter, this raises an interesting point: much of the history of Wales's Others is submerged, marginalized and forgotten.

[3] One could make a similar argument with regard to slavery in the New World. Many of my own family members, descended from a plantation in Tyler County, East Texas, have the last name 'Owens' – i.e. are tellingly called by a name that signifies not only Welshness but ownership. Indeed, Welsh family names are very common among African-Americans, all of whom are descended from slaves.

[4] From a videotaped interview with Nora Glasgow Richer, Butetown, Cardiff, 8 June 1987. Recorded by the Black Film and Video Workshop in Wales. Interviewers: Marcia Brahim Barry, Glenn Jordan and Ian Tweedale. This was the first recorded interview done by the group that would soon become Butetown Community History Project and, later, Butetown History & Arts Centre.

⁵ On 24 February 1998, at the Court of Appeals in London, forty-six years after he was hanged, Mahmood Mattan was finally exonerated.

⁶ The reference to Hegel is to his well-known discussion of the master–slave dialectic in the chapter on 'self-consciousness' in *Phenomenology of Spirit*. Jean-Paul Sartre appropriates this concept in various writings, most notably in *Being and Nothingness* (New York: Philosophical Library, 1956); and *Critique of Dialectical Reason* (London: New Left Books, 1976). The appropriation of the concept in postcolonialist discourse tends to come via Lacan and Fanon.

⁷ The classic elaboration of Homi Bhabha's concept of *ambivalence*, which he adopts from Freud, is contained in Bhabha, 1984.

⁸ I have written, in some detail, about Howard Spring's representation of 'racial mixing' and 'Tiger Bay' in Jordan, 1988.

⁹ Rita Hinds Delpeche, interview document: transcript of interview conducted in Butetown, Cardiff by Glenn Jordan, 1 August 1984.

¹⁰ For an excellent recent exploration of the myth of racially tolerant Wales, see Williams, Evans and O'Leary, 2003.

¹¹ Originally published in 1903, this book, W. E. B. Dubois's *The Souls of Black Folk*, remains a seminal text on the subject of racism.

¹² See Fletcher, 1930; see also Drake, 1954 and 1955.

¹³ Unfortunately, this sort of racist language was and is still used – sometimes in ways that encompass a wide range of phenotype. I have a Greek friend, now in her forties, who was called 'nigger' as a schoolgirl in Cardiff.

¹⁴ On the 1919 race riots in south Wales, see also Evans, 1980 and 1985.

¹⁵ Thus some 'coloured' families that had moved out of Tiger Bay before the First World War moved back as a result of the riots. Some of their descendants are still there.

¹⁶ I have borrowed the phrase 'common skies, divided horizon' from the subtitle to Chambers and Curti, 1996.

¹⁷ I borrow the term 'speaking to power' from Edward Said, the Palestinian postcolonial theorist, who often says that intellectuals have a responsibility to 'speak truth to power'. (I am not so sure about truth . . .) See Said, 1994.

¹⁸ *Black Orpheus*, Sartre's famous essay on race and the dialectics of recognition, was originally written as an introduction to a collection of poetry by French African and Caribbean writers, edited by the *négritude* poet Léopold Sédar Senghor, *Anthologie de la nouvelle poésie nègre et malgache de le langue française*, Paris: Presses Universitaires de France, 1948.

REFERENCES

Bakhtin, M. (1981). 'Discourse in the novel', in Michael Holquist (ed.), *The Dialogic Imagination: Four Essays by M. M. Bakhtin*, Austin, Tex.: University of Texas Press.

Bhabha, H. (1984). 'Of mimicry and man: the ambivalence of colonial discourse', *October*, 28 (Spring), 125–33. Reprinted in Bhabha (1993), pp. 85–92.

Bhabha, H. (1993). 'The Other question: stereotype, discrimination and the discourse of colonialism', in *The Location of Culture*, London: Routledge, pp. 66–84.

Chambers, I. and Curti, L. (eds) (1996). *The Post-colonial Question: Common Skies, Divided Horizon*, London and New York: Routledge.

Childs, P. and Williams, P. (1997). *An Introduction to Post-colonial Theory*, London: Prentice-Hall.

Dirlik, A. (1994). 'The postcolonial aura: Third World criticism in the age of global capitalism', *Critical Inquiry*, 20, 328–56.

Douglas, M. (1966). *Purity and Danger: An Analysis of the Concepts of Pollution and Taboo*, London: Routledge.

Drake, St Clair (1954). 'Value systems, social structure and race relations in the British Isles', unpublished Ph.D. thesis, Department of Anthropology, University of Chicago.

Drake, St Clair (1955). 'The "colour problem" in Britain: a study in social definitions', *Sociological Review*, New Series, 3, 197–217.

DuBois, W. E. B. (1989; orig. 1903). *The Souls of Black Folk*, Harmondsworth: Penguin Books.

Dyer, R. (1997). *White*, London and New York: Routledge.

Evans, N. (1980). 'The south Wales riots of 1919', *Llafur: Journal of the Society for the Study of Welsh Labour History*, 3, 1, 5–29.

Evans, N. (1985). 'Regulating the reserve army: Arabs, blacks and the local state in Cardiff, 1919–45', *Immigrants and Minorities*, 4, 2, 68–115.

Evans, N. (2003). 'Through the prism of ethnic violence: riots and racial attacks in Wales, 1826–2002', in Williams, Evans and O'Leary (eds), *A Tolerant Nation? Exploring Ethnic Diversity in Wales*, Cardiff: University of Wales Press, pp. 93–108.

Fanon, F. (1967). *Black Skin, White Masks*, New York: Grove Press.

Fletcher, M. (1930). *Report on an Investigation into the Colour Problem in Liverpool and Other Ports*, Liverpool: Association for the Welfare of Half-Caste Children.

Foucault, M. (1991). 'The Discourse on Power', in Foucault, *Remarks on Marx: Conversations with Duccio Trombadori*, New York: Semiotext, pp. 147–81.

Hall, C. (1996). 'Histories, empires and the post-colonial moment', in Chambers and Curti (eds), *The Post-colonial Question: Common Skies, Divided Horizon*, London and New York: Routledge, pp. 65–77.

Hall, S. (1996). 'When was the "post-colonial"? Thinking at the limit', in Chambers and Curti (eds), *The Post-colonial Question: Common Skies, Divided Horizon*, London and New York: Routledge, pp. 242–60.

Hall, S. (1997). 'The spectacle of the "Other"', in S. Hall (ed.), *Representation: Cultural Representations and Signifying Practices*, London: Open University and Sage, pp. 223–90.

hooks, b. (1990). 'Marginality as site of resistance', in R. Ferguson,

M. Gever, T. Minh-Ha Trinh and C. West (eds), *Out There: Marginalisation and Contemporary Cultures*, New York: New Museum of Contemporary Art, and Cambridge, Mass., MIT Press, pp. 341–3.

Jordan, G. (1988). 'Images of Tiger Bay: did Howard Spring tell the truth?', *Llafur: Journal of Welsh Labour History*, 5, 1, 53–9.

Jordan, G. and Weedon, C. (1995). *Cultural Politics: Class, Gender, Race and the Postmodern World*, Oxford: Blackwell.

Kristeva, J. (1991). *Strangers to Ourselves*, London: Harvester Wheatsheaf.

Kumar, A. (2000). *Passport Photos*, Berkeley: University of California Press.

Memmi, A. (1968). *Dominated Man: Notes towards a Portrait*, Boston: Beacon Press.

Rushdie, S. (1991a). 'The new empire within Britain', in *Imaginary Homelands: Essays and Criticism, 1981–1991*, London: Granta Books, pp. 129–38.

Rushdie, S. (1991b). 'Home front', in *Imaginary Homelands*, London: Granta Books, pp. 143–6.

Said, E. (1978). *Orientalism*, Harmondsworth: Penguin Books.

Said, E. (1994). *Representations of the Intellectual: The 1993 Reith Lectures*, London: Vintage Books.

Sartre, J.-P. (n.d.). *Black Orpheus*, Paris: Présence Africaine.

Spring, H. (1939). *Heaven Lies About Us: A Fragment of Infancy*, London: Constable and Company.

Trinh, T. M. (1991). *When the Moon Waxes Red: Representation, Gender and Cultural Politics*, New York: Routledge.

Williams, C. (2002). *Sugar and Slate*, Aberystwyth: Planet.

Williams, C., Evans, N. and O'Leary, P. (eds) (2003). *A Tolerant Nation? Exploring Ethnic Diversity in Wales*, Cardiff: University of Wales Press.

II

A QUIET REVOLUTION?
DEVOLUTION AND
POSTCOLONIALITY

5

'Maîtres chez nous'? Awaiting the Quiet Revolution in Wales

ALYS THOMAS

INTRODUCTION

Parallels between the political system of post-devolution Wales and postcolonial independent nation-states are spurious. The National Assembly for Wales is a devolved corporate body with executive powers; thus it has no tax-raising powers, still relies on Westminster for primary legislation, and some functions remain the responsibility of Whitehall either on a UK-wide basis (defence, social security, broadcasting) or on a Wales-and-England basis (police, prisons). Furthermore, forty Welsh MPs continue to sit at Westminster and some Westminster ministers sit for Welsh seats, including the secretary of state for Wales who has a seat at the Cabinet table. The post-devolution political system in Wales, therefore, presents a complex picture which does not have obvious resonance with post-independence states.

Nevertheless, the language of colonialism has been part of the political discourse surrounding devolution. In the late 1980s and 1990s it became commonplace for successive Conservative secretaries of state to be described as 'viceroys' or 'governor generals' by critics of Welsh governance (Osmond, 1995). The old Welsh Office effectively represented administrative devolution on a territorial basis but in practice there was little divergence from the Whitehall line, there being little incentive for politicians from outside Wales to pursue a distinctive Welsh line. Moreover, the principle of collective cabinet responsibility prevailed. The apparent 'democratic deficit' was a central rationale for devolution in 1997, especially for those who had changed their minds

since the referendum of 1979. To a certain extent, therefore, the
objective of devolution was to give Wales autonomy over decision-making within the limits of the settlement, or, in the parlance
of the Quiet Revolution in Quebec, for the Welsh to become
'*maîtres chez nous*' – 'masters in our own house'.

There may be some useful comparative lessons, therefore, to be
learnt from literature dealing with postcolonialism, particularly
that pertaining to the experience of the former dominions and the
experience of the Irish Republic. Some commentators have
argued, for example, that Ireland suffered a 'mental colonization'
which impinged across life and society, perpetuating a 'mono-
maniacal obsession with "Britain"' (Fennell, 1983: 136–7). While
this analysis might be disputed, not least because of far-reaching
economic and social changes which have occurred in the last
decade, the framework provides an interesting starting-point in
looking at Wales. Similarly, the Quiet Revolution in Quebec
represented a decisive break with a conservative 'fortress nationalism' which had fostered cultural autonomy yet maintained
economic dependence, when the Quebec Liberals came in with a
programme for economic modernization, secularization of social
welfare, and state development. It was not the political structures
that had changed, it was the culture and ethos of the would-be
decision-makers. In the Welsh context, therefore, the question is
to what extent have Welsh policy actors developed a self-confident approach to the new political environment. The chapter will
consider the *governance* of Wales since 1999 in the context of
relevant comparative postcolonial perspectives.

POSTCOLONIALISM

The term 'postcolonial' is one over which there has been much
debate, so much so that one commentator suggests that it is
'always open ended', designed to begin a discussion rather than
end it (Landow, 2000). It suggests that former colonies share
certain qualities and experiences which provide a framework for
study and investigation across a range of disciplines. However,
with regard to political science, the concept of post-colonialism,
or post-independence, has an explicit meaning, as 'empire' and
'colony' describe power relationships which are fundamentally
the essence of the study of politics. The colonial state had the
hybridity of 'an alien executive instrument of a culturally different

community'. On the one hand there remain the legacies of the colonizers' models of government, the legal systems and, of course, languages. On the other, there is the experience of post-independence nation-building, characterized by the transformation of political culture (Smith, 1991: 106–16).

The notion of what constitutes a 'colony' is not without dispute. In the context of the British Empire, the Indian subcontinent and Africa loom large in images of empire transmitted through fiction, film and TV drama in the UK. Similarly, the post-independence political order in places such as Zimbabwe and Pakistan is played out nightly on news bulletins. Historically, however, relations with the dominions were of a different order. Post-colonialism has a different resonance there. Unlike India and Africa, where the notion of liberation and winning independence are powerful nation-building myths, Australia and New Zealand have dealt with the historic 'cultural cringe' or subservience towards the mother country through adapting to new spheres of influence and through developing internal relationships with indigenous communities. A key issue for political scientists in such contexts is the detailed understanding of each specific political culture. In spite of having achieved independence, the emergence within a post-colony of a political culture in which citizens and elites put the relations of colonizers and colonized behind them can be a long time coming.

With regard to the changing relationships between the constituent nations of Britain and Ireland, there has been a recent 'rediscovery', by historians such as Norman Davies, of 'the Isles' as having a history which goes beyond the traditional narrative of English history writ large (something less of a revelation to historians of Scotland, Wales and Ireland) (Davies, 1999). It remains debatable, however, whether the relationship between dominant England and the other territories can be described as colonial. It is a question of perception and identity. What in Britain is described as the Irish Troubles of 1919–21, in the Republic is known as the War of Independence. From an Irish perspective, Ireland's development from Free State to Republic to 'Celtic Tiger' has been a process of decolonization. In 1975 Michael Hechter attempted to explain the persistence of difference between the constituent nations of the UK through the theory of internal colonialism, exploring the historic and economic relationship of Scotland, Ireland and Wales to the British state. Peripheral areas are kept dependent and are disadvantaged due to the exploitative nature of their relation to the core. The nature of the Western economic structure is such that the core feeds advantageously off the labour and resources of the periphery. Celtic nationalism emerged, according to the internal colonial model, as a reaction to this regional underdevelopment (Hechter, 1975). However, Hechter's critics have argued that the model fails to take account of core and periphery relations within England, and the existence of regional elites; they have also pointed out that such an overemphasis on economic determination underplays cultural, linguistic and religious factors (Smith, 1991). Furthermore, given that much reflection on the postcolonial experience focuses on the British Empire, the involvement of the Scots, Welsh and, indeed, the Irish as participants in that project cannot be ignored.

'FIRST WORLD' COMPARISONS

In a 1977 article entitled 'Neo-colonial Wales', Ned Thomas pointed out that 'if a third world comparison means anything, it means that united and full independence in no way puts an end to the problems created in the colonial period, but in some cases exacerbates them' (N. Thomas, 1977: 1). Issues related to neo-colonialism can also prove problematic in 'First World' contexts. Ireland and Quebec offer examples of a 'First World' postcolonial experience which may be compared to that of post-devolution Wales. Quebec, one of the ten provinces of the Canadian federal state, narrowly lost a referendum on cessation in 1995. The Republic of Ireland came into being in 1949, although independence had been achieved in 1920 with the creation of the Free State, accompanied by the legacy of partition and civil war.

Quebec is the strongest territorial expression of the 'French fact' in Canada and developed as a political entity as the ultimate loser in the scramble for imperial dominance between Britain and France, when the former beat the latter on the Plains of Abraham in 1759. Concerned that it was best for the colony to return to normal as quickly as possible so that the profitable business of fur trading could continue unhindered, the British administration granted the continuance of the French civil code, although English Common Law was to prevail in the area of criminal law, and gave the Catholic Church virtually the position of an established church in the province. Quebec, therefore, became a Francophone, Roman Catholic enclave within Canada.

By the middle of the twentieth century the dominant political culture of Quebec was that of a conservative 'fortress nationalism', as characterized by the premier Duplessis and his party, the Union Nationale. This party based its support on small businessmen and rural professionals who were Francophone, closely associated with the Catholic Church, and strongly suspicious of big business and industry, seen as connected with Anglophone interests. The dominance of the Church gave it control of education and maintained its sure hold upon French Canadian society. In the 1950s, however, this status quo began to be challenged. The Asbestos Strike in 1949, and strikes such as those at Louiseville in 1952 and Murdochville in 1957, showed that Duplessis's concern with conciliating Anglophone business interests outweighed any cultural allegiances. When the Parti libéral came to power in 1960 under Premier Jean Lesage its slogan was '*Maîtres chez nous*', and the policies followed during its period of office came to be known as the Quiet Revolution. These policies included the control and reform of education in the province and the nationalization of hydro-electricity.

In the Republic of Ireland the emergent political culture of the new state was conservative, Roman Catholic, Gaelic in sympathy and traditionalist. The ideological and cultural dominance of Eamonn de Valera was secured through his party Fianna Fail, founded in 1926, which emerged as the dominant party throughout the twentieth century. Its stated aims were the reunification of Ireland and the restoration of the Irish language. A third implicit aim was a Roman Catholic state for a Roman Catholic people (1937 constitution, see Allen, 2000: 151). In some ways the culture resembled that of Quebec before the Quiet Revolution. But post-independence Ireland, arguably, in common with the Quiet Revolution in Quebec, embarked on policies of economic nationalism intended to dismantle its 'neo-colonial' status (Allen, 2000: 154–5; O'Sullivan See, 1986: 138–41). Some Irish commentators, however, were of the view that even post-independence Ireland had failed to throw off the mindset of the colonized. Desmond Fennell identified what he termed Ireland's 'mental colonization', which he put down to its lack of 'world image' and its tendency to regard the Irish experience as unique, and lacking anything to contribute to the wider human experience. His analysis of the causes of Ireland's 'mental colonization' is evocative of similar thought patterns in Wales:

> A factor which encourages this mental habit is our geographical situation in combination with our history. The fact that we have only one other country – in the sense of nation-state – adjacent to us means that we have habitual contact with it alone. On top of that, we have had a colonial relationship with Britain and are therefore habituated to regarding it – or more particularly England, and actually the English south east – as the human norm. This combination of circumstances is reflected in that familiar Irish way of criticising something in Ireland which begins by saying that such and such is scandalous and then goes on: 'Elsewhere, in Britain, for instance, it's done differently, it's done better', etc. (Fennell, 1983: 134)

Fennell's critique comes from a perspective which decries the 'imperial world image of London–New York–Washington' with its liberal and consumerist paradigms. However, the concept of 'mental colonization' does raise interesting questions for emergent political entities, questions which echo the concept of acculturation mentioned above. While the symbolism of independence is celebrated, mentally the 'colonized' still accept the view that their strengths lie in creativity, while the real business of making money, organizing government or developing policy ideas comes from the colonizers. For example, it has been argued that the Roman Catholic Church acted as an agent of 'cultural inversion' in Quebec (Kahn, 1986: 31). In the French Canadian case, and, it could be argued, in the Welsh and Irish cases as well, this 'cultural inversion' (connected in Wales with Nonconformist culture rather than with the Catholic Church, perhaps) traditionally took the form of an aversion to technical, scientific and commercial subjects, and an emphasis instead on the humanities, with an eye to the professions or the clergy as the pinnacle of success.

Of course, Fennell was writing in the early 1980s. The last decade has witnessed an economic and social transformation in the Republic partly due to the injection of EU Objective 1 funding. A country in which emigration to Britain or the US used to be the norm for graduates is now one of net in-migration, with a young, well-educated workforce. Contemporary Ireland has enjoyed its own 'quiet revolution'.

A 'POSTCOLONIAL' WALES?

By the time John Redwood took over at the Welsh Office in 1993 it had become commonplace to hear the succession of Conservative secretaries of states for Wales sitting for English seats described as viceroys, with the colonial analogy to the fore (Osmond, 1995). Interestingly, Redwood's Welsh political adviser, Hywel Williams, recommended E. M. Forster's *A Passage to India* to him, as the best description of the Welsh relationship with the English: 'A subjugated race wished to please, and, in over-egging the pudding, succeeded in annoying both the conquerors and in exacerbating its own latent self-disgust' (Williams, 1998).

Through developing postcolonial analogies and drawing comparisons, particularly with the Republic of Ireland, the particularity of the Welsh situation becomes evident. Pre-Celtic Tiger days, Ireland combined an overt opposition to its former rulers and an elevation of the symbols of the new nation-state with their emphasis on Catholicism and Gaelicism. If Fennell's analysis is taken on board, the combination promoted the continuance of a mental deference to the British way of doing things in those spheres not covered by culture or religion. Wales, however, has at once a much closer relationship to England (being deemed part of it for certain periods of its history) and yet it is also, in some ways, especially due to the presence of the language, a much more 'foreign' place to the English, a point made by the first minister, Rhodri Morgan, on a number of occasions. The language, of course, will often have a bearing on how the Welsh individual perceives his or her relationship with England. Historically, some parts of society in Welsh-speaking rural Wales may be said to have manifested the kind of cultural 'fortress nationalism' found in Quebec before the Quiet Revolution. At the same time, other largely non-Welsh-speakers, particularly – in the middle years of the twentieth century – those on the left, labelled the Welsh language and the focus on a Welsh cultural dimension as anti-progressive forces. These tensions have been well analysed elsewhere: they are referred to here but as an indication of the many ways in which Hywel Williams's account of his 'subjugated race' to its new 'viceroy' failed to take into account the diversity and specificity of Welsh opinions and attitudes.

Nevertheless, it is the brief of this chapter to consider the functioning of the devolution settlement in Wales in the context of patterns of response observed in other political units which have undergone a 'postcolonial' experience. Of course, a striking difference between the Welsh situation and that of many other nations is the modesty of its self-government ambitions. Some would argue that the limited nature of the Welsh devolution settlement is in itself evidence of a Welsh 'cultural cringe', or self-mistrust. While the road to the creation of the Scottish Parliament began with the Claim of Right, and the Scottish Constitutional Convention built a broad consensus around the values and structure of the Scottish Parliament, the proposals for Welsh devolution emerged from a Welsh Labour Party contemplating devolution once again after successive Conservative election victories, and having to accommodate a range of views from the minimalist 'devosceptics' to the advocates of a Welsh Parliament (A. Thomas 1995, 1996). The Welsh settlement reflected what its architects deemed possible to sell to the party and to the electorate. Accordingly the original Labour Party consultation paper, *Shaping the Vision*, rejected primary legislative powers, tax-raising powers, any form of proportional representation (PR), and recommended a local government-style committee structure. A rethink occurred on PR (central direction), and the Additional Member System (AMS) was adopted. The committee system, 'part of a compromise . . . to ensure support within the Labour Party', was effectively ditched by Ron Davies, using the National Assembly Advisory Group and making common cause with other parties: during the parliamentary passage of the Government of Wales Bill a delegation clause was inserted allowing for a de facto cabinet system which made the Assembly more 'parliamentary' (Laffin and Thomas, 2000).

Whether or not this very cautious approach to the devolution settlement in Wales is indicative of a Welsh 'cultural cringe' can be assessed by examining the relationship of Wales with England, Scotland and, to some extent, the Republic of Ireland. The historic, economic, political and administrative integration of Wales with England ('for Wales, see England', as used to be said in encyclopaedias) underscores the Welsh self-image of dependence and supports the argument of those who would insist that Wales is 'too small' or 'too poor' to aspire to the autonomy of Scotland. A more pejorative mindset sees Wales as 'too divided' to rule itself; such a view clearly carries echoes of a colonialist paradigm, and involves the internalization by Welsh people of an external perspective which sees Wales as ungovernable without the assertion of an outside authority. Further, those affected by a self-image of dependence can see Wales as 'too parochial' for self-government, in a genuflection towards metropolitan received wisdom rather than colonialism per se. It is fair to say that many of these views have permeated Welsh politics and society during the last century, and have formed part of the 'mental maps' of Welsh policy actors and the Welsh public.

In this context, and given the uncertain mandate delivered by the referendum in 1997, there was a pressure on the Assembly to offset such negative assessments of its potential and justify its existence by 'adding value' to the pre-devolution political arrangements (Laffin and Thomas, 2000). The Welsh administration, or Welsh Assembly Government (WAG) as it came to be known, talks of the pursuit a 'Welsh Way' in policy. On the other hand, there is also a view that the Assembly should not pursue distinct Welsh policies 'for the sake of it', and that not all policies need to be stamped 'made in Wales'. In considering the development of policy in Wales, post-devolution, the pressures imposed by the 'cultural cringe' factor are by no means irrelevant, however. The rest of this chapter will consider the development of policy in Wales post-devolution, and the question of how far the Assembly has succeeded in 'making a difference' within the context of these negative viewpoints.

On close reflection the protestation that Wales is 'too small' to pursue certain policies or to enjoy autonomy is not so much to do with size (numerous autonomous polities exist which are significantly smaller than Wales) as with the historic level of integration with England. Scotland, for example, with its separate legal and education systems, always appeared to have the potential for autonomy, for not being part of 'England and Wales'. The very nature of the settlement locks the National Assembly for Wales into a situation where it must remain aware of developments in Westminster, must petition central government if it requires primary legislation, and is unclear about the distribution of responsibilities between the Assembly and the centre (Laffin, Thomas and Thomas, 2003). Moreover, the de facto and mental permeability of the border with England can act as a constraint.

With regard to the view that Wales is too poor to run itself, it is certainly the case that the National Assembly for Wales, as currently established, is almost entirely dependent on central funds received through the Barnett formula, and on other grants

from the Treasury. Thus WAG has to prioritize its policy object-
ives and spending within a fixed budget. It cannot simply pass the
costs of new policy initiatives on to Welsh taxpayers or central
government. On the other hand, it is largely free of hypotheca-
tion, though some would argue that this means that it ultimately
lacks the crucial financial accountability to the electorate. Yet it
could be argued that WAG would face potential electoral consequences if its spending trade-offs produced outcomes which
adversely affected significant parts of the electorate – for example,
if it switched spending away from health so that waiting-lists
lengthened significantly, then it could be expected that the electorate would exact punishment (Laffin, Thomas and Thomas,
2003: 5). Furthermore, the spending announcements by Whitehall
departments can lead to expectations for comparable expenditure
from stakeholders. Some pressure groups have already learnt to
cherry-pick – praising and supporting Welsh divergence if they
oppose English policy but happy to demand comparable spending
commitments to England's should it suit them.

The Barnett formula automatically passes spending increases or
decreases on to the devolved administrations. A decision to
impose user charges for a service, accompanied by a cut in public
subsidy in England, would be likely to place considerable pressure
on the devolved administrations to follow the centre. There is no
doubt that Welsh devolution operates within a financially
constrained environment. It is debatable, however, whether
attaining tax-raising powers would relieve those constraints in the
short term. As I have argued elsewhere,

> given the relative poverty of Wales compared with the wealthier
> English regions, that proportion [of tax revenue] would be quite small
> and Wales would still require considerable financial assistance from
> central government through some equalisation formula. Thus the
> acquisition of limited tax powers would not significantly correct the
> imbalance. (Laffin, Thomas and Thomas, 2003: 5)

What weight should we attach to the notion that Wales is too
divided to govern itself? It is true that Wales is characterized by
multiple political identities reflecting its recent history of concentrated industrialization and subsequent Anglicization in linguistic
terms, and the persistence of a Welsh-speaking society focused on
the rural areas. Moreover, there is a geographical divide between
north and south, historically reinforced by lines of communication

that ran east–west rather than north–south, and meant that in north Wales Cardiff was perceived as more distant than London. An element of distrust of devolution related to geography remains a feature of Welsh life. Despite the design of the Assembly it is still widely perceived as south-Wales-dominated, especially in the north. People in north-east Wales in particular stress a greater closeness and integration with north-west England. Numerous commentators have pointed out that this is exacerbated by the fact that many people watch television news from north-west England. In the 2003 Assembly election, the Electoral Commission found that

> Only one person in four felt that newspapers gave enough coverage to the election while a plurality (41%) said that there was insufficient information. Fluent Welsh-speakers, the youngest respondents and those living in the North were most likely to claim under-coverage by newspapers. (Electoral Commission, 2003)

Head teachers in the north east, for example, found themselves being asked why their schools were not receiving additional money directly from the Treasury like their English colleagues across the border. This was because the Welsh Assembly Government took a different approach to its funding arrangements, but many people were only aware of what was being reported in the English context.

Lastly, with regard to the accusation of parochialism it could be argued that WAG finds itself in a 'no-win' situation. The powers of the Assembly militate against the grand gesture. In some cases the Assembly has been able to achieve all or part of what it wanted, but it has had to resort to complex arrangements to get things done. One example is student hardship grants, which depend on voluntary cooperation by LEAs; the policy cannot be enforced by the Assembly. Nevertheless, it can be argued that the Assembly has considerable 'policy space' despite its lack of primary legislative powers (Laffin, Thomas and Thomas, 2003: 9). Westminster has passed Welsh-only legislation such as the Children's Commissioner Act 2001, and legislation with Welsh-specific clauses such as the Learning and Skills Act 2000 and the Care Standards Act 2000. These create policy space in allowing clear divergence from English policy, for example, the retention of Community Health Councils in Wales and their abolition in England. Furthermore, some significant Assembly policy goals do not require formal legislative powers. WAG policy papers, such as *The Learning Country* (2002) for education and *Freedom and Responsibility* (2002) in local government, included significant policy proposals not requiring primary legislation (Laffin, Thomas and Thomas, 2003). Paradoxically, the accusation of parochialism is implicit in the assertion that WAG is diverging from Westminster in terms of policy 'for the sake of it', the implication being that WAG at one level might be choosing to diverge from central government simply in order to flex its devolved muscles.

CONCLUSION

In the Introduction, the question was posed as to the extent to which Welsh policy actors had developed a self-confident approach to the new political environment, and whether any parallels could be identified with the 'postcolonial' experiences of the comparable polities of the Irish Republic and Quebec. What is clear is that Welsh policy-makers are operating within a devolved settlement that is more complex and imposes greater constraints than the Canadian federal system does on Quebec. However, the thrust of the argument about postcolonialism in the context of this chapter is the extent to which it imposes *mental* constraints – or what Fennell terms 'mental maps'. Welsh political culture has historically had a self-image of dependence, seeing itself as 'too small' or 'too poor' to aspire to autonomy. There has also been a mindset that Wales is 'too divided' or 'too parochial', which implies that Wales is ungovernable without the assertion of an outside authority. On the other hand, an impetus exists to pursue a distinctive Welsh policy agenda to 'justify' devolution.

The *contested* nature of Welsh devolution remains a key factor in charting 'mental maps'. The *petit oui* of the 1997 referendum led to the view that devolution is not the 'settled will' of the Welsh electorate. The Electoral Commission report on the 2003 election revealed that only a little over a third of survey respondents claimed to 'know a great deal or a fair amount' about the work of the Assembly (Electoral Commission, 2003: 17). Political culture in Wales is 'bi-focal' with people continuing to engage with Westminster on one level and local/Welsh politics on another (A. Thomas, forthcoming). At this early stage the new political landscape is unclear: Welsh policy-makers are operating within a political environment where the public are still attuned to the Westminster agenda and other policy actors are often pursuing a rational choice strategy which plays the Assembly off against Westminster.

While it would be untrue to say that all traces of the 'cultural cringe' have completely departed from the Welsh political landscape, the defining characteristic of policy-makers within the new Wales would appear to be pragmatism. The old maxim about politics being the 'art of the possible' is writ large in a complex Welsh devolution settlement which rests on a delicate framework of intergovernmental relations with Westminster and Whitehall and within the political parties (Laffin, Thomas and Webb, 2000; Laffin, Taylor and Thomas, 2004). Of course, WAG finds itself accused of timidity by the opposition parties, yet if part of the motivation is to build up a body of achievement to 'justify' devolution, WAG has to set itself goals that are achievable. Furthermore, the requirement to carve out distinctive policies in a constrained framework can provide an opportunity for innovation which militates against the 'mental colonization' of the newly decolonized as identified by Fennell, who seek merely to ape the former colonizer.

So to what extent can the Welsh in Wales be deemed *maîtres chez nous* – 'masters in our own house'? There is no simple answer to this: the structure of the Welsh devolution settlement does not suggest anything as straightforward as a self-contained dwelling – something more like sheltered housing perhaps? Unlike Ireland and Quebec, where 'postcolonial' developments took place within clearly defined political and legal structures, devolution in the UK, and particularly Welsh devolution, is seeing a recasting of the UK constitution in terms of legal innovation and the emergence of new rules (Rawlings, 2003). There is evidence that those engaged with the political process within Wales are willing to seize whatever levers present themselves to develop policies distinctive to Wales, although eager to avoid the sort of confrontation that could threaten the whole settlement. But other evidence, not least recent Electoral Commission findings, suggests that much of the Welsh public have not fully taken on board the new political environment.

Is Wales 'postcolonial'? It is certainly undergoing a period of constitutional transformation within its borders but it also exists in the wider political context of the UK, the European Union and a globalized world. These present complex challenges for the modern polity which go beyond the historical relationship between the colonizer and the decolonized.

REFERENCES

Allen, K. (2000). *The Celtic Tiger: The Myth of Social Partnership in Ireland*, Manchester: University of Manchester Press.
Davies, N. (1999). *The Isles*, London: Macmillan.
Electoral Commission (2003). National Assembly for Wales Election 2003 Opinion Research Report, Cardiff.
Fennell, D. (1983). *The State of the Nation: Ireland since the Sixties*, Dublin: Ward River Press.
Hechter, M. (1975). *Internal Colonialism: The Celtic Fringe in British National Development*, Berkeley: University of California Press.
Kahn, L. S. (1986). 'The impact of cultural identity on Quebec education', *Quebec Studies*, 4.
Laffin, M., Taylor, G. and Thomas, A. (2004). 'Devolution and party organization: the case of the Wales Labour Party', *Contemporary Wales*, 16, 53–74.
Laffin, M, and Thomas, A. (2000). 'Designing the Welsh Assembly', *Parliamentary Affairs*, 53, 3, 557–90.
Laffin, M., Thomas, A. and Thomas, I. (2003). *Future Options for the Welsh Assembly: An Assessment of the Powers of the National Assembly for Wales*, submission to the Richard Commission, Glamorgan Policy Centre, University of Glamorgan, Pontypridd.
Laffin, M., Thomas, A. and Webb, A. (2000). 'Intergovernmental relations after devolution: the National Assembly for Wales', *Political Quarterly*, 71, 2, 223–33.
Landow, G. P. (2000). 'Why I use the term "Postcolonial" or some words from your webmaster', *Political Discourse – Theories of Colonialism and Postcolonialism*, *http://www.scholars.nus.edu.sg/landow/post/polidiscourse/themes/gplpoco.html*.
Osmond, J. (1995). *Welsh Europeans*, Bridgend: Seren.
O'Sullivan See, K. (1986). *First World Nationalisms: Class and Ethnic Politics in Northern Ireland and Quebec*, Chicago: University of Chicago Press.
Rawlings, R. (2003). *Delineating Wales*, Cardiff: University of Wales Press.
Smith, A. D. (1991). *National Identity*, Harmondsworth: Penguin Books.
Thomas, A. (1995). 'The Welsh Assembly debate: 1979 re-visited?', *Public Money and Management*, 15, 2, 6–8.

Thomas, A. (1996). 'Wales and devolution: a constitutional footnote?', *Public Money and Management*, 15, 4, 21–9.

Thomas, A. (forthcoming). 'Political culture and civil society in Wales', in D. Dunkerley and A. Thompson (eds), *Civil Society and Policy Making in Wales*, Cardiff: University of Wales Press.

Thomas, N. (1977). 'Neo-colonial Wales', *Planet*, 36, February/March.

Williams, H. (1998). *The Guilty Men*, London: Aurum Press.

6

A New Beginning or the Beginning of the End? The Welsh Language in Postcolonial Wales

DYLAN PHILLIPS

On Tuesday evening, 13 February 1962, the following warning was issued over the BBC Wales airwaves:

> [P]e ceid unrhyw fath o hunan-lywodraeth i Gymru cyn arddel ac arfer yr iaith Gymraeg yn iaith swyddogol . . . byddai tranc yr iaith yn gynt nag y bydd ei thranc hi dan Lywodraeth Loegr.

> (If any kind of self-government for Wales were obtained before the Welsh language was acknowledged and used as an official language . . . its demise would be quicker than it will be under English rule.) (Lewis, 1962: 30; trans., 141)

These were the final words of Saunders Lewis's seminal radio broadcast *Tynged yr Iaith* ('Fate of the Language'). This broadcast has repeatedly been celebrated as the most influential action by any one individual in the Welsh language's fortunes during the last half-century. It was the catalyst for the formation of the Welsh Language Society (Cymdeithas yr Iaith Gymraeg) and has been the inspiration for generations of language activists and campaigners in Wales. During those past four decades, however, the main thrust of Lewis's doom-and-gloom polemic has been proved completely wrong, namely his prediction 'y bydd terfyn ar y Gymraeg yn iaith fyw, ond parhau'r tueddiad presennol, tua dechrau'r unfed ganrif ar hugain' ('that Welsh will end as a living language, should the present trend continue, about the beginning of the twenty-first century') (Lewis, 1962: 5; trans., 127). The disproving of this prophecy has occurred in part as a consequence of his lecture, rather than in spite of it. But his warning about the demise of Welsh coming about more quickly in a 'postcolonial', or at least, post-devolution, Wales is only now in the process of being put to the test.

Elsewhere in this volume it is evident that there are conflicting opinions as to in what context Wales can, or even should, be considered a 'postcolonial' country. Many dispute the use of such a term as 'postcolonial' to describe the Welsh experience, and much uncertainty remains as to its actual meaning. However, within Welsh-language political discourse it would appear that terms such as 'colonial' and 'postcolonial' hold no such uncertainties. The idea that Wales has been colonized has been a central theme in Welsh-language politics for many years, and has manifested itself in numerous articles and discussions in Welsh political journals such as *Y Ddraig Goch*, *Barn* and *Tafod y Ddraig*. The semantics of the 'language struggle' discourse has been particularly loaded with references to colonization, from the description of Whitehall policy in Wales as 'colonial policy', to the ironic labelling of the secretary of state for Wales as the 'governor general'. From the 1960s to the present day, protest speeches made by language campaigners from the dock of various court-houses around Wales, emotive at the best of times, have consistently made reference to Wales as a subjugated country and to English law as the tool of a colonial power protecting its own interests of possession and control. When the popular singer Dafydd Iwan stood before the magistrates of Builth in September 1967 for his part in the bilingual road-fund campaign, for example, he used all the patriotic rhetoric he could muster in an attempt to dissuade his betters from finding him guilty of mindless law-breaking:

> Nepell o'r stafell hon saif carreg i nodi'r fan lle syrthiodd Llywelyn, yr olaf o'n tywysogion. Trwy ryw ryfedd wyrth, goroesodd ei bobl a'i iaith i'n dyddiau ni. Ond os gweinyddir cyfraith sy'n amddiffyn trais Lloegr ar ein treftadaeth ni lawer yn hwy, fe fydd carreg Cilmeri yn garreg fedd nid i dywysog yn unig, ond i'n hiaith ac i'n cenedl hefyd.

> (Not far from this room stands a stone marking the place where Llywelyn, the last of our princes, was slain. By some strange miracle, his people and his language have survived unto this day. But if the law that protects the onslaught of English violence on our heritage is upheld for much longer, then not only will the stone at Cilmeri be a gravestone for our prince, but for our language and nation as well.) (Iwan, 1967; my translation).

Since the publication of its first manifesto in 1972, the Welsh Language Society has consistently referred to Wales as a colonized country in its main policy documents. Cynog Dafis (then Davies), in that first manifesto, linked the inferior status of the language during the 1960s to the country's economic exploitation by England:

> Fel y diraddiwyd y Gymraeg yn ei gwlad ei hun er mwyn clymu y Bobl Gymreig yn dynnach wrth Loegr, a suddo o'u hunaniaeth yn yr hunan-iaeth 'Brydeinig' newydd, yn yr un modd hefyd y clymwyd Cymru wrth economi Lloegr, gwthio arni swyddogaeth drefedigaethol: ei gwneud yn gloddfa defnyddiau crai, yn lo a llechi a haearn a dur a dŵr, a'i throi yn awr yn faes chwarae, yn anialwch lliwgar a gwyllt a blodeuog at wasanaeth y conwrbasiynau anferth sy'n gorwedd ar hyd ei chyrion. Un yw darostyngiad Cymru – ei threisio'n ddiwylliannol a'i hegsbloetio'n economaidd.

> (Just as the Welsh language has been downgraded in its own land in order to bind the Welsh people closer to England and to lose their own identity in the new 'British' identity, so also the Welsh economy has been bound to that of England. A colonial function has been forced on it. It has been a source of raw materials, coal, slate, iron, steel and water. Now it is being turned into a playground, a picturesque wilder-ness at the service of the sprawling conurbations along its borders. The subjection of Wales is all one and the same – its ravished culture and its exploited economy.) (Davies, 1972: 39; trans., 124)

Within Welsh-language culture, this sort of discourse has been evident since the 1960s not only in weighty articles and editorials but also in popular protest, as expressed through the medium of pop songs, cartoons, and satirical poetry and prose. It enjoyed its heyday during the build-up to the investiture of Charles Windsor as 'Prince of Wales' in Caernarfon in 1969 – the ultimate symbol in nationalist eyes of colonial rule. As the editor of *Tafod y Ddraig* pointed out on the eve of the investiture, what right had the Queen of England's eldest son to call himself the Prince of Wales? – 'Teitl anrhydeddus a ddygwyd oddi ar y Cymry yn awr eu gwendid ydyw a thra arfer ef gan aelod o genedl arall, erys yn symbol o ddarostyngiad y genedl Gymreig' ('It is an honourable title stolen from the Welsh people in their hour of weakness and while it is used by a member of another nation, it will remain a badge of our nation's conquest') (*Tafod y Ddraig*, 1969). The painstaking and weary grind of having to wrestle for each slight concession to the language in terms of another bilingual leaflet or sign also deepened this sense of being governed by an unsympathetic alien government, under which the indigenous people had to fight for a begrudging acceptance of their difference by their colonial masters and a tokenistic tolerance of their vulgar vernacular. Consequently, colonial terminology and references were endemic in Welsh-language political discourse, especially during the 1960s and 1970s, as a collective sense of being treated as a tiresome nuisance that stood in the way of a homogeneous, monolingual British society and culture found expression in the rise of a popular nationalist movement that swept from Caernarfon to Caerffili.

After generations of common usage, this type of discourse holds very strong connotations for Welsh speakers today. It is hardly surprising, therefore, that the advent of devolution was frequently hailed as a watershed between the 'colonial' and 'postcolonial' periods in Welsh history; this was a recurring theme in Welsh-language political discourse following the success of the 'Yes' vote in the 1997 referendum. The historical significance of the result was dwelt upon over and over again. As John Davies, Bwlchllan, remarked in his role as one of S4C's pundits the night the votes came in and the outcome was announced, this was the most significant day in the Welsh nation's history since the collapse of Owain Glyndŵr's rebellion in the fifteenth century. A semblance of sovereignty had been returned to the people. Neither is it surprising, given that Welsh speakers seemed to be more in tune with this sense of 'casting off the English yoke', that they were proportionally much more likely to have cast an affirmative vote in both the 1979 and 1997 referenda on devolution than their English-speaking compatriots. Indeed, in the numerous studies on indicators of national identity that have been conducted in recent years, it would seem that Welsh speakers have consistently been more aware of their Welshness than English speakers in Wales, and much less likely to consider themselves as British (see, for example, Balsom, 1985; Jones and Trystan, 1999). To many Welsh speakers in particular, therefore, the terms 'post-devolution Wales' and 'postcolonial Wales' are synonymous.

Over the years, many people in Wales have considered the battle for the survival of the language and the battle for political freedom as being two sides of the same coin. This was particularly true of the fathers of modern nationalism in Wales, including Michael D. Jones, Emrys ap Iwan and Saunders Lewis. They were convinced that political freedom and self-government would be the saving grace of the Welsh language, which in their eyes was the most important element of Welsh national identity. Emrys ap Iwan, in a characteristically emotive address in 1895 that links language survival to political freedom, stated that 'y Gymraeg yw'r unig wrthglawdd rhyngom a diddymdra' ('the Welsh language is the only barrier between us and extermination'); in order to preserve the language and Welsh nationhood he calls upon his countrymen to form an unified political party to 'rhydd-hau'r Dywysogaeth oddi wrth yr ormes Seisnig' ('free the principality from English oppression') (ap Iwan, 1937: 23–41). However, his appeal fell on deaf ears until Saunders Lewis, a generation later, led the creation of Plaid Genedlaethol Cymru in 1925, a party which despite having as its main objective the attainment of self-government for Wales, had as much interest in language issues as it had in political affairs, if not more so during its first few years of existence (Lloyd, 1988: 225, 245).

But as the twentieth century progressed, and as the language slowly but surely lost ground and became critically threatened even in its heartlands, a number of nationalists came to the conclusion that saving the Welsh language was more important than gaining self-government. Again, Saunders Lewis became the main proponent of this argument and *Tynged yr Iaith* the most famous expression of the revised priority in the debate concerning language and political autonomy. Indeed, Lewis even argued that '[y] Gymraeg yw'r unig arf a eill ddisodli llywodraeth y Sais yng Nghymru' ('Welsh is the only weapon that can dislodge English rule in Wales') (Lewis, 1963). Moreover, in addition to the increasing concerns about the viability of Welsh as a living community language, some leading figures in Wales also began voicing their anxieties about the implications of language loss to national identity. One of the most influential and respected political thinkers in Wales at the time was J. R. Jones, professor and head of the Philosophy Department at University of Wales College, Swansea. In his classic book *Prydeindod* ('Britishness'), published in January 1966, he warned that the very existence of the Welsh as an identifiable people was in severe jeopardy, and was being slowly eradicated. He argued that there were two inter-twined (or interpenetrative) elements to a *people*, namely a territory and a language. However, if the tie between these two elements were to be broken, the Welsh would surely lose their identity and cease to exist as a people (Jones, 1966: 9–33). Consequently, in his unswerving support for Welsh-language activists, particularly the members of the Welsh Language Society at the height of their opposition to the Investiture in 1969, J. R. Jones argued fervently that the Welsh language was the ideal weapon in the battle for the 'Welsh cause' and an instrument to awaken in the Welsh people 'cynddaredd eu gwahanrwydd' ('a furious sense of their difference') (Jones, 1964).

Thereafter, using Welsh as an instrument to bring about political autonomy became a feature in the writings of many language campaigners, particularly during the 1960s and 1970s. It was apparent that notions of freedom and language maintenance still travelled together hand in hand, although having reversed positions in terms of priority. But there was also a danger, as Saunders Lewis pointed out, if political freedom were to be gained before the language had been saved. In the light of his warning, we must now ask ourselves to what extent has devolution impacted upon the language thus far, and what future can we expect for Welsh in a 'postcolonial' Wales?

There is no denying the fact that the creation of the National Assembly for Wales in 1999 was a momentous milestone in the history of the Welsh language. As well as being an important achievement in itself, providing Wales at last with its first taste of self-government in 700 years, it also established a new political forum which would have tremendous power and influence over the future of the language. During the last few centuries the history of the Welsh language has included a number of such milestones – with most of them, however, pointing the way towards its terminal decline. This trend was rampant during the first half of the twentieth century as growing numbers of observers foretold the fate of the language – some with despair, but others with great satisfaction. According to the editor of *The Times* on the occasion of the publication of the 1961 census results, the time had come for the Welsh people to free themselves from the shackles of the past and join the modern world by finally letting the language go (*The Times*, 12 September 1962). By the 1960s its future did indeed look very bleak. The total number of Welsh speakers in Wales had fallen dramatically since the turn of the century, disappearing at a rate of one every three-quarters of an hour by the 1950s. It seemed as if the objective of the Act of Union of 1536 was about to be realized, namely that the 'sinister Usages and

Customs' of Wales – including most particularly the Welsh language – were to be utterly 'extirp[ed]' (Bowen, 1908: 75–6). Since the Union, the language in effect had been completely ostracized from the political, administrative and legislative life of Wales, and added to the enforced inferior status of Welsh were all the pressures of a new age, which included an English educational system, modern communications, the mass media, deindustrialization and population migration.

Despite all these pressures, however, the Welsh language had survived long enough to see its second millennium. In fact, Welsh is still spoken today by over half a million people in Wales, representing 20.5 per cent of the population aged three and over, according to the latest 2001 census figures. These figures include an increase in overall numbers of 13.3 per cent since 1991, an increase described by John Aitchison and Harold Carter as nothing less than 'momentous' (Aitchinson and Carter, 2003/4). The decline of the language seems to have been finally reversed and there are positive signs of a particularly substantial rise in the number of young people between the ages of three and fifteen who can speak the language, especially in the Anglicized south-east. Districts such as Monmouthshire, Torfaen, Newport and Blaenau Gwent have seen staggering increases in excess of 300 per cent in the numbers of Welsh-speakers during the last decade. Indeed, of the twenty-two local authority areas in Wales, fifteen experienced a rise in the percentage of Welsh speakers since 1991. The district that experienced the greatest decrease in the percentage of speakers was Ceredigion in the rural west (a significant reduction of 7.3 per cent), prompting the pressure group Cymuned, in particular, to maintain that this was the direct result of a renewed process of colonization in the Welsh-speaking heartland. After the local authority unveiled its plans to permit over 7,000 new homes to be built during the next fifteen years in Ceredigion, despite the fact that there is very little natural growth in the net population to warrant such large-scale developments, Dafydd Ieuan, a leading Cymuned member in Ceredigion, warned that 'Bellach mae'r mewnfudo wedi cyrraedd y fath ryferthwy nes bod hyd yn oed y caerau mwyaf cadarn ar ddadfeilio' ('Inmigration has now reached such epic proportions that even the most robust bastions of the language are on the brink of ruin') (Ieuan, 2001: 26–7).

At the same time, the more general reversal of the decline has also seen the status of Welsh increase in many spheres previously closed to the language. Since the 1960s Welsh has enjoyed a marked increase in its use in central and local government administration and in the legal system; its official status has been the subject of two Acts of Parliament; it has gained a Welsh-medium radio station and television station; and every child in Wales receives instruction in Welsh up to the age of sixteen. It is even possible to savour the gastronomic delights of a Welsh-language version of the famous Big Mac in Wales – namely the 'Mac Mawr' – possibly the only instance throughout the world where the corporate giant has conceded to rename its flagship product in any language other than American. Moreover, on a much more significant note, whereas many Welsh men and women in the early twentieth century saw no purpose in transmitting the language to their children, Welsh now enjoys colossal good will and growing support from those unable to speak it. The results of a study undertaken on behalf of the Welsh Language Board in 2000 by Beaufort Research showed that 61 per cent of even the non-Welsh-speakers surveyed supported the increased use of Welsh. The survey also showed that 75 per cent of all the respondents believed that the language would survive for the foreseeable future (Beaufort Research, 2000: 8–10).

But one of the most important developments in recent years in the language's situation remains the creation of the National Assembly itself. That Welsh survived long enough to witness the inception of that institution was remarkable enough; during the consultation period that preceded the Assembly's coming into being in 1999, there was even talk of giving it the heady status of one of Wales's two 'official languages' (*Recommendations*, 1998). That recommendation (number 22) by the Advisory Group under the leadership of John Elfed Jones was, however, one of the very few that sadly went astray; it never featured amongst the Assembly's final standing orders. On a more positive note, a declaration was made in February 2000 by the Post-sixteen Education and Training Committee, in reply to evidence presented before it the previous autumn by the Welsh Language Board, that it 'strongly supports the aim of creating a bilingual Wales' (Welsh Language Board, 2000: 1). Two years later, following a lengthy period of consultation and evidence-gathering, the Assembly's Culture and Education Committees launched a 'ground-breaking' joint report entitled *Our Language: Its Future*. The report spoke, in grandiose terms, of committing the Assembly to a serious and concerted effort at holistic language planning which would: 'promote language growth and ultimately lead to a truly bilingual Wales'. This 'truly bilingual Wales' was defined thus:

> In a truly bilingual Wales both Welsh and English will flourish and will be treated as equal. A bilingual Wales means a country where people can choose to live their lives through the medium of either or both languages; a country where the presence of two national languages and cultures is a source of pride and strength to us all. (NAW, 2002)

With that incontrovertible declaration of intent already agreed upon across the four parties at the Assembly, Jenny Randerson, the minister for culture at the time, had a clear sense of what was expected of the Welsh Assembly Government. By the beginning of 2003, the minister had drafted a National Action Plan entitled *Iaith Pawb* ('Everybody's Language') that was a major break-through in terms of bringing language planning into mainstream policy-making in Wales (WAG, 2003). The document was far from unflawed, not least in that it severely underestimated the funds that would be required actually to fulfil its ambitious task, and completely omitted any attempt at tackling the thorny issues of out-migration and in-migration. However, it still represented a first step on the road towards a national strategy for the language to be implemented by a democratically elected Welsh government.

So, seemingly at least, the future of Welsh in a 'postcolonial' Wales appears promising, and understandably many optimistic observers have predicted that the creation of the Assembly marks a new dawn in the history of the language. This complete turn-around in the position of Welsh, however, has not been achieved overnight and cannot be attributed to the effect of devolution. Instead, it is the culmination of a long-drawn-out struggle to wrest from various tiers of authority representing the old 'colo-nial' Wales an increasing number of concessions for the language. It has yet to be seen whether or not the new 'postcolonial' regime in Wales will be more pliable. What is certain, nevertheless, is that with the powers – albeit limited – of devolved government and self-determination at their disposal, the new political representa-tives of Wales can now build a future for the language. The Assembly has the power to develop the process of bilingual normalization, to improve and evolve Welsh-language education and to instigate measures designed to promote greater use of the language in the public and private sectors. It also has the power and the opportunity to tackle some of the economic and social forces that have so long militated against the prosperity of Welsh. Probably the most heartening aspect of the National Action Plan is the commitment to make Welsh a permanent cross-cutting subject for all policy areas within the Assembly, rather than leaving it compartmentalized and cut off from all other aspects of life, or dealt with as if it existed within a vacuum (WAG, 2003: 12). And as an 'added value' to this new governmental policy, the potential positive repercussions for the language in the populace are also tremendous. It is to be hoped that the new awareness of all things Welsh, and the growth in awareness of national identity that seems to have accompanied devolution, will also promote Welsh cultural identity and inspire many to learn and use the language, as has happened in other countries, such as Finland, in the wake of political autonomy.

However, supporters of the language will have to be very careful not to pin too many of their hopes on the Assembly and its National Action Plan. After all, not every country that has gained political self-determination has also witnessed a revival in the fortunes of its native language and culture. The establishment of the Irish Free State in 1921, for instance, proved to be a major milestone in the decline of the Irish language. Even though the constitution of *Saorstat Éireann* made Irish the official national language of Ireland, and made provisions for the establishment of a minister for language and culture in the Dáil, self-government actually had a negative effect on the fortunes of Irish (see Ó hAilin, 1969: 90–1000). Since 1921, Irish has suffered great losses in the numbers of its speakers, even in the officially defined Gaeltacht, which has been struggling against massive economic and social problems since its creation. The experience of Ireland should serve as a warning to Wales. Given the emphatic nature of the commitment to creating a bilingual Wales declared in *Iaith Pawb*, it hardly seems likely that Welsh will be reserved for ceremonial duties only, as was the Irish language by the Irish government. It will surely not be kept as an ornament to be admired now and again, rather than actively used and fostered as a legitimate medium of communication and expression, and as a living community language. None the less, it is far too soon for the language movement in Wales to set aside its campaigning. According to contemporary analysis, the Gaelic-language supporters of the

1920s in Ireland, headed by Conradh na Gaelige, were as much to blame as the politicians for the demise of Irish: 'by foolishly presuming that the establishment of an Irish State ensured the preservation of Irish culture, the League left the State with no effective critic, with no permanent prodder of its conscience' (Mac Aodha, 1972: 20–30). It seems that having managed to realize the age-old dream of *Éire saor*, the leaders of the Irish movement forgot that they had also intended to strive for an *Éire Gaelach*.

The Welsh-language movement will need to keep its wits about it for the foreseeable future. Many problems still face the language, even within the new devolved set-up of government in Wales. Despite the cross-party agreement to support it, the language is still all too frequently used by the political parties as a stick to wield against each other in an attempt to score some petty points. Ironically, the Assembly has given various enemies of the language a platform upon which to voice their opposition to official support for it. Even before the first elections in 1999, three prospective candidates for the Assembly immediately declared their intention to campaign on a ticket opposing compulsory Welsh-language education. Since then, the contentious issue of the effect of in-migration on Welsh-speaking heartland communities certainly poured petrol on the whole language problem, and unfortunately the debate became increasingly sinister as some contributors deliberately tried to confuse issues of language with those of race (for a discussion of the race debate, see McGuinness, 2003). For Plaid Cymru, the insinuations undoubtedly contributed to their heavy losses in the second Assembly elections; as Richard Wyn Jones and Roger Scully point out, there were obvious problems with being perceived as being 'too Welsh' (Jones and Scully, 2003: 32–4). One possible consequence may be that Plaid Cymru leaders will desperately seek to shed the language yoke in order to distance themselves as much as possible from the conception that theirs is a party mainly for Welsh speakers, whilst Labour, on the other hand, will revel in every opportunity to bolster that very notion. In the end, the only real victim of such tactics is the language itself.

But perhaps the most potent threat for the language in 'post-colonial' Wales is an ironic one. The creation of the Assembly may have given Welsh people a new focus for their national identity strong enough to leave them without further need of the language as a defining characteristic of their uniqueness and singularity.

Welsh could become sidelined as a 'marginal and optional' marker of identity, as Fishman puts it (Fishman, 1997, quoted in Aitchinson and Carter, 2000: 154). After all, when the Irish Free State was created it gave the Irish people a new badge for their identity, which replaced the language as the main marker of their nationhood. When *Our Language: Its Future* was put before the plenary session of the Assembly in July 2002, Peter Black AM argued that 'Language and nationhood are two separate concepts; one is linked to a clearly defined geographical area, and the other facilitates communication between individuals. Language is not a national issue' (NAW, 2002).

This misconception on the part of one of the country's elected members serves as a blatant warning that despite all the best efforts of the Assembly in mainstreaming the language, and aspiring to a bilingual country, the process of building a new civic society in Wales could still, somehow, omit the language. What the Assembly needs to bear in mind is the fact that although 2.2 million people in Wales according to the 2001 census are unable to speak the language, they remain Welsh. The very existence of Welsh, despite it not being the first, or even the second, language of the vast majority of the Welsh people, is the one remaining factor that identifies them as such – a people. The Welsh language's survival has been a key factor in the continuance of the Welsh nation between the Union in 1536 and today – a period when, for the most part, Wales was devoid of any national institutions to help sustain and succour its national identity. As J. R. Jones argued in another of his landmark addresses, *A Raid i'r Iaith ein Gwahanu?* ('Need the Language Divide Us?'), first delivered as a lecture in 1967 to Undeb Cymru Fydd's annual conference in Aberystwyth,

> Daliaf fi nad yw cysylltiad Pobl â'u hiaith – na'u rhwymedigaeth, gan hynny, iddi – yn darfod pan beidiant hwy mwyach a'i medru. Canys y mae eu cysylltiad ffurfiannol â hi yn aros, ac yn weladwy yn y ffaith eu bod hwy'n bod fel Pobl wahanol. Hi yw'r iaith, mewn cydymdrei-ddiad â'u tir, *a adeiladwyd i mewn i'w gwneuthuriad hwy* fel Pobl wahanol.

> (I maintain that neither a People's connection with their language nor their attachment to it come to an end when they cease to speak the language. Because their structural connection with it remains, and is visible in the fact that they exist as a separate People. That language, along with their land, *has been built into their structure* as a separate People.) (J. R. Jones, 1978: 14; my translation)

The reverse in the fortunes of the Welsh language during the course of the twentieth century has been dramatic. Now, with the dawn of the new millennium, Wales has its own democratic political forum that is responsible for, among other things, the future prosperity of the Welsh language. Does this mark the opening of a new, buoyant chapter in its history? It is certainly too soon to celebrate the salvation of Welsh in a 'postcolonial' Wales just yet. We can but hope that devolution marks a new beginning for the language, rather than the beginning of the end.

REFERENCES

Aitchison, J. and Carter, H. (2000). *Language, Economy and Society: The Changing Fortunes of the Welsh Language in the Twentieth Century*, Cardiff: University of Wales Press.

Aitchison, J. and Carter, H. (2003/4). 'Turning the Tide?', *Agenda* (Winter), 55–8.

Balsom, D. (1985). 'The three Wales model', in John Osmond (ed.), *The National Question Again*, Llandysul: Gomer Press.

Beaufort Research (2000). *State of the Welsh Language Research Report* (March/April).

Bowen, I. (ed.) (1908). *The Statutes of Wales*, London: T. Fisher Unwin.

Davies, C. (1972). *Maniffesto Cymdeithas yr Iaith Gymraeg*, trans. Harri Webb, *Planet*, 26/7 (1974/5).

Fishman, J. A. (1997). 'Language and ethnicity: the view from within', in F. Collins (ed.), *The Handbook of Sociolinguistics*, Oxford: Blackwell.

Ieuan, D. (2001). 'Y De Penfro Newydd?', *Barn*, 461 (June).

Iwan, D. (1967). 'Address at Builth magistrates court', 12 September, *Tafod y Ddraig*, 2.

ap Iwan, E. (1937). 'Paham y gorfu'r Undebwyr', in D. Tecwyn Lloyd (ed.), *Erthyglau Emrys ap Iwan – (I): Gwlatgar, Cymdeithasol, Hanesiol*, Dinbych: Gwasg Gee, pp. 23–41.

Jones, J. R. (1964). 'Strategiaeth brwydr Cymru', *Baner ac Amserau Cymru*, 3 December.

Jones, J. R. (1966). *Prydeindod*, Llandybïe: Llyfrau'r Dryw.

Jones, J. R. (1978). *A Raid i'r Iaith ein Gwahanu?* (Aberystwyth), trans. John Phillips, *Planet*, 49/50 (January 1980), 23–33.

Jones, R. W. and Scully, R. (2003). 'The importance of Welshness', *Agenda* (Summer), 32–4.

Jones, R. W. and Trystan, D. (1999). 'The 1997 Welsh referendum vote', in Bridget Taylor and Katarina Thomson (eds), *Scotland and Wales: Nations Again?*, Cardiff: University of Wales Press, pp. 73–82.

Lewis, S. (1962). *Tynged yr Iaith*, trans. G. Aled Williams, in Alun R. Jones and Gwyn Thomas (eds), *Presenting Saunders Lewis*, Cardiff: University of Wales Press, 1983.

Lewis, S. (1963). 'Tynged Darlith', *Barn*, 5 (March).

Lloyd, D. T. (1988). *John Saunders Lewis: Y Gyfrol Gyntaf*, Dinbych: Gwasg Gee.

Mac Aodha, B. S. (1972). 'Was this a social revolution?', in Seán Ó Tuama (ed.), *The Gaelic League Idea*, Cork and Dublin: Mercier, pp. 20–30.

McGuinness, P. (2003). '"Racism" in Welsh Politics', *Planet*, 159, 7–12.

National Assembly of Wales Culture and Education and Lifelong Learning Committee (2002). *Our Language: Its Future: Policy Review of the Welsh Language* (July).

National Assembly of Wales (2002). *The Record*, 9 July.

Ó hAilín, T. (1969). 'Irish revival movements', in Brian Ó Cuív (ed.), *A View of the Irish Language*, Dublin: Stationery Office.

Recommendations of the National Assembly Advisory Group (1998) August.

Tafod y Ddraig (1969). Editorial, 22 (June).

The Times (1962). 'The pedigree of nations', 12 September.

WAG (2003). *Iaith Pawb: A National Action Plan for a Bilingual Wales*, Cardiff.

Welsh Language Board (2000). *Annual Report and Accounts, 1999–2000*, Cardiff.

7

Women's Political Participation and the Welsh Assembly

PAUL CHANEY

The history of colonialism in Wales was central to the thinking of organizers of the most significant public rally held by the pro-devolution group Women Say Yes. Billed as 'a gathering of women from across Wales to support the campaign for equality for women through a Welsh Assembly', it was not a mass demonstration; participants put the attendance figure in the hundreds. The gathering took place in late summer, on Saturday 30 August 1997, in Hendy-Gwyn-ar-Daf – or Whitland – in west Wales. Chosen because of its connection with Hywel Dda, it was, the organizers stated, 'the place where Welsh women were first granted rights'. The publicity sheet for the rally went on to say that the Acts of 'union' with England had effectively 'swept away' these rights. Campaigners in Women Say Yes resolved to 'plan for a women's campaign to ensure that equality is at the heart of the Assembly's activities'. The Whitland publicity 'flyer' ended by saying: 'join us to ensure that women's voices are heard in the new Wales.'[1] Whilst acknowledging the ongoing debate around notions of Welsh postcolonialism (see Chapter 1), the following discussion takes the perspective offered by Women Say Yes and elides the creation of the National Assembly for Wales with the idea of a postcolonial country. Using original research findings[2] – including interviews with participants in the recent reframing of Welsh governance – we now explore whether the aspirations of 1997 have been realized and women's voices *are* being heard in the revised political structures of a 'new' Wales.[3] Accordingly, initial focus will be placed on the way that women influenced the process of constitutional change. Later in this chapter, subsequent analysis will examine women's political participation in devolved government from the 'internal' and 'external' perspectives offered by politicians, policy-makers and women in civil society.

Research examining the transition from administrative to elected devolution lends further salience to the postcolonial paradigm. The Welsh Office era is widely seen as one with 'overtones of colonialism' (Rawlings, 1998: 466; Rawlings, 2003). It was at once exclusive, 'centralizing and anti-democratic' (Hanson, 1995; Bradbury, 1998: 127; Morgan and Mungham, 2000: 65). One Permanent Secretary stated that, in her view, the Welsh Office performed a 'colonial' role in implementing London policy in Wales (Laffin and Thomas, 2001: 47), whilst a recent study dubbed it a 'Raj' style of administration (Morgan and Rees, 2001: 161). According to Peter Hain, the current secretary of state, devolution was about reforming 'the old British state – quintessentially centralised, elitist, secretive . . . not so much a *British* as an *English* state, defined above all by hostility to regional or local autonomy' (1998: 20, original emphasis).

Such shortcomings in the accountability and legitimacy of government under the Welsh Office were reinforced by the under-representation of women in all tiers of government and the public sector. During the period, women comprised just 28 per cent of public appointments (Welsh Office, 1999), under a fifth of local councillors and – prior to 1997 – there had only ever been four Welsh women MPs returned to Westminster. Gender activists recall that requests to meet secretaries of state were turned down because equality of opportunity was not seen as the responsibility of the territorial ministry that served Wales. This is borne out by official sources. One states that most Welsh Office civil servants 'ha[d] received no training or awareness raising at all on equality matters' (NAW, 2001: para. 3.1).

The marginalization and exclusion of Welsh women from politics and public administration has a long history. Describing the suffrage movement, Cook and Evans conclude that 'feminist consciousness certainly existed in turn of the century Wales but it could not resonate in the social and economic structure which so confined women' (1991: 184). According to Beddoe (2000: 108), throughout the period before the Second World War 'women made little headway' in the political sphere. Williams (1996) explains that the labour movement, from which the Labour Party in Wales emerged, reflected the patriarchal attitudes of society as a whole, whilst Plaid Cymru remained cautious and reticent in its adoption of positive action for women (McAllister, 2001). Writing in the mid-1970s and reflecting on the progress made since the suffragettes, one activist pointed to consistent failing by the political parties. She concluded that 'in politics the situation is bathetic . . . it seems to me that the feminist position in both parties [Plaid Cymru and the Welsh Labour Party] has been steadily eroding' (Lipman, 1973: 35). In the early 1990s, Feld (1992: 81) observed that women's inequality in Wales 'comes together in an underlying alienation of women from legislative institutions, in particular what can be perceived as male institutions, male agenda, male political methods . . . '. As Beveridge et al. (2000: 401) conclude, the post-1997 programme of constitutional reforms represented a 'window of opportunity which appeared for gender mainstreaming advocates in the context of devolution'.

Despite long-standing marginalization in 'formal' party politics, as Aaron (2001: 201) observes, 'women's contribution to grass roots politics was . . . vital during the second half of the last century'. It included: shaping and leading the equality agenda, the defence of the Welsh language, campaigning for peace and nuclear disarmament (cf. Aaron, 1994), Welsh Women's Aid, the predominantly female-led Wales Congress in Support of Mining Communities that grew up in response to the hardships of the 1984 miners' strike, and, more recently, the pro-devolution campaign group Women Say Yes.

In the first half of the 1990s gender equality activists were already exerting an influence in the Parliament for Wales Campaign (PWC). At the March 1994 Democracy Conference equality issues were originally absent from the 'Draft Democracy Declaration' – the Campaign's blueprint for a future Welsh Parliament. After this conference, addressed by the future Assembly Members (AMs) Jane Hutt (then director of Chwarae Teg) and Val Feld (then director of the Equal Opportunities Commission in Wales), the following clause was added to the Declaration and subsequently approved: 'a future Welsh Parliament will ensure, from the start, that there is a gender balance in its elected representatives, and will ensure that its procedures will enable women, men and minority groups to participate to the fullest extent' (PWC, 1994).

Subsequently, the PWC broadened out from its party political origins in the Welsh Labour Party (see Andrews, 1999) and developed a number of affiliated campaign groups including Women Say Yes. The latter organization comprised a diverse range of groups – from those representing women employed in agriculture to the Minority Ethnic Women's Network (MEWN) Cymru. Organizers in Women Say Yes were concerned that support for constitutional reform might be undermined if it were seen as a party political campaign group. In response, as an activist recalls, 'one of our mantras was that "devolution is too important to be left to the politicians" – which brought in people who hadn't been involved in mainstream political parties'. The group's aims were stated in the following terms:

> We believe that the Assembly offers a real opportunity for a new kind of politics. Women in Wales have been seriously under-represented in political life for generations . . . We want an Assembly where women's contributions can be heard and valued . . . we want to ensure that equal opportunities are built in from the start – it will not work if it is an add-on later.[4]

Women Say Yes succeeded in raising the profile of gender equality in the context of the devolution campaign. It arranged a number of public meetings around Wales, and on its launch day – 23 June 1997 – supporters 'urg[ed] the Secretary of State to make known his proposals for ensuring that equal opportunities are part of the Assembly's activities and the way Assembly Members are selected'.[5] Reflecting on this period, participants describe 'an enormous feeling of optimism and hope – and a tremendous feeling that we were actually about to change things'. According to one of those involved, this confidence was based on the belief that constitutional reform would mean that

> there would be somewhere that we would count on, in a way that hadn't happened in Westminster – that women would actually have a say in a way that they haven't had before in Wales. That was a sort of feeling really that you were carving your own destiny and you actually had the power to do that, which probably had been lacking in formal politics before. I think that the devolution movement brought in women to be active in that sort of way and that was very, very important.

According to another participant, 'it was one of those "can do" moments, empowering moments, when you knew you couldn't go backwards.'

However, women's role in influencing the initial process of constitutional change in Wales differed from broad-based mobilization and engagement witnessed in the pro-devolution campaigns in Scotland and Northern Ireland (see Brown et al., 2002; Dobrowolsky, 2002). Rather it relied on a small network of influential gender equality activists in Women Say Yes, the left-of-centre political parties and individuals in gender equality organizations such as the Equal Opportunities Commission and Chwarae Teg.

Welsh Labour Party activists also lobbied for the issue of gender balance to be addressed within a wider 'commitment that the Assembly should have a responsibility to drive forward equality issues' (Feld, 2000). This idea fitted neatly into the prevailing concept of 'inclusiveness' that became the buzzword of the devolution campaign (cf. Chaney and Fevre, 2001). Subsequently, the secretary of state for Wales invited key figures in the Equal Opportunities Commission to draft equality of opportunity clauses that were later endorsed by the National Assembly Advisory Group (NAAG) and ultimately found their way into the Government of Wales Act (1998). One of these clauses (section 120) is an example of a 'fourth generation' equality duty (cf. Fredman, 2000) and it is unique amongst the devolution statutes (cf. Chaney and Fevre, 2002b) for it requires government to take a proactive stance and promote equality for *all* persons and in respect of *all* Welsh Assembly Government functions. According to law academics this equality duty is a development of 'potentially greater significance' than the Human Rights clauses in the Government of Wales Act. The result of these changes in equality law means that, 'the people of Wales are the first in the UK to be given a series of positive rights to exercise, and if necessary, to enforce through the courts in Wales' (Clements and Thomas, 1999: 10). Reviewing post-devolution equality law Squires (2003) concurs and notes that 'this approach has a series of significant benefits . . . it gives citizens legally enforceable rights in relation to elected representatives' actions thereby empowering citizens vis-à-vis the state.' This development shows that the pro-devolution gender equality activists' invocation of the effect of colonialism on native Welsh law was more than symbolic.[6] The repatriation of some government functions to Wales has afforded the opportunity to re-establish greater legal rights for women compared to those applying across the border in England.[7,8]

Interviewed in 1999, the late Val Feld AM summarized the activists' impact on the pro-devolution campaign by saying:

I think that we have succeeded in putting in place every structural measure that we could reasonably expect to try to create a new framework and ethos that means equality has a good chance of flourishing in the way that the Assembly carries out its business and in the way that it works internally and externally.

The views of other participants – supported by academic analysis (cf. Breitenbach et al., 2002) – concur with Feld's assessment, namely, that devolution has presented Wales with 'an important enabling context within which equalities work can develop' (Mackay and Bilton, 2000: 109). The evidence of women's role during the Assembly's first term also provides empirical evidence that supports the principal arguments about why women's presence matters in contemporary politics (see, for example, Phillips, 1995; Lovenduski, 1997; Mansbridge, 1999). Childs (2001: 319) summarizes these as 'the style argument; the symbolic argument; the substantive argument; and the justice argument'. All are linked to wider political science debates about democratic legitimacy and the nature of deliberative democracy.

Progress was made in the symbolic – or descriptive – representation of women (viz. the situation where women directly represent women) following the clear statement contained in the devolution White Paper that 'the Government attaches great importance to equal opportunities for all ... It believes that greater participation by women is essential to the health of our democracy' (Welsh Office, 1997: 24). The three main left-of-centre parties heeded this message in their preparations for the first Assembly elections in 1999. As a result the Assembly secured the second highest proportion of women elected to a national government body in Europe (41.7 per cent)[9] (for a full discussion see Russell, Mackay and McAllister, 2002).

The second national elections saw a consolidation of this earlier progress when the Welsh Assembly became the first example of a national government body in the world to achieve gender parity. During election campaigning party activists ensured that gender balance remained an issue for competition between the two main parties. Each used positive-action measures, and ultimately the following numbers (and percentages) of women representatives were elected: Welsh Labour 19 (63), Plaid Cymru 6 (50), Welsh Conservatives 2 (18), and the Welsh Liberal Democrats 3 (50).

The emerging evidence suggests that during the Assembly's first term the 'critical mass' of 42 per cent of women AMs has made a significant impact, although it is too early in the Assembly's history to gain a full understanding of this effect. According to Norris and Lovenduski (2001: 3): 'once the group [of women] reaches a certain size, critical mass theory suggests that there will be a qualitative change in the nature of group interactions, as the minority starts to assert itself and thereby transform the institutional culture, norms and values.' In short, this marks the progression from marginalized minority to a mainstream voice for women by women. According to one woman AM, 'Having a critical mass of women parliamentarians has made a difference to what we talk about, what we prioritize, what we do, and it's made a big difference about how we do it.' A male Assembly Member described its effect in the following way: 'The Assembly's gender make-up is a crucial start. In this Chamber, I am aware of the palpable difference that a strong representation of women makes. It is the Assembly's most distinctive feature. In due course, it will inform every aspect of Welsh life.'[10]

Despite the sometimes acrimonious politicking between the parties during the Assembly's first term, some AMs are reluctant to dismiss the notions of a 'cross-party sisterhood' that were expressed during the Assembly's initial months (see Betts, Borland and Chaney, 2001). One noted, 'It's not nonsense . . . if you look at the committees that have succeeded in working in an inclusive way, they are predominately committees where women are ministers and feminist women that make a difference.' Yet women AMs are cautious about the idea that the new gender settlement is, in any way, becoming 'normalized'. Referring to the way that male colleagues have returned to the issue of abandoning family-friendly working hours, one observed that 'there is a big risk that people get complacent about this.' Notwithstanding the evident need for such vigilance, the fact that increased gender equality amongst elected representatives has been achieved from the outset of the new legislature means that, at least in terms of the Assembly's rules and mode of operating, there is some evidence of 'normalization'. In the wake of constitutional change this aspect of the 'new politics' once again highlights the importance of the way that equality was built into the original institutional blueprint of the Assembly. Such 'normalization' is evident in the institution's working hours[11] and rules on the language permitted in political debate.[12] However, the transfer of the Welsh Office civil service to the National Assembly with its attendant underrepresentation of women amongst its staff and its poor record in promoting equality of opportunity means that much further work is necessary before gender equality is normalized in the bureaucracy.

Identity, affinity and the 'role model effect' are also salient factors in attempting to understand the post-1999 developments. From inside the Assembly one woman AM stated: 'We've now got some brilliant role models, some people who are not traditionally obvious supporters; people who can look at [the Assembly] and say "they are like me, she cares about the same things I care about."' Interviewees outside the new legislature echoed this view. One key gender equality activist spoke of 'the positive role models that physically exist in terms of the number of AMs and ministers . . . [they] deal with a very diverse agenda and this makes sure that equality of opportunity is considered across the work of the Assembly'. A comparative perspective of the differences between Westminster and Cardiff Bay was forthcoming from a Welsh woman MP who said:

> I think the women Ministers in Wales are giving good role models for women and I think their type of politics on the whole are the non-confrontational type of politics where you're working hard to achieve change and you do it in a 'hands-on', constructive sort of way; and the cut and thrust of the debating chamber is a secondary sort of thing really.

The experience of the Assembly also supports the findings of recent research in relation to Westminster (Childs, 2002) and Edinburgh (Mackay et al., 2003), namely, that there are differences in ways of working that are at least partly attributable to gender. However, a cautionary note is necessary here for it is hard to separate the influence of the institutional design of the Assembly with its emphasis on committee work from the way that women have influenced the style of politicking. Nevertheless, participants have supported a link between gender, constitutional change and putative 'consensual politics'. For example, the chair of the Assembly's Health and Social Services Committee referred to the committee's gender dynamics and concluded: 'It is true – we have worked really, really hard in my committee to work in a way that is consensual. And I think that in the three and a half years that we have been running we have only failed to come to a consensus twice.' Other women AMs spoke of their 'determination to break down tribal, confrontational politics'. Reflecting upon this development, managers of women's groups that are participating in the new post-devolution equality agenda have pointed to the ideological background of a number of women AMs as underpinning this shift. In the words of one, 'Quite a lot of the women in the Assembly have come up through feminism.' According to another interviewee, this has 'made a difference because they're more "people-centred" . . . because compared to male AMs – they're more used to working with consensus'.

Descriptive representation and the ability to draw directly upon life experiences inextricably linked to the ascriptive characteristics of the individual, in this case derived from gender, provide a link between the benefits of symbolic and substantive representation. This has been a central feature of post-devolution politics (see Chaney and Fevre, 2002b). It also supports the arguments of those advocating the merits of a pluralist conception of 'deliberative democracy'. In short, this theory highlights the problems that arise in democratic systems, such as in the male-dominated politics prior to constitutional change, when participants represent the interests of groups fundamentally different to themselves (see, for example, Gutmann and Thompson, 1996).

The way in which descriptive representation of women strengthens and enhances political debate – or the deliberative aspects of democracy – has been evident during the Assembly's first term. Women AMs have brought a direct female perspective to political debate; this was not previously possible in the male-dominated Welsh Office and was difficult to achieve in Westminster with the small number of women representing Welsh constituencies. This aspect of gender and constitutional change has been highlighted by a number of AMs. According to one, 'If we bring our experience into politics, we know how important things are, therefore we give them priority in our discourse and in terms, then, of how we've gone about things.' Another asserted:

> Without women taking part in decision-making, their views and needs are bound to be overlooked to a certain extent. It means that the life circumstances and perspective of 52 percent of the population are inevitably ignored, played down or tackled inappropriately. This does not assume that all male politicians are chauvinist pigs, although sometimes those in the House of Commons may manage to give us that impression. It simply recognises that one sex, however sympathetic, cannot fully and fairly represent the interests of the other.[13]

According to Mackay et al. (2003), substantive representation refers to 'the opportunities for the concerns and interests of women to be heard and taken into account in the policy-making process – through the institutionalisation of channels and mechanisms'. As recent research has concluded, 'in the devolved institutions of Wales and Scotland the proportion of women is substantially greater, and their ability to determine the agenda correspondingly more effective' (Ward, 2000: unpaginated). The most prominent, but by no means only, example of this is the way that women have shaped and reprioritized the political agenda in order to promote equality of opportunity during the Assembly's first term. Wales has a poor historical record in this respect. As Feld observed,

> cultural expectations and attitudes represent only one of the barriers to real equality between the sexes, but here in Wales they play a crucial part and, I would argue, make the difference that means we consistently fare worse than England or Scotland when it comes to the indices of equality. (Feld, 1992: 41)

Analysis of the transcripts of political debates and policy documents during the Assembly's first term shows how women have repeatedly been able to intervene to mainstream gender equality into proceedings across all areas of government. This is typified by the interjection of a woman AM during one of the Assembly's plenary debates: 'in the spirit of equality of opportunity, to which we have a *statutory obligation, all* our reports should have a feminist eye cast over them . . . to pick out the prejudices of white, middle-aged, middle-class men in grey suits.'[14] In addition to their 'critical mass' in the legislature as a whole, women continue to form a majority in the Assembly Government's cabinet (five out of nine ministers). This is something that, according to Feld (2000: 76), is 'unparalleled in the Western world'. Analysis of the published minutes and policy documents of the executive's ministerial Cabinet meetings over a three-year period provide further evidence of how women government ministers have mainstreamed gender (and other strands of equality) into the executive's policy-making and debate. Examples include interventions in relation to funding for a Muslim women's centre,[15] policy initiatives to achieve equal pay for women,[16] promoting gender balance in public appointments,[17] and securing gender equality in the work of the Cabinet's Economic Research Advisory Panel.[18]

During the first four years of devolved governance women AMs have formed the majority of the eleven-member cross-party Standing Committee on Equality of Opportunity. The committee made greatest progress when it was chaired by a succession of two women Cabinet ministers. In the post-1999 framework, the Assembly's equality duty has effectively removed equality issues from the list of competing priorities of party political agendas, for AMs have no choice in this matter; they are *legally obliged to promote equality.* The executive's initial actions in responding to the Assembly's statutory equality imperative have mainly concentrated on the public sector and government itself, for, as the minister responsible for equality matters observed, 'only once it gets its own house in order can the Assembly take the lead in addressing th[e] enduring barriers to equality' (WAG, 2001: 2). One AM expressed a widely held view when she described the Equality Committee's responsibilities as 'a huge remit'. This follows because the statutory duty applies to all Assembly government functions. The committee has been proactive in meeting this challenge and a wide range of reforms are now being implemented across government, and the public and voluntary sectors (for a full discussion, see Chaney and Fevre, 2002a; Chaney, 2004).

Notable examples of the reforms aimed at promoting equality for women (and other groups) include those that have been applied to the Assembly civil service. These have involved: the introduction of a new work scheme to enable those with domestic and family responsibilities greater flexibility; a survey on childcare needs in the Assembly; mandatory equality of opportunity awareness training for all civil servants; measures to ensure that the salaries of women taking maternity leave or staff taking career breaks do not fall behind; and the funding of a 22 per cent increase in the Assembly's pay bill in order to move towards ending the gender pay gap. These developments have received widespread attention. According to one commentator they placed the Assembly at the 'centre of the universe' in developing good equality practice (MacErlean, 2002: unpaginated). The Welsh executive has also introduced measures to mainstream equality in the policy process. These include equality impact statements used by civil servants in the preparation of policy, and funding for a women's consultative policy network with over 100,000 members (see Chaney 2003, for a full discussion). However, analysis of these reforms shows that there is unevenness in the way that the legislature is responding to the equality imperative and that much further work will be necessary before full gender mainstreaming in government becomes a reality.

In order to understand the post-1999 developments it is also necessary to look outside the Assembly. As Paterson and Wyn Jones (1999: 193) have observed, the civic culture into which the new legislature has been inserted is crucial to its future performance. Proponents of devolution acknowledged this fact and set out the aim of creating a 'participatory democracy' (cf. Hain, 1999). For members of Women Say Yes this meant 'bringing decision making closer to home . . . so that women can participate'.[19] Accordingly, 'we can set our own priorities on the services that matter most to women . . . the Assembly can use the talents and abilities of all our citizens.'[20] At the beginning of the Assembly's second term it is therefore pertinent to ask to what extent this aspiration has been achieved. Is the Assembly engaging with, and affecting the lives of, women across Wales? The emerging findings from new research[21] provide some answers. A survey of 1,100 women was completed at the end of the Assembly's first term in 2003. This theoretical sample was designed to reflect differences of language, age, sexual orientation, geographical location, class, ethnicity and (dis)ability. Detailed questionnaires were distributed via a range of women's organizations including: Merched y Wawr; MEWN Cymru; Lesbian, Gay and Bisexual Forum Cymru; and Welsh Women's Aid.

The findings present a mixed picture. They show that the underlying motives for women's membership of groups and organizations – the civil associations that the pro-devolution campaigners hoped to engage – are diverse. Almost half of respondents cited social reasons as underpinning their associative activities (44 per cent). A broadly similar number said that they belonged to a women's organization in order to promote the rights of women (41 per cent), with a lesser number concerned to advance the rights of lesbian and bisexual people (10 per cent). Just 14 per cent of respondents cited political factors. Whilst this shows that gender equality, as well as the desire to socialize, appear to be more important than political motivations per se in explaining the patterns of activism in civil society, there is significant evidence of a willingness on the part of women to participate in the work of the Welsh Assembly. A clear majority of those surveyed saw this as a worthwhile objective. Just 26 per cent agreed with the statement: 'It makes no difference: government would be the same whether women's organizations worked with the Assembly Government or not.' In addition, just over a third of respondents (35 per cent) felt that members of women's organizations have some sort of *responsibility* or duty to work with the Assembly.

In terms of general awareness of the new devolved structure of governance, a fifth of respondents were able to name their local or regional Assembly Member but only a minority (13 per cent) were able to identify an Assembly Government policy implemented over the previous twelve months. These 'grassroots' views also show that a majority (53 per cent) have a generally positive assessment of the developing working relationship between women's organizations and the new Welsh government body.[22] Moreover, there was evidence of comparatively high levels of political engagement, for a majority of respondents said that their organization had lobbied the Assembly at some point during its first term (51 per cent).[23] In addition, a quarter of those surveyed felt that one of the benefits of belonging to a women's organization was that it facilitated contact with the National Assembly. The recent data indicate that constitutional reform has also made progress in addressing one of the principal criticisms of the pre-1999 system of governance for, again, over a half of respondents (53 per cent) said that the Assembly *is* accountable to the members of their organizations.[24]

When questioned about a variety of post-devolution innovations in governance, the answers showed that, overall, many have yet to make a significant impact. In questions with a straight 'yes'/'no' alternative, the extent to which the following innovations were perceived as having improved the level of communication between women's organizations and government was as follows: having a local AM, 35 per cent; having a regional AM, 14 per cent; the existence of regional Assembly committees, 15 per cent; the Voluntary Sector Partnership Council, 13 per cent; the Assembly cross-party Equal Opportunities Committee, 17 per cent; and the Assembly's main policy fora – its subject committees, just 9 per cent. These findings show that much further work is necessary if a majority of women are to regard key aspects of the new system of governance as either effective or beneficial.

Based on the experience of the first four years of devolved governance, just under a half of the women surveyed (42 per cent) were undecided as to whether the National Assembly had actually made *any* difference to the organization to which they belonged; only 17 per cent felt that it had made some impact. In the view of respondents, two key areas where an improvement in the working relationship between women's organizations and the Cardiff-based government might be effected were the provision of better information on Assembly Government policies (41 per cent) and better opportunities to meet AMs locally (50 per cent). Interestingly, the recent findings also show significant variations in trust between the UK government and the Welsh Assembly Government. A fifth of respondents had absolutely no trust in the UK government compared with 9 per cent in the case of the Assembly. Overall, 44 per cent of women had a generally positive assessment of their trust in the Welsh Assembly compared with 32 per cent for Westminster.

In summary, this snapshot of women's views suggests that the young Assembly has positive resources to draw upon in terms of gender activism, a willingness to participate and increased levels of trust in government; factors that are, in part, based on greater democratic accountability. However, these findings also reveal that a significant proportion of women remain to be convinced about key aspects of the new system of governance and its ability to both effectively engage with – and deliver tangible outcomes for – women. The danger for politicians and policy-makers is the potential undermining effect that this may have on the aforementioned 'positive resources'.

CONCLUSION

When viewed in the context of the postcolonial paradigm, the evidence of the past decade would suggest that, in several respects, Wales has resisted the experience of other nations. For example, analysis has shown how in twentieth-century Ireland 'women were silenced and excluded within the process of nation building' (Gray and Ryan, 1998: 134). In addition, whilst acknowledging the 'slippage' between 'independence' and the limited self-government thus far achieved in Wales, Jahan's international assessment of the relationship between women, politics and colonialism has salience to the Welsh case. She concludes that

> after independence was won, the postcolonial states did very little to push for gender equality in public life. What is worse, the nationalist

ideology in many states in recent years has turned more extremist and reactionary defining women's place in society in a more restrictive way. Thus, while nationalist movements created a space for women in public life, when the movements achieved their goals women's space was again restricted. (Jahan, 1999)

The early evidence of constitutional change in Wales shows that, to date, these historical precedents have not been followed. The establishment of limited self-government has led to a profound change in women's participation in national politics. In a manner that often contrasted with events in the UK's other devolved polities, activists successfully used the opportunities presented by constitutional change to secure advances in gender equality. It is too early to fully understand all the implications of the increased rights and representation secured by women – as well as the effectiveness of the new post-devolution equality agenda. Arguably, the new gender settlement may be seen as the most significant impact of Welsh devolution to date. The experience of the Assembly's first term provides clear empirical evidence of discontinuity with the former, pre-devolution mode of politics – and supports the principal theoretical arguments for gender equality in contemporary politics. The presence of a 'critical' mass of female elected representatives has enabled women to influence and manage the political agenda. This marks a major development over the earlier system of governance when gender equality was not seen as the responsibility of the territorial ministry that served Wales. At that time women had to rely on male politicians to represent their viewpoints. Proportional descriptive representation – or gender parity – has changed matters and effected an improvement in the deliberative function of democracy. Women representatives have been able to engage in and shape the political debate and discourse through direct reference to gendered life experiences. Whilst these achievements should not be understated, further and formidable challenges remain. In particular, whereas constitutional change has had a major impact on women's role in national politics, it remains to be seen whether similar progress will be made at a subnational level. In addition, it is uncertain whether the new devolved legislature will be successful in engaging with, and serving the needs of, the broader mass of women citizens in Welsh society.

Despite these remaining uncertainties, the move towards a 'postcolonial' Wales has had a transformative effect. The aims expressed in the pro-devolution campaign by gender equality activists are being realized and women's voices are beginning to be heard. This lends credence to the assessment by Rawlings (2003) that 'devolution may now be accounted a positive experience, one that has already served to generate and release new potentials . . . given the peculiar history of this little country – including as England's "first colony" – [it] is nonetheless worth repeating: there is no going back'.

NOTES

[1] Quotations from: Women Say Yes (1997) Whitland Rally Publicity 'flyer', National Library of Wales Archive and Manuscript Collection, Aberystwyth, 'Yes For Wales Referendum Campaign Records', Box 6/G12/1/4.
[2] Undertaken during the Economic and Social Research Council-funded projects 'Gender and Constitutional Change: Transforming Politics in the UK?' (Devolution and Constitutional Change Programme, L219252023).
[3] All quotations that appear in this discussion are taken from original research interviews unless otherwise attributed.
[4] Women Say Yes, fax of launch press conference running order and introductory speech, NLW (as n. 1), Box 6/G12/1.
[5] Women Say Yes, NLW (as n. 1), Box 6/G12/1/6.
[6] Cf. Jenkins and Owen, 1980.
[7] The appropriateness of describing the Assembly's equality duty as conveying legal rights is borne out by accepted legal analysis, such as: 'the counterpart and correlative of a legal right is a legal duty, in that if one person has a legal right of a particular kind some other person or persons must be subject to a legal duty' (D. M. Walker, *The Oxford Companion to Law*, Oxford: Clarendon Press, 1980, p. 1070).
[8] According to Schedule 8 of the Government of Wales Act, the National Assembly may be subject to judicial review if it is felt that it has failed to comply with the provisions of Section 120 of the same Act.
[9] International Parliamentary Union (2000). International Classification of Parliaments, *http://www.ipu.org/wmn-e/classif.htm*.
[10] R. Edwards, Official Record of Proceedings, 8 March 2000.
[11] See National Assembly Standing Order 5.2 (2002).
[12] Office of the Presiding Officer of the National Assembly for Wales (1999), Protocol on conduct in the Chamber/Rules of Debate, Key Principles.
[13] J. Randerson, debate to mark International Women's Day, Official Record, 8 March 2000, Cardiff: NAW.
[14] J. Randerson, Official Record of Proceedings, 16 January 2001.
[15] Record of Cabinet meeting, 8 October 2001.
[16] Record of Cabinet meeting, 26 June 2001.
[17] Record of Cabinet meeting, 15 January 2001.
[18] Record of Cabinet meeting, 25 November 2002.
[19] Women Say Yes, press release, NLW (as n. 1), Box 6/G12/1/6.
[20] Women Say Yes, campaign poster, NLW (as n. 1), Box 6/G12/1/11.
[21] 'Social capital and the participation of marginalized groups in government' (ESRC Funded project R000239410).

[22] 7 per cent said it was 'strong', 23 per cent 'good', and 23 per cent 'fair' – with 38 per cent saying that they did not know.

[23] 41 per cent said 'Don't Know'.

[24] 27.5 per cent said 'Don't Know'.

REFERENCES

Aaron, J. (1994). 'Finding a voice in two tongues: gender and colonization', in J. Aaron, T. Rees, S. Betts and M. Vincentelli (eds), *Our Sisters' Land: The Changing Identities of Women in Wales*, Cardiff: University of Wales Press.

Aaron, J. (2001). 'A review of the contribution of women to Welsh life', *Transactions of the Honourable Society of Cymmrodorion*, New Series, 8, 188–204.

Andrews, L. (1999). *Wales Says Yes*, Bridgend: Seren.

Beddoe, D. (2000). *Out of the Shadows: Women in Twentieth Century Wales*, Cardiff: University of Wales Press.

Betts, S., Borland, J. and Chaney, P. (2001). 'Inclusive government for excluded groups: women and disabled people', in P. Chaney, T. Hall, and A. Pithouse (eds), *New Governance – New Democracy? Post-Devolution Wales*, Cardiff: University of Wales Press.

Beveridge, F., Nott, S. and Stephen, K. (2000). 'Mainstreaming and the engendering of policy-making: a means to an end?', *Journal of European Public Policy*, 7, 3, 385–405.

Bradbury, J. (1998). 'The devolution debate in Wales during the Major governments: the politics of a developing union state?', *Regional and Federal Studies*, 8, 1, 120–39.

Breitenbach, E., Brown, A., Mackay, F. and Webb, J. (eds) (2002). *The Changing Politics of Gender Equality in Britain*, Basingstoke: Palgrave.

Brown, A., Barnett Donaghy, T., Mackay, F. and Meehan, E. (2002). 'Women and constitutional change in Scotland and Northern Ireland', *Parliamentary Affairs*, 55, 71–84.

Chaney, P. (2003). 'Social capital and the participation of marginalized groups in government: a study of the statutory partnership between the third sector and devolved government in Wales', *Public Policy and Administration*, 17, 4, 20–39.

Chaney, P. (2004). 'The post-devolution equality agenda: the case of Welsh Assembly's statutory duty to promote equality of opportunity', *Policy and Politics*, 32, 1, 63–77.

Chaney, P. and Fevre, R. (2001). 'Ron Davies and the cult of inclusiveness: devolution and participation in Wales', *Contemporary Wales*, 14, 21–49.

Chaney, P. and Fevre, R. (2002a). *The Equality Policies of the Government of the National Assembly for Wales and their Implementation: July 1999 to January 2002: A Report for: the Equal*

Opportunities Commission, Disability Rights Commission, Commission for Racial Equality, and Institute of Welsh Affairs, Cardiff: IWA.

Chaney, P. and Fevre, R. (2002b). 'Is there a demand for descriptive representation? Evidence from the UK's devolution programme', *Political Studies*, 50, 897–915.

Childs, S. (2001). 'Attitudinally feminist? The New Labour women MPs and the substantive representation of women', *Politics*, 21, 3, 78–85.

Childs, S. (2002). 'Hitting the target: are Labour women MPs "acting for" women?', in Karen Ross (ed.), *Women, Politics and Change*, Oxford: Oxford University Press.

Clements, L. and Thomas, P. (1999). 'Human rights and the Welsh Assembly', *Planet*, 136, 7–11.

Cook, K. and Evans, N. (1991). '"The petty antics of the bell-ringing boisterous band"? The Women's Suffrage Movement in Wales 1890–1918', in A. John (ed.), *Our Mothers' Land: Chapters in Welsh Women's History 1830–1939*, Cardiff: University of Wales Press.

Dobrowolsky, A. (2002). 'Crossing boundaries: exploring and mapping women's constitutional interventions in England, Scotland, and Northern Ireland', *Social Politics: International Studies in Gender, State and Society*, 9, 293–340.

Feld, V. (1992). 'What chance for women?', *Planet*, 93, 39–43.

Feld, V. (2000). 'A new start in Wales: how devolution is making a difference', in A. Coote (ed.), *New Gender Agenda*, London: IPPR.

Fredman, T. (2000). 'Equality: a new generation?', *Industrial Law Journal*, 30, 145–68.

Gray, B. and Ryan, L. (1998). 'The politics of Irish identity and the interconnections between feminism, nationhood and colonialism', in R. R. Pierson and N. Chaudhuri (eds), *Nation, Empire, Colony: Historicizing Gender and Race*, Bloomington: Indiana University Press.

Gutmann, A. and Thompson, D. (1996). *Democracy and Disagreement*, Cambridge, Mass.: MIT Press.

Hain, P. (1999). *A Welsh Third Way?*, Tribune Pamphlet, London: Tribune Publications.

Hanson, D. (1995). *Unelected, Unaccountable and Untenable: A Study of Appointments to Public Bodies in Wales*, Cardiff: Wales Labour Party.

Jahan, R. (1999). *The Practice of Transformative Politics*, paper presented to the Fourth Asia-Pacific Congress of Women in Politics held on 1–3 September 1997 at Taipei. Published by the Center for Asia-Pacific Women in Politics, *www.capwip.org*.

Jenkins, D. and Owen, M. E. (1980). *The Welsh Law of Women*, Cardiff: University of Wales Press.

Laffin, M. and Thomas, A. (2001). 'New ways of working: political–official relations in the National Assembly for Wales', *Public Money and Management*, 21, 2, 45–50.

Lipman, B. (1973). 'Diary of a Welsh liberationist', *Planet*, 15, 1, 33–6.

Lovenduski, J. (1997). 'Gender politics: a breakthrough for women?', *Parliamentary Affairs*, 50, 4, 708–19.

McAllister, L. (2001). 'Gender, nation and party: an uneasy alliance for Welsh nationalism?', *Women's History Review*, 10, 1, 51–69.

MacErlean, N. (2002). 'Why can't a woman be (paid) more like a man?', *The Observer*, 20 January.

Mackay, F. and Bilton, K. (2000). *Learning from Experience: Lessons in Mainstreaming Equal Opportunities*, Edinburgh: University of Edinburgh/The Governance of Scotland Forum.

Mackay, F., Myers, F. and Brown, A. (2003). 'Towards a new politics? women and constitutional change in Scotland', in A. Dobrowolsky, and V. Hart (eds), *Women Making Constitutions: New Politics and Comparative Perspectives*, Basingstoke and New York: Palgrave.

Mansbridge, J. (1999). 'Should blacks represent blacks and women represent women? A contingent "yes"', *Journal of Politics*, 61, 3, 628–57.

Morgan, K. and Mungham, G. (2000). *Redesigning Democracy: The Making of the Welsh Assembly*, Bridgend: Seren.

Morgan, K. and Rees, G. (2001). 'Learning by doing: devolution and the governance of economic development in Wales', in P. Chaney, T. Hall and A. Pithouse (eds), *New Governance – New Democracy? Post-Devolution Wales*, Cardiff: University of Wales Press.

National Assembly for Wales (NAW) (2001). *Equality Training and Raising Awareness Strategy – ETAARS*, Cardiff: NAW.

Norris, P. and Lovenduski, J. (2001). *Blair's Babes: Critical Mass Theory, Gender, and Legislative Life*, Cambridge, Mass.: John F. Kennedy School of Government, Harvard University Faculty Research Working Papers Series, RWP01–039.

Parliament for Wales Campaign Democracy (PWC) (1994). *Parliament for Wales Campaign Democracy Conference Programme 5–6 March 1994*, Cardiff: PWC.

Paterson, L. and Wyn Jones, R. (1999). 'Does civil society drive constitutional change?', in B. Taylor and K. Thompson (eds), *Scotland and Wales: Nations Again?*, Cardiff: University of Wales Press.

Phillips, A. (1995). *The Politics of Presence*, Oxford: Oxford University Press.

Rawlings, R. (1998). 'The new model Wales', *Journal of Law and Society*, 25, 4, 461–509.

Rawlings, R. (2003). *Delineating Wales: Constitutional, Legal and Administrative Aspects of National Devolution*, Cardiff: University of Wales Press.

Russell, M., Mackay, F. and McAllister, L. (2002). 'Women's representation in the Scottish Parliament and the Welsh Assembly: party dynamics for achieving a critical mass', *Journal of Legislative Studies*, 8, 2, 49–76.

Squires, J. (2003). 'The new equalities agenda: recognising diversity and securing equality in post-devolution Britain', in A. Dobrowolsky and V. Hart (eds), *Women Making Constitutions: New Politics and Comparative Perspectives*, London: Palgrave.

Ward, M. (2000). *The Northern Ireland Assembly and Women: Assessing the Gender Deficit*, Belfast: Democratic Dialogue.

Welsh Assembly Government (2001). *The National Assembly for Wales: Arrangements to Promote Equality of Opportunity 2000–2001 – Annual Equality Report*, Cardiff: Welsh Assembly Government.

Welsh Office (1997). *A White Paper: A Voice For Wales/Papur Gwyn: Llais Dros Gymru*, London: Stationery Office, Cm. 3718.

Welsh Office (1999). *The Government's Expenditure Plans 1999–2000 to 2001–2002: A Departmental Report by the Welsh Office and the Office of Her Majesty's Chief Inspector of Schools in Wales*, Cardiff: Welsh Office.

Williams, C. (1996). *Democratic Rhondda: Politics and Society 1885–1951*, Cardiff: University of Wales Press.

III

A POSTCOLONIAL CULTURE?
WELSH CULTURAL DIFFERENCE

8

Bardic Anti-colonialism

JANE AARON

In his chapter in this volume, Stephen Knight suggests that it is in the fiction of Welsh writing in English, rather than in any of its other genres, that we find the most consistent exploration of post-colonial experience. As theorists of nation-building have argued, the most appropriate literary form for the imagining of a nation would appear to be the realist novel, for no other genre can represent so effectively the idea of a 'special community' 'moving calendrically . . . through time' which constitutes the modern nation (Brennan, 1990; Anderson, 1983: 25–6). Given also the capacity of fiction to probe in detail and depth the multiform social and psychological effects on individuals and communities of such a phenomenon as postcolonialism, it is not surprising that it is primarily the novelists of a nation who have hitherto traced the literary record of its encounter with colonization or imperialism, and Welsh culture in English would appear to constitute no exception. Within Welsh-language literature, however, the role played by another genre in the history of Wales's relation to its colonizers has resulted, it may be argued, in a different pattern, one in which poetry takes central place. And by the second half of the twentieth century, a growing awareness of Welsh poetry's historic role in resisting cultural colonialism can also be said to be influencing the work of English-language poets in Wales as well.

Of course, this is not to say that no Welsh-language fiction is of relevance to the postcolonial debate; on the contrary, some of the most influential twentieth-century novels, such as Islwyn Ffowc Elis's *Wythnos yng Nghymru Fydd* ('A Week in Future Wales', 1957) or Angharad Tomos's *Yma o Hyd* ('Here Still', 1985), engage directly with the struggle for Welsh cultural survival against the odds, while others are concerned with such problematic issues as

neo-colonialism in the contemporary Welsh Establishment
(Gruffudd, 1986 and 1997), the eighteenth-century involvement
of the Welsh in the British imperial slave plantations (Roberts,
2001), and Welsh military service in Northern Ireland (Miles,
2002). But the Welsh-language novel is a relatively recent
phenomenon; it has not played the same long-term part as poetry
in resisting cultural colonization. The genre which has historically
worked most effectively to keep Wales Welsh, in cultural terms, is
poetry, or so, at least, this chapter on Welsh poetic traditions and
contemporary Welsh identities will suggest.

A MUSIC OF THE TONGUE

What makes the Welsh case unusual is the earliness of its primary
colonial experience. No vernacular language includes in its literature contemporary records of what it felt like to undergo Roman
imperial rule, but sixth-century Welsh-language poetry does speak
of the gradual erosion of territories and cultural influence under
the next invaders of Britain. The Britons were losing ground to the
Saxons as the Welsh language evolved from British; from its
beginnings, therefore, Welsh literature reflected the experience of
conquest and the resultant cultural, social and psychological
disarray. An anonymous ninth-century poem, for example, ostensibly narrated by Heledd, sister of Cynddylan, a seventh-century
Prince of Powys, laments his death and the massacre of his retinue
after the sacking of Pengwern Court, near present-day
Shrewsbury; the traumatized survivors of the attack have lost the
foundation of their identity as well as their home, and Heledd
fears for her sanity (see Conran, 1976: 127, for an English-
language translation of this poem). In a 'Britain' dominated by
Saxons, first-millennium Welsh speakers may not have found 'a
viable political form for their highly individual polity' (G. A.
Williams, 1985: 60), but they did forge as an expression of their
experience a highly individual poetic form.

The eventual thirteenth-century conquest of Wales by the
Anglo-Normans incorporated many of the tactics later to mark
more modern Western imperialism. Under the protection of those
Norman-built castles which feature so large in the list of twentieth-century Wales's tourist attractions, settlers from England and
the Marches were established in the walled towns of the new
colony, and used as front lines of defence against the possible

insurgence of the indigenous population, herded outside the town walls. The imposition of tax and legal rights which differentiated the Welsh from the English also made of the Welsh subordinates in territories previously their own. In the struggle to come to terms with, or at least to survive, such humiliations, the main recourse of Welsh culture, from the sixth to the sixteenth century, was its long-established bardic tradition. As professionals employed by the dynastic princes and nobles of Wales, it was the job of the bards to maintain and develop, in so far as they could, the good name of their lords and the esteem in which they were generally held. The idea of art as having the capacity to construct as well as represent its subject was thus already an appreciated aspect of the poet's role. As they performed their compositions, Welsh bards made their princes noble rulers through the spell of language, the sign system. But the death of lords and princes in battles and the fall of their dynasties spelt disaster also for their bards; fear of the devastation to come after a leader's death forms the subject of many of their most moving and memorable works. Not surprisingly, perhaps, the death of Llywelyn, the last Prince of Wales, killed by Edward I's soldiers at Cilmeri in 1282, provoked the most resonant of all these poems of traumatic loss. 'I've lost a lord, long terror is on me,' grieves the poet, Gruffudd ab yr Ynad Coch. 'The heart's gone cold, under a breast of fear':

> Poni welwch-chwi hynt y gwynt a'r glaw?
> Poni welwch-chwi'r deri'n ymdaraw?
> Poni welwch-chwi'r môr yn merwinaw'r tir?
>   Poni welwch-chwi'r gwir yn ymgyweiriaw?
> Poni welwch-chwi'r haul yn hwylaw'r awyr?
>   Poni welwch-chwi'r sŷr wedi r'syrthiaw?
> Poni chredwch-chwi i Dduw, ddyniadon ynfyd?
>   Poni welwch-chwi'r byd wedi r'bydiaw?
> Och hyd atat-ti, Dduw, na ddaw môr dros dir!
>   Pa beth y'n gedir i ohiriaw!
>   Nid oes le y cyrcher rhag carchar braw;
>   Nid oes le y triger: och o'r trigaw!

> (See you not the way of the wind and the rain?
> See you not the oak trees buffet together?
> See you not the sea stinging the land?
>   See you not truth in travail?
> See you not the sun hurtling through the sky,
>   And that the stars are fallen?

Do you not believe God, demented mortals?
Do you not see the whole world's danger?
Why, O my God, does the sea not cover the land?
Why are we left to linger?
There is no refuge from imprisoning fear,
And nowhere to bide – O such abiding!) (Conran, 1976: 163–4)

But despite – or perhaps because of – his dread that he and his culture will be swept away into formlessness after Llywelyn's death, Gruffydd ab yr Ynad Coch's eulogy is actually very highly wrought. Like that of the ninth-century Heledd and the productions of the professional bards generally, it is composed in *cynghanedd* form, making use of patterns of cross-alliteration and internal rhyme organized around the stressed words within each line of verse. After the fall of Llywelyn, this form did not in fact relax or flounder; on the contrary, it underwent new definition and became much more rigorously intricate and demanding in structure. The relatively flexible early patterns of the metre were elaborated into the twenty-four rules of the *mesurau caeth* (or 'strict metres') to produce a verse form in which harmonized or contrapuntal sound patterns were prioritized to an unusual degree, as indicated in the generic Welsh term for poetry written in *cynghanedd*, *cerdd dafod*, 'a music of the tongue' (see G. Jones, 1968: 125–35, and Conran, 1976: 310–39, for English-language accounts of the rules of *cynghanedd*). Thus an epoch of great social and political insecurity in Wales saw its bards working to develop their craft into ever more elaborate form, as if in defiance of that formlessness into which their culture generally had been thrown. They succeeded to such an extent that it is the centuries after Llywelyn's death and the conquest of Wales, and not those before it, which are now generally considered to represent the 'golden age' of the Welsh bardic tradition.

The content of their verse as well as its form also served of course as a reminder of the distinctiveness of Welsh culture, in the face of colonizing attempts to absorb 'the principality' as a member of the English body. Whether berating Saxons as the children of the deceivers Hengist and Horsa who gained ascendancy over the Britons through trickery, or building up as the *mab darogan* (son of prophecy) likely saviours such as Owain Glyndŵr or Henry Tudor, the bards wrote as if conscious of their responsibilities as front-liners in the defence of Welsh difference (see Evans, 1997; R. R. Davies, 1995: 88–92; and G. Williams, 1985).

Figure 1. Thomas Nepal, studio portrait in his uniform, early 1900s. Used by permission of Marcia Brahim Barry, his granddaughter (photograph).

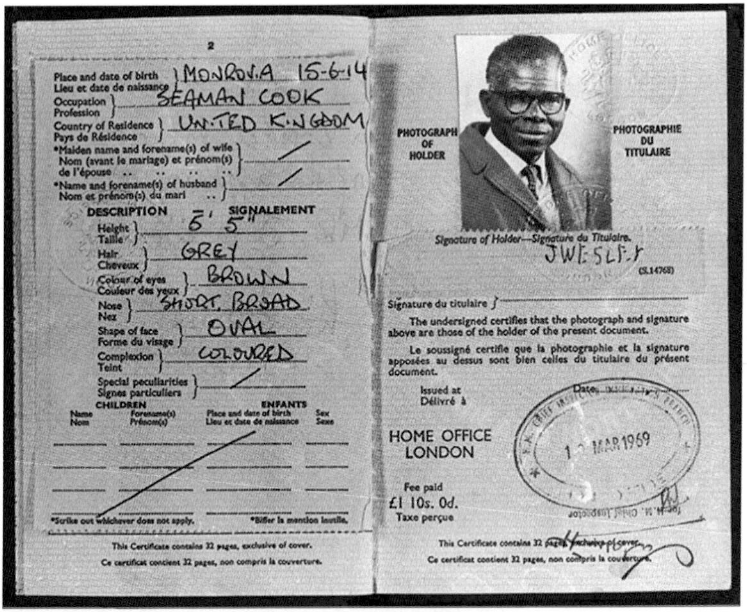

2

Place and date of birth / Lieu et date de naissance: MONROVIA 15-6-14
Occupation / Profession: SEAMAN COOK
Country of Residence / Pays de Résidence: UNITED KINGDOM
*Maiden name and forename(s) of wife / Nom (avant le mariage) et prénom(s) de l'épouse: /
*Name and forename(s) of husband / Nom et prénom(s) du mari: /

DESCRIPTION — SIGNALEMENT
Height / Taille: 5' 5"
Hair / Cheveux: GREY
Colour of eyes / Couleur des yeux: BROWN
Nose / Nez: SHORT, BROAD
Shape of face / Forme du visage: OVAL
Complexion / Teint: COLOURED
Special peculiarities / Signes particuliers: /

CHILDREN — ENFANTS
Name / Nom — Forename(s) / Prénom(s) — Place and date of birth / Lieu et date de naissance — Sex / Sexe

*Strike out whichever does not apply. — *Biffer la mention inutile.

This Certificate contains 32 pages, exclusive of cover.
Ce certificat contient 32 pages, non compris la couverture.

PHOTOGRAPH OF HOLDER — PHOTOGRAPHIE DU TITULAIRE

Signature of Holder—Signature du Titulaire.
J WESLEY
(S.14768)

Signature du titulaire

The undersigned certifies that the photograph and signature above are those of the holder of the present document.

Le soussigné certifie que la photographie et la signature apposées au dessus sont bien celles du titulaire du présent document.

Issued at / Délivré à
HOME OFFICE LONDON
Date
1 MAR 1969
Fee paid £1 10s. 0d. Taxe perçue
for H. M. Chief Inspector

This Certificate contains 32 pages, exclusive of cover.
Ce certificat contient 32 pages, non compris la couverture.

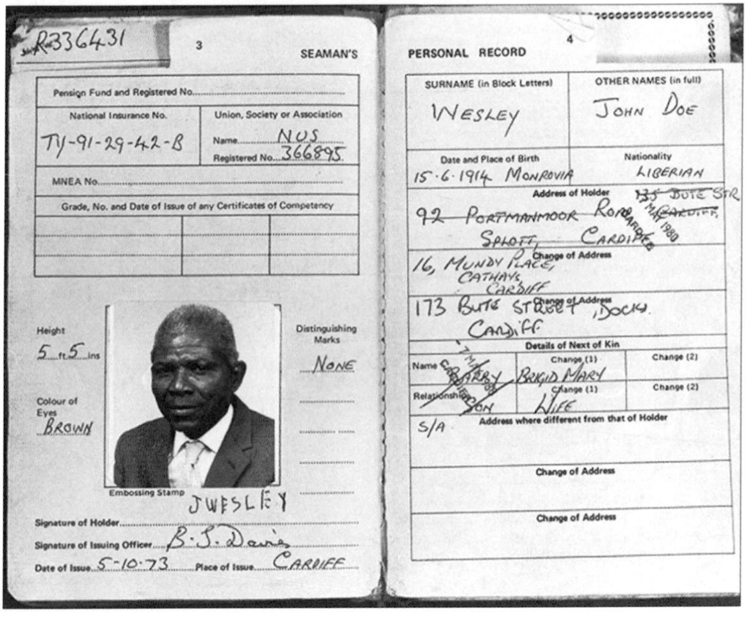

R336431
3
SEAMAN'S

Pension Fund and Registered No.	
National Insurance No. TY-91-29-42-B	Union, Society or Association — Name NUS — Registered No. 366895
MNEA No.	
Grade, No. and Date of Issue of any Certificates of Competency	

Height 5 ft. 5 ins
Colour of Eyes BROWN
Distinguishing Marks NONE
Embossing Stamp
Signature of Holder J WESLEY
Signature of Issuing Officer B. J. Davis
Date of Issue 5-10-73 Place of Issue CARDIFF

4
PERSONAL RECORD

SURNAME (in Block Letters)	OTHER NAMES (in full)
WESLEY	JOHN DOE
Date and Place of Birth: 15-6-1914 MONROVIA	Nationality: LIBERIAN

Address of Holder: ~~135 BUTE STR CARDIFF~~
92 PORTMANMOOR ROAD, SPLOTT, CARDIFF
Change of Address: 16, MUNDY PLACE, CATHAYS, CARDIFF
Change of Address: 173 BUTE STREET, DOCKS, CARDIFF

Details of Next of Kin
		Change (1)	Change (2)
Name	~~HARRY~~	BRIGID MARY	
Relationship	~~SON~~	WIFE	

S/A Address where different from that of Holder
Change of Address
Change of Address

Figures 2a and 2b. Pages from John Doe Wesley's certificate of identity and seamen's discharge book. Used by permission of Butetown History & Arts Centre, Cardiff (photograph).

Figure 3. Mr Wesley, in cook's uniform, with a shipmate. Used by permission
of Butetown History & Arts Centre, Cardiff (photograph).

Figure 4. Young Somali men in Berlin's Milk Bar, Butetown, 1950. Photograph by Bert Hardy. Used by permission of Hulton Getty (photograph).

Figure 5. Two girls in a Cardiff children's home, 1954. Photograph by Bert Hardy. Used by permission of Hulton Getty (photograph).

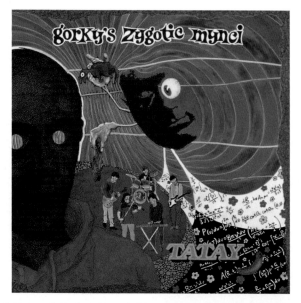

Figure 6. Cover of Gorky's Zygotic Mynci's *Tatay* (Ankst, 1994): the spirit of independence. Used by permission of Ankst and Alan Holmes.

Figure 7. Ivor Davies, *The Writing on the Wall. Destruction of Language and Community XI*. 2001. Three books including a family bible and the artist's grandfather's antique shotgun (*c*.1840) cloven and fixed on hessian. 4' x 5'.

Figure 8. Cerith Wyn Evans, *Cleave 03* (*Transmissions: Visions of the Sleeping Bard*), 2003. Venice Biennale. Searchlight, shutter, computer transmitting Morse code, text by Ellis Wynne. Dimensions variable. Photograph: Polly Barden, Wales Arts International.

Figure 9. Shani Rhys James, *Colander 1*. Oil on linen, 4' x 3', 2000.
Photograph: Graham Matthews.

Figure 10. Tim Davies, *Postcard Series 2*.
Cut postcards (1 in series of 12), 2002.

Figure 11. Iwan Bala, *Gwalia ar y Gorwel II/Horizon Wales II*.
Mixed media on canvas, 51 x 61cm, 2000. Photograph: Pat Aithie.

According to the British historian Norman Davies, 'one could not hope for a better example of colonial cultural policy' than the 1536 Act of Union which sought 'utterly to extirpate all the singular sinister uses and customs' by which Wales differed from England, and decreed that 'no person or persons that use Welsh speech or language shall have or enjoy any manner of office or fees' (N. Davies, 1999: 493). As a result, 'a largely monoglot people were made aliens in their own lawcourts and cultivated a corresponding alienation', a situation which did not change in legal terms until the Welsh Language Act of 1967 (G. A. Williams, 1985: 121). For the bards in particular, whose livelihood depended on the gentry's continuing loyalty to the Welsh language and customs, the granting of increased civil rights to the Welsh only if they abandoned their cultural distinctiveness could only have exacerbated rather than eased the felt humiliations of conquered status. As far as they were concerned, language and culture were all in all; the option of following the Tudors to rich pickings in England was no compensation when one had no official right to one's own language, and was granted access to it only as suited the needs of the English state – e.g., in 1588 'the Crown was forced to accede to pressure and authorize Welsh translations of the Bible' in order to make Wales Protestant (G. A. Williams, 1985: 121). By the seventeenth and eighteenth centuries, the accumulative Anglicization of the Welsh nobility was leading to the attrition of a bardic system which had historically depended on its patronage: 'twice better than the *cywydd*'s muse / Is the pampered note of the English tongue' complains Owen Gruffydd (1643–1730) of the changing taste of his erstwhile patrons (see Conran, 1976: 227 for this translation). In the mid-eighteenth century, Ieuan Brydydd Hir describes as derelict and abandoned the homesteads which supported Welsh poetry in its heyday: thorns and brambles reign over the ruins of Ifor Hael's court, where Dafydd ap Gwilym once sang (see Conran, 1976: 238).

However, Ieuan Brydydd Hir, or Evan Evans to give him his baptismal rather than bardic name, through his publication of such volumes as *Some Specimens of the Poetry of the Ancient Welsh Bards* (1764), also contributed to that cultural revival which in the second half of the eighteenth century helped to give birth to the modern concept of Welsh nationhood. The revival relied heavily upon the rediscovery of Welsh medieval and first-millennium poetry. According to the mid-twentieth-century

Algerian analyst Frantz Fanon, whose work has proved seminal
for later postcolonial theorists such as Homi K. Bhabha, for a
colonized people to claim a literature as their own, and label it
'national', is fighting talk; the discovery of such literature constitutes a vital step towards their freedom:

> It is a literature of combat, because it moulds the national conscious-
> ness, giving it form and contours and flinging open before it new and
> boundless horizons; it is a literature of combat because it assumes
> responsibility, and because it is the will to liberty expressed in terms of
> time and space. (Fanon, 1967: 193)

During the Romantic period a number of London-based societies founded with the express aim of rediscovering and
supporting Welshness – the Cymmrodorion, the Gwyneddigion
and the Cymreigyddion – busied themselves with making early
Welsh poetry accessible to the general public. Antiquarians, historians and Celtic scholars edited and published for the mass
audiences of the printing presses bardic 'specimens' whose
survival had hitherto depended on manuscript collectors (see
Morgan, 1983; G. A. Williams, 1988). The poet Iolo Morganwg,
who notoriously contributed forgeries as well as originals to the
manuscript collections published by the Gwyneddigion, also
helped to bring about a revival of the eisteddfod, or bardic competition, and established its rituals, again on dubious historical
grounds. National and local, large and small, the eisteddfodau, as
much as the printing presses, became the patrons and publicists of
new generations of nineteenth- and twentieth-century bards. Of
course, a renewed interest in the poetry of the past also meant
renewed knowledge of its predominant themes; the medieval
bards' concern with cultural survival in the face of colonization
became part of Welsh self-consciousness. In the 1830s one of the
Rebecca rioters of the period, protesting against high tolls on
country roads, pens a warning to a tollgate keeper, who appears
to have been English, referring to the betrayals of Hengist and
Horsa as if they had been enacted but the day before and were still
ripe for revenge (see D. G. Jones, 1945: i, 31). It is unlikely that
this daughter of Rebecca acquired such a sense of her national
history from any weekday or Sunday schooling she received;
rather, she probably picked it up from direct or indirect acquaint-
ance with the work of the old bards.

During the nineteenth and twentieth centuries in Wales, epochs of heightened national consciousness were marked by further renewals of cultural interest in *cerdd dafod*, and by the successive emergence of new poets capable of reviving the old bardic metres and making them meaningful and resonant once again to new generations. The so-called 'Welsh Renaissance' of the *fin de siècle* period can be linked to the rise and fall of the Cymru Fydd, or Young Wales, movement with its aim of achieving Home Rule for Wales. By 1896 the political movement had failed, because the south Wales Liberals refused to unite with the north Walians and make the cause their own, but the cultural movement it gave rise to did not perhaps peak until T. Gwynn Jones won the National Eisteddfod chair in 1902 with 'Ymadawiad Arthur', or 'Arthur's Passing'. The *cynghanedd* of this *awdl*, and that of subsequent poems by T. Gwynn Jones, was considered to be startlingly original and accomplished, and the themes of his poems too echoed anew calls to resistance in the face of cultural colonization (see Conran, 1976: 257–66, and Elfyn and Rowlands, 2003: 31–44, for translations of T. Gwynn Jones's poetry). Similarly, in the middle years of the twentieth century, a build-up of anger at the drowning of Welsh valleys to provide water for English cities, along with resentment at the investiture in 1969 of a Prince of Wales not recognized as such by some members of his principality, led to another resurgence in the use of *cerdd dafod* as a political weapon. When Gerallt Lloyd Owen in his 1972 volume *Cerddi'r Cywilydd* ('Poems of the Shame'), for example, speaks of the death of the last Welsh Prince of Wales as if it happened but the day before, the fact that the form which he employs with such sparse eloquence closely echoes that in which contemporary eulogies to Llywelyn were sung in the thirteenth century helps to substantiate his and his readers' sense of connection with the past. His poem 'Cilmeri' reads:

> Fin nos, fan hyn
> Lladdwyd Llywelyn.
> Fyth nid anghofiaf hyn . . .
>
> Fan hyn yw ein cof ni,
> Fan hyn sy'n anadl inni,
> Fan hyn gynnau fu'n geni. (Owen, 1972: 23)
>
> (At nightfall, in this place
> Llywelyn was killed,
> Never will I forget this . . .

In this place is our memory.
In this place is our life's breath.
In this place just now our birth.) (Elfyn and Rowlands, 2003:
283–4)

The overt aim of a poetry collection like *Cerddi'r Cywilydd* is
to waken a nation from the lassitude and passivity imposed by the
experience of colonization. Since the days of Iolo Morganwg its
bardic tradition has historically been Wales's primary weapon in
this cultural 'combat', and for many it remains so to this day.
Listening to and composing verse in *cynghanedd* is currently very
much a popular part of Welsh-language culture: the rules of *cynghanedd* are taught to children in schools and to adults in
well-attended evening classes and poetry clubs; radio and television *Talwrn y Beirdd* (bardic contests) are held regularly with
packed live audiences, and also feature as pub entertainment, and
as part of the programme in national and local eisteddfodau;
every Welsh region has its team of local bards. It would appear
that the medieval developers of *cerdd dafod* succeeded in
producing a form with a singular and persistent appeal. Through
its sound-patterning, *cynghanedd* can serve to sensitize the ear to
the particular aesthetic effects of the Welsh language, its open
vowels and crisp consonants. To leave their audience peculiarly
alive to the beauty of their own language, so that they would
cleave to it even to the detriment of their material advance, may
have been part of the bards' intention, as they constructed a
music 'for the delectation of the ear, and from the ear to the heart'
(E. Williams, 1829: 195).

According to various testimonies, poetry, as opposed to any
other literary form, is the cultural medium most evocative of
Wales. 'More than the springtime in Wales, I remember her poets',
says the contemporary critic and poet Bobi Jones, of his home
thoughts during one period of exile: 'they scratch at my hiraeth
[nostalgia] oftener than the hills.' In his poem 'To the Poetry
Clubs of Wales' he stresses the oddity and singularity of the
Talwrn, the bardic contest: 'America doesn't know – no, nor any
country of Europe – of that contention, / Why they have it, those
farmers, postmen, garage hands, ministers.' But of course 'they
have it', and have had it since at least the sixth century, in part
precisely because it is not known in American or other European
cultures, because it is unique and resists incorporation into
another culture. A modern-day practitioner of the craft includes

in one of his *cywyddau* (that is, a poem made up of seven-syllabled rhyming couplets, with *cynghanedd*) a debate between a 'trad-itional' poet and modernists who deride the poet's loyalty to the old metres. But the poet is aware of his craft as a weapon in a 'literature of combat': the tight framework of rules within which he writes frees him and his co-bards rather than constrains them:

> . . . rŷm ni yn ein cerddi caeth
> yn hawlio ymreolaeth,
> eu sain parhaus yw'n parhad,
> geiriau rhydd ein gwareiddiad. (E. Lewis, 1995: 19)

> (. . . we in our strict poems
> lay claim to independence,
> their constant music's our survival,
> the free words of our culture.) (Elfyn and Rowlands, 2003: 358)

In the twentieth century, this unique 'literature of combat' began also to be heard in English-language poetry. I have argued else-where that when poets whose first language had been Welsh first began to write verse in English, the patterns of *cynghanedd* often sounded in their lines (Aaron, 1995). The coal-mining poet Huw Menai, for one, acknowledged what he called 'my *cynghanedd* habit' in his English poems, attributing it to 'the secret storage of memories asserting themselves'. 'Poetry', he says, 'has more cunning tools, more secret weapons in its armoury than prose ever dreamt of' (Menai, 1958). Even in second-generation cases, where it was the parents of the poet who stopped speaking Welsh or did not pass it on, echoes of *cerdd dafod* sometimes feature. It is famously to be heard in some of Dylan Thomas's most familiar and resonant lines: 'Ann's bard' in 'After the Funeral', for example, calls 'the seas to service' to sing her praise and 'babble like a bellbuoy over the hymning heads' (D. Thomas, 1988: 73). Thomas was ambivalent about his relation to traditional Welsh metre, at one moment saying he knew nothing of it, at another emphasizing that his own experiments in metre were influenced by *cerdd dafod*. But whether or not the effect was deliberate, the persistent chime of the *cynghanedd* in his alliterative English-language verse leaves it sounding 'other' and hybrid, a combination of two cultures. And his friend Glyn Jones had no qualms about deliberately experi-menting with *cynghanedd* in his English-language verse to produce a 'music' which, to a Welsh ear, very clearly echoes his mother tongue (see, for example, G. Jones, 1988: 28).

Further, in English as well as in Welsh verse, a '*cynghanedd*
habit' can also be the means by which direct anti-colonial protests
are voiced, in terms of content as well as form. A poet and trans-
lator like Tony Conran, who has worked closely for many years
with Welsh medieval poetry, refers as frequently and as naturally
as the Welsh-language poets to figures like Gruffydd ab yr Ynad
Coch, the Last Prince's eulogizer. In Conran's poem 'Referendum
1979' 'Gruffydd the beak's son' ('ynad' means judge') tells the
poet, after the abysmal collapse of the 'Yes' vote in the first Welsh
Devolution referendum, to 'Keep your head down, boy . . . I've
been here before': the medieval poet advises his modern successor
how to survive a situation experienced as devastating defeat,
similar to his own at the death of Llywelyn (Conran, 2004: 86).
Conran not only translates many of the Welsh classical poems for
new English-language audiences, but employs *cynghanedd* in his
own English-language verse in poems which protest against Welsh
cultural losses. In the 1967 poem 'Trippers to Aberffraw', for
example, a verse in *englyn* form speaks of cultural impoverish-
ment superficially glossed over: Aberffraw, seat of the dynasty of
Gwynedd kings whose last heir was mourned so bitterly by
Gruffudd ab yr Ynad Coch, has become a spot on the map which
does not know itself:

> This village has come, somehow, all our glib
>   Lies to disallow
> Not free to be Aberffraw
> Names our sickness to us now. (Conran, 2004: 31)

But Aberffraw both knows itself and speaks of that knowledge in
Conran's poem, written in a metre the function of which could be
said to be to ensure that Wales remembered what it had been and
named it to itself. The old bards consciously and deliberately
made princes princely and nobles noble through their descriptions
and praise; since the eighteenth century their poetry and that of
their modern successors has been used consciously and deliberately to make Wales Welsh and resist the effects of English cultural
colonization.

Unlike the majority of its medieval precedents, however,
Conran's poem primarily criticizes the Welsh, not the English; it is
we with 'our glib lies' who disavow the Welsh past and betray
what is distinct about Welsh identity. To attack the attitudes not
so much of the colonizers as of the colonized, and to denounce

their part in that cultural decay which results from colonization, has also frequently been the aim of Welsh poets. In this context, bards function not so much as 'prince-creators' or 'nation-builders' but as satirists and accusers of their own people, for anti-colonial ends. The next section of this chapter examines this phenomenon, and its occurrence in both Welsh- and English-language poetry, in greater detail.

DIC SIÔN DAFYDD

Cynghanedd is not the only verse form in which Welsh poets have sought to resist the insidious effects of cultural colonization. During the last years of the eighteenth century, a radical balladeer, using a simple ballad metre no doubt influenced by English-language popular ballads of the period, created one of the most ubiquitous symbols of the English colonization of the Welsh and one of the most effective tools against it – the figure of 'Dic Siôn Dafydd'. Dic Siôn Dafydd was the central character in a series of satirical ballads, which also featured his cousin, Parri Bach, and various female relatives. The series was composed by Jac Glan-y-Gors, or John Jones of Cerrigydrudion, Denbighshire, who went to London in 1796 to became a tavern-keeper and a central figure in both the Gwyneddigion and Cymreigyddion London-Welsh societies. Like his author, Dic also leaves his Welsh home for London, where he bluffs his way up from shopkeeper's assistant, to shopkeeper, businessman, capitalist and gentleman, in debt every inch of the way, only to be exposed at last and left in abject poverty at the close of his story. As part of the process of his gentrification, he pretends to forget his Welsh origins and the Welsh language, but is laughed at for this presumption when he returns home hoping to excite envy (Millward, 2003: 26–9). The name and image of Dic Siôn Dafydd entered Welsh consciousness as the archetype of the native betrayer. He represents those who succumbed to the cultural pressure to leave behind all the 'singular sinister uses and customs' of Wales in order to promote their social advancement in a Britain under English domination. His image continued to inform some of the satirical pop songs of twentieth-century Welsh protest singers, such as Huw Jones's 'Dwi Isie Bod yn Sais' ('I want to be an Englishman') or Dafydd Iwan's 'Croeso Chwedeg-Nain' ('Welcome '69') or 'Mae 'Na Le yn Tŷ Ni' ('Such a State our House is In'), and references to him

abounded throughout nineteenth-century popular culture. An
1864 poem by R. J. Derfel, for example, conveys the artifice of the
Dic Siôn Dafydd pose by suggesting jocularly that,

> Mae'r adar yn canu Cymraeg
>   Yn siarad Cymraeg â'u gilydd;
> Ni welwyd un deryn erioed
>   Yn myned yn Dic Siôn Dafydd. (Derfel, 1864: 56)

> (The birds sing Welsh,
>   In Welsh they speak to one another;
> No bird was ever seen
>   Becoming a Dic Siôn Dafydd.) (my translation)

Dic Siôn Dafydd was a figure of fun but also at the same time an
effective weapon in the struggle to keep Wales Welsh. The
message his image conveyed to the aspiring nineteenth-century
Welsh was that if they attempted to 'pass' as English in order to
improve their fortunes, then their natal communities would scorn
them.

But the original Dic Siôn Dafydd betrayed his people not only
by disavowing his Welshness but also by becoming a capitalist. He
and his relatives are all avid moneymakers to the detriment of
their humanity: of his cousin Parri Bach it is said,

> Caiff undyn gan hwn fawr gysur,
> Mae'n hynod o brysur am bres

> (Nobody gets much comfort from him,
> He's so busy making money.) (Millward, 2003: 38)

Another of Jac Glan-y-Gors's ballads, 'Y Ffordd i Fyned yn Ŵr
Bonheddig yn Llundain' ('How to Become a Gentleman in
London'), refers to the buying of stocks and shares as a game in
which players deceive one another as to their actual assets in order
to inveigle money out of the less wary. The Welsh who would be
London gentry are satirically advised to remark at every possible
opportunity, 'O what a glorious news! / I see the stocks are rising'
– that is, as if they owned shares galore (Millward, 2003: 40; in
English in the original). Jac Glan-y-Gors was a follower of Tom
Paine; his prose tracts *Seren tan Gwmmwl* ('A Star Under a
Cloud', 1795) and *Toriad y Dydd* ('The Break of Day', 1797), as
well as arguing against English rule in Wales, also preach against
Britain's undemocratic institutions generally, particularly the
Royal Family, the House of Lords, and the House of Commons as

it was before the extension of the franchise and the securing of the secret ballot (J. Jones, 1923: 14–15, 22–3, 33–4). No person has a right to wield power over any other person unless democratic-ally elected to do so, he insists in *Toriad y Dydd*, where he also takes up arms against such hierarchical impositions of English law on the spirit of egalitarianism as the practice of primogeniture (J. Jones, 1923: 8, 19–22). In the Dic Siôn Dafydd ballads he was composing during the same years as he penned these political tracts, Jac Glan-y-Gors presents the Welsh as more community-spirited and democratic than the English. They may succumb to the lure of filthy lucre but they do so because they have been drawn away from the influence of their indigenous culture. To speak the language of capitalism is just as much to speak a foreign language as to speak English, in these poems.

In many of the later nineteenth-century poems which make reference to Dic Siôn Dafydd, this combination of anti-colonial and anti-capitalist satire remains prevalent. In his English-language collection, *Songs for Welshmen* (1865), for example, R. J. Derfel includes a poem which shows Dic Siôn Dafydd in hell, doing his best even there to 'find a bidder' to whom he can sell the place: that is, Dic Siôn Dafydd's only interest in his environment and community is in what he can get for them (Derfel, 1865: 28). R. J. Derfel originally trained as a Nonconformist preacher but he left the pulpit in later life, finding it incompatible with his de-veloping socialism. The fusion of anti-capitalism and anti-colonialism evident in his poems also features in the popular verse of Evan Pan Jones, another Nonconformist minister who frequently castigates the Welsh for their readiness to admire and emulate the English. In a poem such as 'Ymrestrwch i'r Fyddin' ('Enlist in the Army'), for example, written at the time of the Mahdi uprising in the Sudan, Pan Jones satirizes those Welsh soldiers who volunteered for British imperial wars without connecting the plight of the conquered people with their own past (represented here by the reference to the 'ghosts of the Normans'), and without realizing that the wars were fought in the interests of British trade (in this case, a quick route to India), not for the dissemination of Christianity, as the pro-imperialists preached:

> Nawr i'r gâd ni awn dan ganu,
>   Fechgyn teyrngar Cymru i gyd;
> Clywch ysbrydion y Normaniaid
>   'Nawr yn cyfarth megis cwn, –

Eisiau llarpio y barbariaid
    O'r Soudan i ben Kartoun . . .

De'wch i ddial angeu Gordon,
    O! yr oedd e'n Gristion mawr:
Lladdai'r neb ymddygai'n greulon, –
    '*Come to smash the Mahdi*' nawr . . .

Rhuthrwch arnynt am y cynta' –
    Tân o'u cylch fo megis ton;
Rhaid i ni gael ffordd i'r India,
    Pe drwy uffern elai hon. (E. P. Jones, 1912: 94–5)

(Now to battle we'll go singing
all of us loyal Welsh lads;
hear the ghosts of the Normans
barking like dogs –
eager to devour the barbarians
from the Sudan to the top of Khartoum . . .

Come to avenge the death of Gordon,
O! he was a great Christian:
He killed anyone who behaved cruelly, –
'Come to smash the Mahdi' now . . .

Let's rush upon them eager to be first –
let there be fire about them like a wave;
for we must have a route to India,
even were it to go through hell.) (my translation)

The notion that nineteenth-century Welsh people happily
profited from the British Empire without ever critically assessing
imperialism in the light of their own history of colonization is a
misconception based on too little knowledge of Welsh-language
culture. On the other hand, it is of course true that many did
profit, and that the second half of the nineteenth century saw the
growth of a Welsh middle class, which fragmented the image of
the undivided Welsh community, that necessary judge in the background of the Dic Siôn Dafydd satires.

In the twentieth century, the naturalness with which earlier
Welsh radical poets had connected anti-capitalist and anti-colonialist themes seemed more difficult to arrive at: there are poems
which condemn the Welsh for forgoing socialism, and others which
attack them for neglecting the Welsh language, but few which do
both at the same time. For Idris Davies, for example, a Welsh
person who betrays socialism betrays his or her national identity.

'Who loves not these derelict vales / Is no true son of eternal Wales', he says in 'The Angry Summer' (1943) of the south Wales Valleys during the 1926 miners' strike (I. Davies, 1994). But for another group of poets, of whom R. S. Thomas is perhaps the best-known English-language example, it is Welsh people's neglect of their language that arouses the greatest anxiety. In 'Reservoirs' Thomas berates the Welsh for digging a grave for their language, while the narrator of the poem 'Welsh' blames his parents and their generation for

> bringing
> me up nice,
> No hardship
> Only the one loss,
> I can't speak my own
> Language.
> (Thomas, 1993: 129)

Lack of sympathy with the working classes is not considered a loss which imperils Welsh identity in this poem, but loss of the Welsh language is. This splitting of the original two-pronged attack of course reflects the political life of Wales in the twentieth century, with Plaid Cymru – a party considered to be particularly supportive of the Welsh language – at odds with and competing against the Labour Party. Nevertheless, it renders vulnerable the concept of a distinctively democratic Welsh national identity, as it was envisaged by the nineteenth-century radicals.

But the element of turning upon oneself, of tearing oneself apart, so clearly manifested in twentieth-century Welsh politics, could be said to be from the first an aspect of this type of bardic anti-colonialism which focuses on attacking the internal betrayer, the fellow-countryman who lets the side down. The Dic Siôn Dafydd ballads made scapegoats of people caught up in the pressures of their times, and accused them of betrayal without considering to what degree they had the knowledge or opportunity to make better choices. In his 1952 volume *Black Skin, White Masks*, Frantz Fanon analyses this scapegoating of their own members by colonized people as an aspect of their condition created ultimately by the colonizers. 'The feeling of inferiority of the colonized is the correlative to the European's feelings of superiority,' he says (Fanon, 1986: 93). Of course, he is here writing of Third World colonialism, but to those nineteenth-century Welsh people who held on to a sense of themselves as other than the English, the discrepancy between their own self-image and that of the English must also have seemed daunting: few countries ever were more caught up in the illusions of a massive superiority complex than nineteenth-century England. But for the Welsh to retaliate against feelings of inferiority by scapegoating those amongst their members who succumbed to Anglicization cannot have done much to relieve their continuing cultural alienation or self-distaste.

According to R. S. Thomas in his poem 'Gifts', his 'sad country' gave him nothing but 'shame' (1993: 161). More positively one might say that because it did hold on by the skin of its teeth to a distinct, if not 'superior', identity, his 'sad country' at least gave him the tensions which informed much of his poetic output. Today, postcolonial theorists like Fanon's follower Homi K. Bhabha teach that such tensions are at the core of the modern psyche: the old master narratives by which various power groups attempted to hold on to a hierarchical sense of superiority are discredited and it is the tales of the 'conquered' or 'inferior' who yet managed to survive the impositions of history that the world needs to give it renewed hope for the future:

> Where once, the transmission of national traditions was the major theme of a world literature, perhaps we can now suggest that trans-national histories of migrants, the colonized, or political refugees – these border and frontier conditions – may be the terrains of world literature. (Bhabha, 1994: 12)

To what degree it can be said of Welsh poets that they have contributed to this new transnational awareness is a question I turn to in the final section of this chapter.

TRANSNATIONAL VOICES

In 1853, in a passage from his long poem *Y Storm* ('The storm'), the Blackwood poet Islwyn expressed himself of the conviction that every spot on the globe is equally capable of proving the inspiration for art.

> Mae dyfroedd Helicon yn gwyrddu'r byd,
> Yf lle y mynnot, Helicon yw'r cwbl.
> Parnassus? Dacw ef, y mynydd ban
> Y'th anwyd dan ei gysgod . . .
>
> (The waters of Helicon green the globe,
> drink where you will, the whole is Helicon.

Parnassus? There it is, that mountain peak
under whose shadow you were born . . .
(W. Thomas, 1897: 5–6; my translation).

By today, this theme has found frequent expression in the
poetry of colonized people. Because the imperialists' culture
frequently constituted the only art taught within the colony's
educational institutions, its poets first had to convince themselves
and their audiences that artistic creativity was not the exclusive
property of the dominant mother-countries. In 'Another Life', for
example, Derek Walcott represents the West Indian poet as struggling to realize that his immediate environment can also be the
source of high art. Palm trees, he has to persuade himself, are not
in fact 'ignobler than imagined elms', or 'the breadfruit's splayed
leaf / coarser than the oak's', and you can be a poet without
having seen a daffodil (Walcott, 1986: 148). Similarly, the Irish
poet Patrick Kavanagh, in his poem 'Epic', feels dissatisfied with
what he experiences as the petty parochialism of the brawls and
disputes taking place around him in the parishes of Ballyrush and
Gortin till he remembers that Homer 'made the Iliad from such /
A local row' (Kavanagh, 1986: 76). Islwyn's poem was written in
the context of the 1847 Government Report on the State of
Education in Wales, which had largely attributed what it
presented as gross Welsh ignorance, backwardness and
immorality to the principality's retention of the Welsh language,
and its insufficient familiarity with the supposedly civilizing,
improving effects of English-language culture. By writing in
Welsh, Islwyn is demonstrating that, just as all areas of the globe
can provide the inspiration for creativity and culture, so no one
language has a monopoly of civilizing effects. His choice of metre
is also revealing in this context. Instead of writing *Y Storm* in
traditional Welsh *cynghanedd* metres, at which he was in fact
adept, he chooses blank verse, Shakespeare's and Milton's metre,
and a marker of high culture in English terms, thus emphasizing
the translational and transcultural properties of aesthetic forms as
well as more physical sources of inspiration: *Y Storm* is a hybrid
text, incorporating perspectives from more than one culture.
Given the significance of language politics within the imperial
policies of Victorian England, at that time intent upon Anglicizing
half the known world in the name of civilization, Islwyn's protest
contributes to global anti-colonial resistance, not though, but
because it is written in a minority language.

In the twentieth century, many Welsh-language poets have similarly equated their minority perspective with that of other subordinated and oppressed cultures. In the 1930s and 1940s, the communist poet T. E. Nicholas, in such poems as 'Yr Un Baich' ('The Same Burden'), connected the struggles of the Welsh workforce against capitalism and imperialism with those of the indigenous inhabitants of British colonies generally (Nicholas, 1948: 58). A decade later, Waldo Williams in his poem 'Plentyn y Ddaear' ('Child of the Earth') suggests to the 'magically imprisoned' colonized masses that the forces which oppress them have in fact but little substance, could they but see through their delusions (W. Williams, 1956: 68). Amongst contemporary poets, Menna Elfyn in 'Song of a Voiceless Person to British Telecom', uses the common enough Welsh experience of not having one's Welsh recognized by a company professedly offering a bilingual service to sharpen her sense of empathy with other nations who are 'possessors of nothing but their dispossession' (Elfyn, 1995: 6–9). Similarly Grahame Davies in the poem 'Rough Guide' from his and Elin ap Hywel's bilingual collection, *Ffiniau/Borders*, speaks of the way in which wherever he goes he's drawn to identify with the local minority culture, his reaction is always 'Nice city. Now where's the ghetto?' (ap Hywel and Davies, 2002: 42). And Gwyneth Lewis's bilingual meditations on what it means to lose an endangered culture, in her collections *Y Llofrudd Iaith* ('The Language Murderer') and *Keeping Mum*, have implications not only for the speakers of all minority languages but for narrowing global consciousness generally. 'What's in a Name?', for example, reflects on what would be lost with the loss of Welsh bird names:

> *Lleian wen* is not the same as 'smew'
> Because it is another point of view,
>
> another bird. There's been a cull
> *gwylan*'s gone and we're left with gull
>
> and blunter senses till that day
> when 'swallows', like *gwennol*, might stay away.
>   (G. Lewis, 2003: 14)

Since the 1960s in particular, Welsh poets writing in English have made similar transnational connections, connections which also, interestingly, often bridge that destructive gap between anti-colonialist and anti-capitalist politics apparent in early twentieth-century Welsh culture. In 1970 Harri Webb in his poem 'For Frantz Fanon' described the splendour of the statuary and civic buildings the French *mission civilisatrice* left behind in Algiers, comparing it as if idly in the last lines of the poem with the scenery of central Cardiff (Webb, 1995: 136–7). Tony Conran, in the poem with which he welcomed the Cuban poet Pedro Perez Sarduy to the 1985 National Eisteddfod in Rhyl, juxtaposes the 'shanty towns' of industrial Wales, 'at the edge of Capital's shadow', with a South America in which 'the cash flowed north-wards' (Conran, 2004: 92–5). And R. S. Thomas, in one of his later poems, offers as a model to

> a world
> oscillating between dollar
> and yen

a Wales which for all its frailties has not sold itself completely: 'our liquidities . . . are immaterial' (Thomas, 1993: 25).

These poems are transnational communications whose significance is based upon the fact that they represent the point of view and experience of a stateless and historically subordinated nation. But they are not *post*-national voices, and, for all my co-editor's arguments in this volume and elsewhere (C. Williams, 2003/4), I cannot see that in the current situation there would be any gain if they were. While the possibility of constructing human communities capable of cooperation and of maintaining a wealth of cultural diversity while eschewing nationhood may be an ideal worth working for, for contemporary Wales to give up its aspirations to nationhood surely would do little to further that cause. The post-nation people of Wales could not float in limbo in a world otherwise inhabited by nationals without being recategorized: we would all, willy-nilly, be categorized, by others if not by ourselves, as 'British', as unproblematic members of the British nation-state. And in today's Britain, the default position for those who identify, or are identified, as British only, with no qualifiers, remains an unexamined English cultural identity. British Unionists would of course be gratified by such a denouement to Welsh difference but it is difficult to see how it would profit any other group. The Afro-American critic Henry Louis Gates, Jr., remarked in the context of a debate on black identity:

> Consider the irony: precisely when we (and other Third World peoples) obtain the complex wherewithal to define our black subject-ivity in the republic of Western letters, our theoretical colleagues

declare that there ain't no such thing as the subject, so why should we be bothered with that? . . . For anyone to deny us the right to engage in attempts to constitute ourselves as discursive subjects is for them to engage in the double privileging of categories that happen to be preconstituted. (Gates, Jr., 1992: 36, 39)

Much the same point could be made about any attempt to persuade stateless nations to be the first to abandon national status: if they did so they would but doubly privilege nation-states that happen to be preconstituted. No doubt many of the anti-colonial poets whose work has been analysed in this chapter would be happy to abandon the ambivalent contradictions of Welsh nationhood for the sake of equal membership in a global community, free of divisive national allegiances and respectful of cultural difference. But until that day draws nearer, for the Welsh unilaterally to abandon their claims to national difference and become, in national terms, nothing but members of a British nation-state, still very heavily English-dominated, surely cannot be the best way to aim a blow at the more pernicious aspects of nation-building.

REFERENCES

Aaron, J. (1995). 'Echoing the (m)other tongue: Cynghanedd and the English-language poet', in B. Humfrey (ed.), *Fire Green as Grass: Studies of the Creative Impulse in Anglo-Welsh Poetry and Short Stories of the Twentieth Century*, Llandysul: Gomer, pp. 1–23.

Anderson, B. (1983). *Imagined Communities*, London: Verso.

Bhabha, H. K. (1994). *The Location of Culture*, London: Routledge.

Brennan, T. (1990). 'The national longing for form', in H. K. Bhabha (ed.), *Nation and Narration*, London: Routledge.

Conran, T., trans. (1976). *Welsh Verse*, Bridgend: Poetry Wales Press, (Second edn 1986).

Conran, T. (2004). *The Shape of My Country: Selected Poems and Extracts*, Llanrwst: Gwasg Carreg Gwalch.

Davies, I. (1994). *The Complete Poems of Idris Davies*, ed. D. Johnston, Cardiff: University of Wales Press.

Davies, N. (1999). *The Isles: A History*, London: Macmillan.

Davies, R. R. (1995). *The Revolt of Owain Glyn Dŵr*, Oxford: Oxford University Press.

Derfel, R. J. (1864). *Caneuon Gwladgarol Cymru*, Wrecsam: R. Hughes a'i Fab.

Derfel, R. J. (1865). *Songs for Welshmen*, Bangor: J. M. Jones.

Elfyn, M. (1995). *Eucalyptus: Detholiad o Gerddi/Selected Poems 1978–1994*, Llandysul: Gwasg Gomer.

Elfyn, M. and Rowlands, J. (eds) (2003). *The Bloodaxe Book of Modern Welsh Poetry: Twentieth-Century Welsh-Language Poetry in Translation*, Tarset: Bloodaxe Books.

Evans, R. W. (1997). 'Prophetic Poetry', in *A Guide to Welsh Literature 1282–c.1550*, eds. A. O. H. Jarman and G. R. Hughes, rev. D. Johnston, Cardiff: University of Wales Press, pp. 256–74.

Fanon, F. (1986 [1952]). *Black Skin, White Masks*, trans. Charles Lam Markmann, new edn, London: Pluto Press.

Fanon, F. (1967 [1961]). *The Wretched of the Earth*, trans. C. Farrington, Harmondsworth: Penguin Books.

Gates, Jr., H. L. (1992). *Loose Canons: Notes on the Culture Wars*, New York and Oxford: Oxford University Press.

Gruffudd, R. (1986). *Y Llosgi*, Tal-y-bont: Y Lolfa.

Gruffudd, R. (1997). *Crac Cymraeg*, Tal-y-bont: Y Lolfa.

ap Hywel, E. and Davies, G. (2002). *Ffiniau/Borders*, Llandysul: Gwasg Gomer.

Jones, D. G. (ed.) (1945). *Detholiad o Ryddiaith Gymraeg R. J. Derfel*, Aberystwyth: Y Clwb Llyfrau Cymreig.

Jones, E. P. (1912). *Odlau . . . : Cofion Cefnydfa*, Merthyr Tydfil: Joseph Williams.

Jones, G. (1968). *The Dragon Has Two Tongues*, London: Dent; reprinted and ed. T. Brown, Cardiff: University of Wales Press, 2003.

Jones, G. (1988). *Selected Poems: Fragments and Fictions*, Ogmore-by-Sea: Poetry Wales Press.

Jones, J., Glan-y-Gors (1923). *Seren tan Gwmmwl a Toriad y Dydd*, new edn, Liverpool: Hugh Evans.

Kavanagh, P. (1986). 'Epic', in P. Muldoon (ed.), *The Faber Book of Contemporary Irish Poetry*, London: Faber, p. 76.

Lewis, E. (1995). *Chwarae Mig*, Abertawe: Cyhoeddiadau Barddas.

Lewis, G. (2003). *Keeping Mum*, Tarset: Bloodaxe Books.

Menai, H. (1958). 'The bilingual mind', *Wales*, xxxii and xxxiii.

Miles, G. (2002). *Cwmtec*, Llanrwst: Gwasg Carreg Gwalch.

Millward, E. G. (ed.) (2003). *Cerddi Jac Glan-y-Gors*, Abertawe: Cyhoeddiadau Barddas.

Morgan, P. (1983). 'From a death to a view: the hunt for the Welsh past in the Romantic period', in E. Hobsbawm and T. Ranger (eds), *The Invention of Tradition*, Cambridge: Cambridge University Press, pp. 43–100.

Nicholas, T. E. (1948). *Prison Sonnets*, trans. Daniel Hughes, London: W. Griffiths.

Owen, G. L. (1972). *Cerddi'r Cywilydd*, Caernarfon: Gwasg Gwynedd.

Roberts, W. O. (2001). *Paradwys*, Abertawe: Cyhoeddiadau Barddas.

Thomas, D. (1988). *Collected Poems 1934–1953*, ed. W. Davies and R. Maud, London: Dent.

Thomas, R. S. (1993). *Collected Poems 1945–1990*, London: Dent.

Thomas, W. [Islwyn] (1897). *Y Storm* (1853), in *Gwaith Barddonol Islwyn*, Wrecsam: Hughes a'i Fab.

Walcott, D. (1986). *Collected Poems 1948–1984*, London: Faber.

Webb, H. (1995). *Collected Poems*, ed. Meic Stephens, Llandysul: Gwasg Gomer.

Williams, C. (2003/4). 'A post national Wales', *Agenda* (Winter), 2–5.

Williams, E. [Iolo Morgannwg] (1829). 'Dosbarth Simwnt Fychan', in E. Williams (ed.), *Cyfrinach Beirdd Ynys Prydain*, Abertawe: J. Williams.

Williams, G. (1985). '*Y mab darogan*: national hero or confidence trickster?', *Planet*, 52, 106–10.

Williams, G. A. (1985). *When Was Wales?*, Harmondsworth, Penguin.

Williams, G. A. (1988). 'Romanticism in Wales', in R. Porter and M. Teich (eds), *Romanticism in National Context*, Cambridge: Cambridge University Press, pp. 9–36.

Williams, W. (1956). *Dail Pren*, Aberystwyth: Gwasg Aberystwyth.

9

Welsh Fiction in English as Postcolonial Literature

STEPHEN KNIGHT

PROLOGUE

Dylan Thomas, soon to be married and keen for money as much as fame, proposed to a London publisher a book of stories called *The Burning Baby*. Modernist verging on surrealist, they involved the people of a Welsh valley in dark actions and worse fantasies. The publisher's reader, poet and novelist Richard Church, rejected the idea; he said some of the stories were 'obscene', much preferring the quaintly anodyne accounts of a Welsh childhood that first appeared in *A Portrait of the Artist as a Young Dog*. In prose Thomas went on, for a mostly English audience on radio and in print, to create a charmingly written, engagingly humorous Welsh version of the Black and White Minstrel Show.[1]

The constraining, redirecting, damaging influence of London publishers is one of the most striking colonial features of Welsh writing in English, at least in the past. Other examples are the rejection in 1937 by Gollancz's timidly liberal readers of Gwyn Thomas's bitterly radical *Sorrow for thy Sons* and the self-indulgent promoting by David Garnett of the brilliant and tragic Dorothy Edwards in the inherently hostile Bloomsbury Group. These were personal deformations and literary losses, but they are also characteristic instances of the encounter between colonizing power and colonized writers. The impact of English rule on the Welsh language, institutions and values that had been native to Wales for centuries is clear enough – as is the native resistance to it. More complex, and indeed more complicit, is the relationship between English power and language and the people identifying as Welsh who nevertheless used English as their language of speech and writing.[2]

In order to understand that contested literary and sociocultural history it is helpful to identify three phases of Welsh writing in English, a drama in three rather disparate acts. Arguably, the main genre of the encounter has been fiction; the contributions of drama, film and, especially in the work of R. S. Thomas, poetry have been powerful but they are not continuous like the sequences of the fiction. To my mind, they are best read as commentaries on and intensifications of a hundred years of conflicted attempts by Welsh writers in English to create in fiction an account of their society – in both relation and resistance to the language and traditions of English fiction and their political implications.

ACT 1: FIRST-CONTACT ROMANCE

Colonization generates two early cultural formations. Some native writers become absorbed into the culture of the colonizer: from Wales Henry Vaughan, John Dyer and others became ranked among the English poets; Roland Mathias has told this story (Mathias, 1987). There also develop narratives about how sensitive colonial visitors encounter the intriguing and sometimes threatening natives and so enrich their cultural, even amatory, lives – just as the colonizing power profits from the new natural resources. In the case of Wales, like other English colonies, these stories are mostly told in novels and, as scholars have recently shown, they dominate as representations of Wales in English up to the mid-nineteenth century (see Dearnley, 2001; Aaron, 1994 and 1998; A. Davies, 2001).

The grandeur of colonial topography and the alarming and exciting nature and customs of the people are also outlined, often with illustrations; these first-contact features are strong in the colonial novels, but can also appear alone, often called 'sketches'. There is a largely unknown wealth of these from Wales, often provided by Welsh authors: elementary approaches are James Motley's *Tales of the Cymry* (1848) and Alfred Thomas's *In the Land of Harp and Feather* (1896), but a nativist Christian fantasy is called up by H. Elwyn Thomas's *Where Eden's Tongue is Spoken Still* (1904), and the Revd George Tugwell invokes both English leisure and exploitation in *On the Mountain, Being the Welsh Experience of Abraham Black and Jonas White, etc,*

Esquires, Moralists, Photographers, Fishermen, Botanists (1862). Some of these authors published in both London and Wales, often from the presses of newly established English-language Welsh newspapers. Colonized authors frequently both internalize and promulgate external exploitation; a marked example of that from Wales was the fiction by Arthur Machen and the poetry and journalism by Ernest Rhys which, around the turn of the century, offered a 'Celtic twilight' version of Wales, strongly in keeping with Matthew Arnold's influential argument that Welsh and Irish literature could ameliorate the rougher edges of the vigorous English personality (see D. Williams, 2000).

A simpler form of complicity was the main thrust of highly successful writers of nineteenth-century Welsh-set romance like Anne Beale and Rhoda Broughton, who routinely find an English gentry husband for a fertile Welsh girl, so miming colonial appropriation – Aaron discusses both authors at some length (Aaron, 1998: 163–5 and 168–9). But romance, as in the Irish Maria Edgeworth, can be a critical colonial form, and some Welsh women writers, while retaining a first-contact element, nevertheless represent their country with an independent spirit. Amy Dillwyn's *The Rebecca Rioter* interweaves a distinctly sympathetic account of the rural unrest in south-west Wales of the late 1830s with deliberate non-romance (Dillwyn, 1880). The well-born Gwenllian Tudor, a name rich in native tradition, encourages and helps educate Evan Williams, a labourer's son, but Dillwyn is too realistic to permit a romance between them – he dies after being transported for Rebecca crimes to Tasmania. This locally sensitive analysis is surpassed in Welsh patriotism by *A Maid of Cymru* by 'The Dau Wynne', Mallt and Cate Williams (A. M. and C. Williams, 1901). Their previous novel, *One of the Royal Celts* (1889), was a classic colonized text, starring a Welsh gentleman who fights nobly for the empire, but in *A Maid of Cymru* the heroine Tangwystyl Hywel rejects a handsome Englishman to engage in activities that combine the New Woman with a Welsh version of the Gaelic League.

Somewhere between Dillwyn's liberal realism and the excitable patriotism of 'The Dau Wynne' is the very popular series of novels by 'Allen Raine', the pseudonym for Anne Adeliza Puddlecombe. After living in London with her banker husband she returned to Wales and took up writing in her fifties. Her novels are always romances – she equalled Marie Corelli in fame and sales – and some of her recurrent themes fit comfortably with fictions of colonial exploitations: the beautiful peasant girls, quaint and semi-magical customs, an emphasis on the beauty of the west Wales coastline. But where Beale and Broughton merely used the local people for colourful setting, Raine gives her peasants and villagers full lives, in terms of both aspiration and conflict, and she often represents a non-romance world: the hero can be mistakenly married (*Queen of the Rushes*), there can be familial deceit (*Garthowen*), splendid success in London can be rejected (*A Welsh Singer*), madness is recurrent (*Torn Sails*), and a disturbingly real context can combine with symbolic mysteries: *The Welsh Witch* involves both charges of witchcraft and a sojourn in the eastern industrial district; *Queen of the Rushes* combines the story of a dumb native girl with the vociferous disruptions of the 1904 Revival.

Raine was read in England and around the world as a romancer with a quaint setting, and Gwyn Jones dismissed her work as part of 'a sandcastle dynasty' (1957), but the waves of male realism have not in fact effaced her work. Her first novel, *A Welsh Singer*, responds vigorously to a post-colonial reading as both realizing and to some degree rejecting the power of colonization. The talented native boy and girl become, as sculptor and singer, stars in London, but they are never fully appropriated – Mifanwy is especially faithful to her native area and its values and, like Raine herself, finds value back in Wales.

A later and less consistent representer of the impact of colonization on the country was Hilda Vaughan. Born to the gentry near Builth Wells, she became part of London literary life largely through her marriage to Charles Morgan. Her first novel, *The Battle to the Weak* (1925), contrasts two Welsh families from the Powys hills, one Welsh-speaking and backward-looking, the other hybridized and English-speaking, though also having a violent father – gender issues can as in Raine be part of the politics. English-speaking Esther loves Welsh-speaking Rhys, but they are parted by their hostile familial positions. He goes to America and eventually marries; she soldiers on at home. Ultimately they unite, and nativism seems largely rejected as Rhys has himself been hybridized (into Adult Education), but the novel does at least deal with the complexities of a country and a people facing Anglicization. This sense of complex realities seems abandoned in Vaughan's later work which largely reverts to first-contact attitudes. Two novels trace the ferocity of the native Welsh: in *The Invader* (1928) an English woman inherits a farm but is chased out by the rough locals, and in *The Soldier and the Gentlewoman* (1932) another Gwenllian controls, marries and eventually murders an Anglicized and enfeebled Welsh ex-officer who inherits her family's estate. The novella *A Thing of Nought* (1935) combines a sense of magic with a woman's isolation in rural Wales, and Vaughan later reworked the folklore story of Llyn y Fan Fach in *The Fair Woman* (Vaughan, 1942).

Geraint Goodwin, born further north in Powys, near Newtown, who was introduced to the Welsh tradition by his English master at school (a typical piece of colonial complexity), became a London journalist and then writer. His first book, *Call Back Yesterday* (1935), was basically autobiographical, giving high if nostalgic value to the remote native Wales of Goodwin's grandparents, and his first novel, *The Heyday in the Blood* (1936), combines native figures – a pretty girl, her earthy father, a poetry-writing but tubercular miller – with the modernity of English businessmen and a diasporic journalist of Welsh origin. A fairly unsubtle debate about the forces operating in Wales climaxes with a new road driving through the village, and it seems the dice are loaded against survival. The novel was very successful with English readers – an *Evening Standard* Book Club choice – but Goodwin, coming under the influence of his publishers and Mary Webb the border romancer, wrote nothing so searching again. His later novels are set in border towns, and the only Welsh figures are charming but highly colonized young women.

But not all the appropriative traffic was one-way. Peggy Whistler, mostly English and bred near London, was a very talented poet, illustrator and author of fiction who chose to live on the Welsh side of the border and wrote under the name Margiad Evans. Her short stories, published in *The Old and the Young* (1948), are a rich ethnography of the people of her region, Welsh, English and thoroughly mixed, but her major response to colonization is *Country Dance* (1932). Short, potent, finely illustrated by herself, it tells how a shepherd's daughter a hundred years ago is sought by both Evan ap Evans, her father's bullying master, and Gabriel Ford, an English shepherd. In Brontë style they compete and Ann, who seems like a symbol of her country, eventually gives herself to Evans at harvest-time. But she is found murdered; Evans is cleared; Ford has disappeared. Margiad Evans realizes both the drama and the cost of conflict, male and ethnic, and the novella stands as a tragic reverie on the impact of power on ordinary people in the colonial context.

There was always a dark side to first-contact stories, revealing the dangerous and contemptible side to the natives, so implicitly justifying their disempowerment. That was not the motive for Caradoc Evans's deeply satirical stories about the people of 'Manteg', that far-from-fair place through which he represented bitterly his region of birth and the Nonconformity and greed that ruled it. But the welcome the stories received in London and the anguish they raised in Wales show how they could be read as valid-ation to the English for repression of Welshness, and as frustrations for those Welsh who desperately wanted to be admired by their masters, and themselves. Evans was, like Goodwin, a London journalist, and the stories in *My People* are also colonial creations, both complex and complicit (C. Evans, 1915).

ACT 2: WRITING THE INDUSTRIAL SETTLEMENT

The development of the potential industrial wealth of Wales was led by colonial capital but in its early stages mostly used relocated Welsh labour, and so did not at first develop an English-language culture. In the north-west slate industry that process never occurred, but in the booming coal and metal production of south-east and north-east Wales by the end of the nineteenth century labour immigration, largely from England, though also from the fellow-colony Ireland, generated a hybrid culture in the English language. The second major phase of Welsh writing in English is the literature that was developed in this hybrid working-class community to describe itself in a new ethnography, like the bush literature of Australia or black American culture.

The early attempts to chronicle the mining areas could not disen-tangle themselves from the colonial romance. Irene Saunderson's *A Welsh Heroine* (1911) represents with considerable realism the context, language and resistant attitudes of the colliers, but real conflict is romantically dissolved, rather than resolved: Morfudd Llewelyn, beautiful, Welsh and working-class, marries the aristo-cratic captain of the soldiers sent to quell a strike. Similarly Joseph Keating, a Mountain Ash collier turned journalist and novelist, wrote about mining but located his narratives primarily among the coal-owning and professional class in melodramatic contexts – vengeance in *Son of Judith* (1900), tragedy in *Maurice* (1905), his most worker-focused work, and murder in the later and well-structured *Flower of the Dark* (1917).

Rhys Davies went further, but with his own reasons for falling short of a full ethnography. The son of a Clydach grocer, who became, like Henry Vaughan, a respected member of the English literary world, Davies nevertheless continued to write about Wales, if at some distance. His first novel, *The Withered Root* (1927), shows a brutal mining world from which the young hero recoils to be a revivalist preacher – and die from the contradictions this generates for him. In *The Red Hills* (1932) a heroic miner stands outside the mining village world in a positive, Lawrentian position. Yet Davies, despite his personal literary withdrawal to London, which he later represented in *Tomorrow to Fresh Woods* (1941), went on to write a major settlement trilogy. A valley is industrialized in *Honey and Bread* (1935), turn-of-the-century conflicts are dramatized – or melodramatized – in *A Time to Laugh* (1937), and the story is brought up to the thirties in *Jubilee Blues* (1938). Davies never fully identifies his novels with the workers, but he does outline their harsh context and sympathizes to some real degree with their struggles, though he always criticizes violent and disrespectful resistance (see Knight, 2001, for a discussion of Davies's industrial fiction).

Reverting to nativism to criticize the colonizer, Davies used Dr William Price of Llantrisant as a heroic symbol of Welsh resistance to oppressors through time. This move towards allegory as a way of handling anti-colonial feelings – common in many contexts around the world, as Jameson notes (1986) – is more successfully deployed in Davies's later novel *The Black Venus* (1944). Here, as in many of his short stories, he uses a woman's viewpoint that permits him to glance at social realities but move on to other issues of freedom and vitality, which include linking the heroine's real independence and sexual vitality with a colonially looted artefact – a genuine black Venus.

Davies's success in London gave Welsh writers a platform from which to develop fiction that did write the settlement from inside through the 1930s. The growing number of left-wing sympathizers in Britain was a major part of the audience, and it is notable that the leftism of most thirties Welsh fiction in English was itself an import, the dialectical twin of industrialization.

In this context Jack Jones celebrated the Merthyr of his childhood in a draft named, for his mother, 'Saran'. Judged in London
as far too long, it was cut severely to the vigorous, semi-factual
Black Parade (1935). But the publisher produced first the less
sprawling, less powerful *Rhondda Roundabout* (1934), which,
despite its socially focused title, is really a romance about a young,
shy preacher and a shop girl, with digressions, sometimes negative, on Rhondda society. Having established himself as a
chronicler of settlement life, Jones produced his largest novel,
Bidden to the Feast (1938). The first to realize the industrial
context without external evaluative foci like romance or nativism,
Jones emphasizes family and women's centrality, and his work
gave vigorous voice to the oppressed, self-constructed, hybrid
social culture of the southern Valleys. The combination of intim-
acy and naïvety that gives his novels a confessional ethnographic
power was matched in poetry by Idris Davies's poem sequence
about the 1926 strike, *The Angry Summer* (1943), but *Times Like
These* (1936) by Gwyn Jones, a young academic from Blackwood,
is a more class-neutral account of the strike, giving more
sympathy than Jones or Davies can countenance to some of the
bosses and to those who aspire to move out of the area.

These authors, while inherently anti-colonial, dealt little with
the radical activity in south-east Wales, but this was classically
represented in Lewis Jones's *Cwmardy* (1937) and *We Live*
(1939). A communist miner and activist, he consciously set out to
'novelise . . . a phase of working-class history' (Jones, 1937). His
argument is more with capitalism than colonization, seeing, like
most leftists of the period, the struggle as international and class-
based, not that of an oppressed colony. It is the muddled heroic
mine worker, Big Jim Roberts, who recalls the princes of Wales,
not the hero, his son Len, who becomes a communist leader of the
valley, against bosses, against the First World War, and finally
against the fascist insurgents in Spain. Like many in similar positions, Fanon notable among them, Jones reaches for weapons of
resistance forged in the language and culture of the colonizing
country. The effect of Jones's work as both writer and political
organizer was to generate an image of another Wales, not Welsh-
speaking, rural, Nonconformist and traditional, but industrial,
radical, self-conscious and determined to stand up for itself.

This rejection of Welsh tradition was also the position of Gwyn
Thomas, but his work, like his writing and his imagination, is

richer than Jones's and more clearly marked by his position as a colonized writer. A clever Rhondda boy who hated Oxford, Thomas wrote a novel for a Gollancz competition for a prole-tarian novel. *Sorrow for thy Sons* was rejected as lacking 'the relief of beauty that Rhys Davies can give' (Smith, 1986). It is a bitter book: the village is ugly, the life of the three brothers has little positive in it – one is a Tory grocer, one is an educational exile, and the hero is a one-man anarcho-syndicalist movement. Had it been published, a mainstream career as a radical realist might have followed, but as it was, when Thomas's work first appeared in 1946 it emphasized fables and allegories, like many an undercover colonial resister. The finest is 'Oscar', telling how Lewis, the anti-hero, works for a brute, sees his oppressions and eventually arranges his death. But this is less than resistance: Lewis is deeply complicit, and much in Thomas's work expresses the discomfort of living in a hybrid world (see Knight, 2001/2).

Though Thomas often, and with damaging impact, expressed his dislike of the Welsh-language culture that he had as a child found oppressive (and his strongly left-wing position found un-acceptable), his fiction is in fact strongly marked by Welsh native tradition. 'Oscar' is in part a folkloric giant; the Bible is always close to Thomas's titles and his characters' speech; his language is superbly rhetorical. He also consistently represents acquisitive English people – and, worse, the Welsh who imitate them – as the enemies of the embattled communities he depicts. His histor-ical novel *All Things Betray Thee* was warmly praised by Raymond Williams as a fictional realization of Welsh radical history (R. Williams, 1982), but more revealing from a post-colonial viewpoint is the contemporary *The Thinker and the Thrush*. Not published until 1988, this is a potent narrative of complicity and resistance, focusing on a smug and ambitious grocer's assistant trying to prosper in a dissenting Welsh world (G. Thomas, 1988).

Thomas's later work tends to be short stories that are amusing rather than probing, and like Dylan Thomas he came to represent an acceptably comic Wales over the BBC and, worse yet, in *Punch*. The comic image they created fitted comfortably alongside the cosily colonized Wales, created by Richard Llewellyn in his best-selling novel *How Green Was My Valley* (1939) and very widely disseminated by the Oscar-wining film, which hybridized Llewellyn's sentimentality with Irish colonial stereotypes. A story which rejects both industry (the hero leaves the valley at the start of the book) and radical resistance (the family finally become strike-breakers to save the boss's interest), the novel neatly reverses Jack Jones's structure to romanticize a plentiful past and deplore a present disfigured by disobedient workers. Written in a painfully 'lyrical' style, with plenty of fake-Welsh locutions, here the colonized plays the happy peasant for the pleasure – and indeed money – of the colonizer; and very successfully was the trick turned. Until the early 1950s London publishers were still assiduously hunting for the next *How Green* and some dire noble peasant stuff was produced, notably the creaking trilogy by Richard Vaughan starting with *Moulded in Earth* (1951).

Llewellyn and the likes of Vaughan emphasize the risk of publishing to please a condescending imperial taste; the same forces altered Gwyn Thomas's career, redirected Dylan Thomas and Geraint Goodwin, favoured Bert Coombes's essentially English versions of mining life[3] and rejected two Jack Jones novels, as well as causing major cuts to the saga 'Saran'. Nevertheless the energy of the industrial writers and – perhaps ironically – their access to an English audience did realize, in a short time and with long reverberations, a new, colonially constructed kind of Wales.

ACT 3: INTEGRATION AND INDEPENDENCE

Rural romance and industrial self-realizations have not disappeared, especially in nostalgic versions, and the popular writers Alexander Cordell and Iris Gower have essentially condensed the two forms. But in the decades since the Second World War a third movement has occurred in the drama of Welsh fiction in English. Novels and stories have appeared that in tone avoid the quaintly rural and the rhetorically proletarian, and tend to explore forms of integration – integration between rural and industrial, between native and immigrant versions of Welshness and, in recent decades, between women and men, and the multiple ethnicities that exist in modern Wales. In various, and often incomplete ways, seeking to reintegrate the separatenesses created in Wales by colonization, the writers of these fictions also tend, more or less consciously, to see independence as a natural state for Wales. They are neither servile nor embattled in their relation to England; they have not forgotten the impact and the scars of colonization – indeed its economic and social impact remains a major context and theme – but the impact of this third sequence of writing Wales in English is to realize a country that is, in its essential attitude, post-colonial, putting together the pieces of lives and a country in the aftermath of empire.

Glyn Jones, Merthyr-born school teacher, poet and novelist, always wrote about Wales and Welsh people, but he as consistently transcended realism. His early book of stories, *The Blue Bed* (1937), contains some of the best English-language surrealist writing, and in *The Island of Apples* (1965) he transmutes a Merthyr-lad-at-school story into a dreamlike encounter with an aesthetic Galahad, who represents vision and bravura in action and imagination. In the same far-reaching way Jones, who regained the Welsh language that was lost in his family, linked rural and industrial Wales (especially in his short stories), translated early Welsh-language poetry, was notably supportive to all other writers throughout his long life and published the first major account of Welsh writing in English with the consciously integrative title *The Dragon has Two Tongues* (Glyn Jones, 1968).

In a parallel move Menna Gallie extended the traditional south Wales novel in two ways. Brought up in Ystradgynlais, she retained her familial Welsh language and in her first novel, *Strike for a Kingdom* (Gallie, 1959), set in 1926, she makes the miners' leader a bard with the striking name, D. J. Williams – apparently referring to the famous author of *Hen Dŷ Ffarm*, one of the famous three of Penyberth. By representing a pit village of the older sort, where English did not dominate, Gallie tends to defuse colonial issues, and her politics emphasizes the constraints women undergo in the community. This emphasis is stronger in her second 'Cilhendre' novel, *The Small Mine* (Gallie, 1962), which takes place under nationalization and is much more strongly driven by gender concerns, as discussed by Jane Aaron in her Introduction to the recent reprint.

Gallie's integrational instincts in language and gender make her transitional between the Valley novelists and the major work of Emyr Humphreys. The son of a Flintshire Anglican headmaster, like Glyn Jones and Menna Gallie he went to university in Wales: the locally educated elite always play a major role in the move towards cultural reclamation. At Aberystwyth he became a nationalist, then a conscientious objector. His first novel, *A Toy Epic* (1958), was rejected by Graham Greene for Heinemann in 1942 as, it seems, not sufficiently, stereotypically, Welsh, and it only appeared sixteen years later. In modernist stream-of-consciousness style three boys typify modern Wales, the sons of a farmer, a worker and an Anglican minister: the last is committed to nationalism but his motives are sceptically probed by Humphreys. His first published book, *The Little Kingdom* (1946), goes further into the possible errors of commitment – the nationalist hero is also a murderer – and after a detour into English-style novels of moral choice he produced in *A Man's Estate* (1957), his first major Welsh-focused work. Basing the novel on the Orestes myth – as in Glyn Jones, dealing with Wales did not imply international ignorance – Humphreys reveals with bitter power the decayed gentry and the vulgar urban peasantry of modern north Wales. Brilliantly written and deeply negative – the only figures of value are a weak minister and a crushed daughter, though the peasants do retain vulgar vitality – the novel established Humphreys at a level he did not fail to sustain as the major chronicler of modern Wales.

In *Outside the House of Baal* (1965) he combined, with *Ulysses* as a model, a morning in the life of a retired minister and his elderly sister-in-law with a mosaic of flashbacks that traced their lives and, through them, the major events of fifty years, including the wars, the Depression and the many hopes and betrayals of the native Welsh in that time. There is a consistent awareness of the impact of colonial capitalism – the 'House of Baal' of the title is a vulgar modern pub embodying the threat of Englishness. There is little comfort in the narrative: the minister's children are both Anglicized and he has seen his values, which include pacifism and socialism (he spends many years in the south), apparently frustrated; equally his sister-in-law's devotion to family has come to nothing more than housekeeping and memories. Yet the novel also speaks up for their endurance: though Humphreys chooses to write in English, both because of the nature of the novel and because of the larger audience, the characters are usually speaking in a translated Welsh, and the old family home was named 'Argoed' in reference to T. Gwynn Jones's poem about the defiant resistances of historical Celticity (see Humphreys, 1965: 9, 12).

The question of how to perpetuate a native culture concerns Humphreys directly in *The Taliesin Tradition* (1983) and is the dominant theme of his massive novel sequence *The Land of the Living*. Starting with *National Winner* (1971), then meant to complete the series, it focuses on a north Wales solicitor-bard,

John Cilydd More, his two wives, their children, and their many friends and associates over fifty years. The complex technique of *Outside the House of Baal* is simplified and the narrative clarifies a range of characters, positions – and problems.

John Cilydd was a *dadeni* poet, winning the National Eisteddfed just after the war. Always sensitive, he was also persistent and consistent, holding to poetic and native values against material temptations and – a crucial matter for Humphreys – refusing to let his nationalism melt before British patriotism in the Second World War. Increasingly marginalized – Myrddin Wyllt, the all-knowing, all-suffering ancient bard becomes his conscious avatar – he will eventually kill himself through a combination of ostracism and despair. His life and its struggle for meaning are steadily, and with great narrative skill, unfolded over the next volumes which chart the promise and the failures in Wales of the gentry, nationalism, Nonconformist earnestness, southern leftism: the conflicted colonized history of Wales, touched on and symbolized in *Outside the House of Baal*, is here represented in historicized detail.

Amy, John Cilydd's second wife, is a major figure, difficult to assess. In her last years Lady Brangor, a politician's widow, she was born very poor and ascended in part through her beauty, in part through good friends, and to a debatable degree by her fierce and not always honest determination. An enthusiastic nationalist at university (Aberystwyth, of course), a true friend to the tragic, well-born Enid Prydderch, loving the romantic nationalist Val Gwyn who dies of TB, easily seduced by the heroic southern Marxist Pen Lewis, a reliable support at first for the suffering bard John Cilydd, Amy in the chronologically early novels seems neither villain nor victim, but as John Cilydd grows more remotely bardic Amy becomes more like a seeker after power, and finds this in wartime through the Labour Party. She remains enigmatic, in part the exploited fertility of Wales, in part an opportunistic survivor. Humphreys has created in Amy a figure sufficiently complex, and complicit, to represent the social history of Wales under the distorting effects of English colonialism and twentieth-century history.

The only rival to Humphreys in terms of seriousness and productivity is Raymond Williams. His fame as a Cambridge-based literary critic and theorist did not deter him from writing fiction, all in some way dealing with Wales. Born in Pandy on the eastern border, the son of a railwayman, his links were with the industrial novel, not the romances of Powys. His role as part of the colonial diaspora dominates the first two of his 'Welsh trilogy': *Border Country* (1960) creates an imaginative bond between the young Welsh academic and his dying father, focused on the experience of 1926; *Second Generation* (1964) deals with Welsh car workers and students in Oxford, but its prime concern is the Britain-wide working class, and Welsh issues are minor. This changes radically in *The Fight for Manod* (1977), where characters from the previous two novels investigate a European plan to found a new-style, high-technology corridor city in mid-Wales. Corruption is eventually exposed, both local and international, a toll is taken of the brave investigators, but the essence of the book is Williams's high valuing of the Welsh community, a renovated version of the *gwerin*. As in his other work, Williams tends to rely for emotive value on landscape more than native tradition, but here as in his other writing of the period (see R. Williams, 2003), he states a commitment to Wales and its concerns that was pursued in *The Volunteers* (1978), a polished near-future thriller that finds the value of resistance at several levels in Wales, and *Loyalties* (1985), which finds the same virtues and those of familial trust at risk in the world of communism and espionage. In a sophisticated version of nativism, from *The Fight for Manod* on, Williams is clear that capitalist colonialism, though it may be used for profit by some Welsh, is inherently hostile to the country and its values, and late in life he made a commitment to nationalism without in any way rejecting his lifelong left-wing positions (see R. Williams, 1977).

Williams's love of history and landscape and his valuing of community came together in his final, unfinished project, *People of the Black Mountains* in which he was charting all the people who had lived over time in his beloved Black Mountains. A step beyond Humphreys's use of the mythic lens and then the *roman fleuve* to command time, the approach seems less capable of detailed social history than Williams's other work, but though he exploits topographic romance he never reverts to the mere land-taking descriptions of the early colonial material: the people are always present, and respected in terms of their own culture, their own struggles.

In many ways Williams's late engagement with Wales and its issues complements Humphreys's longer commitment to the

country, especially through their different locations and connections, and their combined weight has been one impetus for recent
writing in Wales. Another has been the rise of publishers, often
working with quasi-governmental subsidies, located in Wales: the
days have gone of terrible proof-reading of Welsh-language words
and decisions to publish made entirely on London terms. A third
dynamic has been the very substantial rise of writing by women
in Wales, as around the world.

The motifs of integration and independence have recurred
through this recent work: a combination of modern forces is
evident in Moira Dearnley's *That Watery Glass* (1973). Self-confi-
dently serious, published in Wales, it charts a young woman's
career at university. Not a native speaker herself, she is embraced
by fertile Welshness in the person of a handsome student called –
the name is deliberate rather than ironic – Dafydd ap Gwilym.
That symbolized independence and integration is distant but still
imagined in Christopher Meredith's *Shifts* (1988). He shows
powerfully how the decline of a steel plant in the south-east is
symbiotically integrated with the return to meaningless diaspora
for one man, the first clear feelings of independence in the woman
he has encountered, and for her husband a path is opening to
study the history of local industry in its original language. The
withdrawal of colonial capitalism is more indirectly, but more
poignantly, lamented in the work of Ron Berry and Alun
Richards, while new writers are more savage: Richard John
Evans's *Entertainment* (2000) and Rachel Trezise's *In and Out of
the Goldfish Bowl* (2000) chart the bleak world of the young
Valley unemployed, and Niall Griffiths in *Grits* (1999) identifies
the same desperate lifestyle in west Wales. Yet anarchic as the
characters seem to be, the writers often explicitly evoke writing
itself as a way forward and the energy of fiction in English at the
moment – like that of fiction in Welsh as well – indicates a stage
in post-colonial development where the formerly colonized
country is, through its culture, determinedly considering its
options.

That does not mean the writers are content: very striking is
the recurrent use of a disabled figure to express a sense of difficulty, immobility, in the present context. Both Evans and Trezise
represent physical limitations, as does Lewis Davies in *My
Piece of Happiness* (2000), a subtle exposition of life among the
handicapped. Disability is a powerful and repeated image: its

recurrence among post-colonial writers has been noted by Ato Quayson (1999).

A post-colonial Wales, by recognizing its own status, has become attentive to its innate complexity, recognizing the ethnic varieties found in Wales and previously overlooked in the major battle between England Wales: Trezza Azzopardi's *The Hiding Place* (2000) deals with Maltese people in Cardiff; Stephen Knight's *Mr Schnitzel* (2000) links Swansea and Austria; Charlotte Williams writes *Sugar and Slate* (2002) as both Afro-Caribbean and north Welsh.

The renewed vigour of Welsh fiction in English has – perhaps ironically – led to London publishers again taking up local authors, but it seems that by now Welsh fiction can hold its own, and authors are writing what they choose to say, not what a leisured imperial reading class might feel quaintly diverting. Jonathan Cape, one of the liberal and also constraining London publishers of earlier Welsh writing, now publishes John Williams's novel, *Cardiff Dead*,[4] which takes its title from a localized jingle 'I's Cardiff born and Cardiff bred, And when I dies I'll be Cardiff dead.'

Such defiance, and such irony, is the voice of postcolonialism.

NOTES

[1] Two anthologies with good introductions print a range of the early stories and give an account of their limited success: see D. Thomas, 1971 and 1983.

[2] The arguments of this chapter are elaborated and extended to other writers in my book *One Hundred Years of Fiction: Writing Wales in English* (Knight, 2004).

[3] *These Poor Hands* (Coombes, 1939) was a Left Book Club Book of the Month and Coombes remained in demand in English media as a calm, sad voice for the Welsh miners. See Jones and Williams, 1999, for an account of his work and reception.

[4] (London: Bloomsbury, 2000).

REFERENCES

Aaron, J. (1994). 'A national seduction: Wales in nineteenth-century women's writing', *New Welsh Review*, 27, 31–8.

Aaron, J. (1998). *Pur fel y Dur: Y Gymraes yn Llên Menywod y Bedwaredd Ganrif ar Bymtheg*, Cardiff: University of Wales Press.

Coombes, B. (1939). *These Poor Hands*, London: Victor Gollancz.

Davies, A. (2001). '"The reputed nation of inspiration": representations of Wales in fiction from the romance period, 1780–1829', unpublished Ph.D. thesis, Cardiff University.

Davies, I. (1943). *The Angry Summer*, London: Faber; reprinted (ed. Tony Conran), Cardiff: University of Wales Press, 1993.

Dearnley, M. (2001). *Distant Fields: Eighteenth Century Fictions of Wales*, Cardiff: University of Wales Press.

Dillwyn, A. (1880). *The Rebecca Rioter*, London: Macmillan; reprinted (ed. K. Gramich), Dinas Powys: Honno, 2001.

Evans, C. (1915). *My People*, London: Andrew Melrose; reprinted (ed. J. Harris), Bridgend: Seren Books, 1987.

Evans, M. (1948). *The Old and the Young*, London: Lindsay Drummond; reprinted (ed. C. Lloyd-Morgan), Bridgend: Seren Books, 1998.

Gallie, M. (1959). *Strike for a Kingdom*, London: Victor Gollancz; reprinted (ed. Angela V. John), Dinas Powys: Honno Press, 2003.

Gallie, M. (1962). *The Small Mine*, London: Victor Gollancz; reprinted (ed. Jane Aaron), Dinas Powys: Honno Press, 2000.

Humphreys, E. (1965). *Outside the House of Baal*, London: Eyre & Spottiswoode; reprinted (ed. M. Wynn Thomas), Bridgend: Seren Books, 1996.

Jameson, F. (1986). 'Third World literature in the era of multinational capitalism', *Social Text*, 15, 65–88.

Jones, B. and Williams, C. (1999). *B. L. Coombes*, Cardiff: University of Wales Press.

Jones, Glyn (1968), *The Dragon Has Two Tongues*, London: Dent; reprinted (ed. Tony Brown), Cardiff: University of Wales Press, 2001.

Jones, Gwyn (1957). *The First Forty Years: Some Notes on Anglo-Welsh Literature*, Cardiff: University of Wales Press; reprinted in *Triskel One: Essays on Welsh and Anglo-Welsh Literature*, ed. Sam Adams and Gwilym Rees Hughes, Llandybïe: Christopher Davies, 1978, pp. 75–95.

Jones, L. (1937). *Cwmardy*, London: Lawrence & Wishart; reprinted (ed. D. Smith), London: Lawrence & Wishart, 1979.

Knight, S. (2001). '"Not a place for me": Rhys Davies's industrial fiction', in *Rhys Davies: Decoding the Hare*, ed. Meic Stephens, Cardiff: University of Wales Press, pp. 54–70.

Knight, S. (2001/2). 'The voices of Glamorgan: Gwyn Thomas's colonial fiction', *Welsh Writing in English*, 7, 16–34.

Knight, S. (2004). *One Hundred Years of Fiction: Writing Wales in English*, Cardiff: University of Wales Press.

Mathias, R. (1987). *Anglo-Welsh Literature: An Illustrated History*, Bridgend: Poetry Wales Press.

Motley, J. (1848). *Tales of the Cymry*, London and Llanelli: Longmans; Thomas.

Quayson, A. (1999) '"Looking awry": tropes of disability in postcolonial writing', in *An Introduction to Contemporary Fiction*, ed. Rod Mengham, Cambridge: Polity Press, pp. 53–68.

Smith, D. (1986). 'Introduction', in Gwyn Thomas, *Sorrow for thy Sons*, London: Lawrence & Wishart.

Thomas, D. (1971). *Dylan Thomas: Early Prose Writing*, ed. Walford Davies, London: Dent.

Thomas, D. (1983). *Collected Stories*, ed. Leslie Norris, London: Dent.

Thomas, G. (1988). *The Thinker and the Thrush*, Bridgend: Seren Books.

Thomas, H. E. (1904). *Where Eden's Tongue is Spoken Still*, London and Newport: H. R. Allenson; George Bell.

Tugwell, G. (1862). *On the Mountain, Being the Welsh Experience of Abraham Black and Jonas White, etc, Esquires, Moralists, Photographers, Fishermen, Botanists*, London: Bentley.

Vaughan, H. (1942). *The Fair Woman*, New York; Duell, Sloan and Pearce; published as *Iron and Gold*, London: Macmillan, 1948; reprinted (ed. J. Aaron), Dinas Powys: Honno, 2002.

Williams, A. M. and C. (The Dau Wynne) (1901). *A Maid of Cymru: A Patriotic Romance*, London and Carmarthen: Simpkin and Marshall; Spurrell.

Williams, D. (2000). 'Pan-Celticism and the limits of post-colonialism: W. B. Yeats, Ernest Rhys and William Sharp in the 1890s', in *Nations and Relations: Writing Across the British Isles*, ed. Tony Brown and Russell Stephens, Cardiff: New Welsh Review, pp. 1–29.

Williams, J. (2000). *Cardiff Dead*, London: Bloomsbury.

Williams R. (1977). 'Marxism, poetry, Wales', *Poetry Wales*, 13, 16–34; reprinted in Raymond Williams, *Who Speaks for Wales?*, ed. Daniel Williams, pp. 81–94.

Williams, R. (1982). 'Working-class, proletarian, socialist: problems in some Welsh novels', in H. Gustav Klaus (ed.), *The Socialist Novel in Britain: Towards the Recovery of a Tradition*, Brighton: Harvester, pp. 110–21.

Williams, R. (2003). *Who Speaks for Wales? Nation, Culture, Identity*, ed. Daniel Williams, Cardiff: University of Wales Press.

10
Dramatic Fictions in a Postcolonial Wales

STEVE BLANDFORD

INTRODUCTION

In June 1997 *The Observer* asked the ubiquitous Ed Thomas, arguably the most significant figure in drama across all media in contemporary Wales, to comment on the new possibility of devolved government for Wales. His reply runs through the post-colonial sensibilities of much of the work that I would like to discuss here:

> Old Wales is dead. The Wales of stereotype, leeks, daffodils, look-you-now boyo rugby supporters singing Max Boyce songs in three-part harmony while phoning mam to tell her they'll be home for tea and Welsh cakes has gone . . . So where does it leave us? Free to make up, re-invent, redefine our own versions of Wales, all three million definitions if necessary, because the Wales I know is bilingual, multicultural, pro-European, messed up, screwed up and ludicrously represented in the British press . . . So old Wales is dead and new Wales is already a possibility, an eclectic self-defined Wales with attitude. (quoted in Roms, 1998: 186)

The fact that *The Observer* asked for Thomas's views and that he became one of the most frequently interviewed personalities during the referendum campaign draws attention to the very high profile that dramatic fictions have enjoyed in defining and redefining Wales. By 'dramatic fictions' one does not simply mean drama in a general sense, but more specifically the idea of performance, as Roger Owen has suggested:

> Some of the most important recent general studies of Welsh history have defined Wales and Welshness in terms which make strong (albeit

sometimes implicit) reference to performance. I want to propose that, during the past twenty years, a body of historical and cultural writing has begun to emerge which has characterised Welshness not as a cultural condition but as a cultural act, one that requires invention rather than inhabitation or incantation. (Owen, 2001: 101)

Both Owen and Thomas draw our attention to Wales's need continually to 'perform' its identity, partly because of the non-existence of an actual nation-state:

> The prime factor responsible for inciting this notion of performance is the simple fact that, throughout the epoch of modern history, Wales has not had – and still does not have – its own apparatus of state. The idea of an independent – even separate – Welsh identity is not acknowledged in any real sense by the political system under which the Welsh are governed, and this lends to the political culture of Wales a strong sense of performance, even of theatre. (Owen, 2001: 101)

Owen then goes on to make links not only to the kind of theatre that is emerging in contemporary Wales (though of course he is also talking about 'performance' in a wider sense) but more specifically to ideas about the problematics of postcolonial cultures that seek to mimic the forms of the imperial power in order to aspire to the 'elevated condition of the coloniser' as Homi Bhabha put it (Owen, 2001: 101). This, I would like to argue, is central to debates about the kind of dramatic fictions that have emerged in Wales, not just in the post-devolutionary period itself, but during the period when a pro-devolutionary impetus began to be felt again after the débâcle of the 1979 referendum.

Writers and film makers in the media of theatre, film and television have continually wrestled with this most critical of postcolonial dilemmas: how far to adopt or mimic mainstream Anglo-American forms to write in and about contemporary Wales, or, conversely, how far to engage with the much more complex struggle to create forms that are distinctive. This issue is at the heart of many, often bitter, debates concerning, for example, the pros and cons of a mainstream 'national' theatre based at Theatr Clwyd, the aspirations of Welsh film makers to work with larger budgets and within popular genres, and the seeming impossibility of creating television drama that stands any chance of a network presence on either the BBC or ITV 1.

In the following sections on theatre and film and television drama I attempt to explore the complexities of these dilemmas, their relationship principally to ideas of mimicry and hybridity, and the various answers that appear to be emerging from the artists working in Wales today.

THEATRE

Of the three media considered here theatre has had the most turbulent post-devolutionary history. In this section I explore how both policy-makers and artists working in Wales have sought to respond to the challenge of the raised expectation of a distinctively Welsh theatre.

Appropriately the theatre community in Wales began what we might see as its postcolonial life with a series of impassioned and very public rows over the Arts Council of Wales's now notorious Drama Strategy. The response to this document was in many ways extraordinary and at one point included the parading of a coffin through Cardiff as well as questions in the Westminster Parliament. There are a number of different ways of reading this, of course, but in the context of the immediate post-devolution atmosphere it is tempting to see it optimistically, that is, as a sign of an arts community with a new sense of its own identity, seeking to make policy-makers more open and accountable. To an extent there was some success. Under pressure from the National Assembly the Drama Strategy was partially abandoned and, eventually, the chief executive of the Arts Council resigned. The clearest signals possible had been given that the Assembly would assert its influence through the Arts Council and that it was not afraid of those that fear undue direct political influence in the arts.

How, then, has this seemingly robust official quest for post-devolutionary, postcolonial identity impacted upon the actual dramatic fictions being produced for the stage in Wales? The downside is still the strong sense of loss amongst the Welsh theatre community over the virtual demise of what many felt was Welsh theatre's most distinctive feature, namely the strong concentration of experimental theatre in Wales exemplified by internationally renowned companies such as Brith Gof, Moving Being and Volcano. Ironically, these were often the companies at the forefront of attempts to create a theatre that could have been seen as postcolonial. As Mike Pearson, now professor of performance at Aberystwyth but formerly one of the central figures in the Welsh experimental theatre movement, put it,

The aim of *Brith Gof* is to develop a new, vibrant and distinctive theatre tradition in Wales, one which is relevant and responsive to the perceptions, experience, aspirations and concerns of a minority culture and a small nation and which is more than just a pale reflection of English theatre convention. (quoted in Adams, 1996: 55)

However, Brith Gof's work was not about creating something Welsh in any essentialist sense, but rather about working in a way that has often been central to postcolonial analyses:

Brith Gof deals with subject matter from Welsh literary, historical, social political and mythical sources. But what we've done is to weld on to those sources a form of theatre entirely alien, and made a hybrid. The idea of hybridisation is very important and is entirely opposite to ideas of purity and authenticity. (quoted in Saville, 1997: 104)

Brith Gof's clear understanding of the relationship between form and the politics of identity in Wales is typical not only of their own work, but of a number of other practitioners during the decade immediately preceding devolution.

However, one way of looking at recent Welsh theatre history would be to say that the significant 'events' have moved away from a 'theatre of invention', as Ed Thomas has called it, towards a kind of middle ground. This is a territory that has enabled a number of young Welsh writers to have their work staged at prominent London fringe venues as well as tour in Wales and, perhaps just as significantly, to appeal to different audiences within Wales. Many would see this as ironic, as the production of new writing in Wales has been amongst the most neglected and contentious areas of Arts Council policy, most recently through its decision to close Made in Wales, formerly the English-language new-writing company, and to create one company only to produce new work in both Welsh and English.

In the introduction to the first of two published volumes of Made in Wales plays from the late nineties, the ex-artistic director, Jeff Teare, makes his vision of the function of new work in Wales quite explicit:

Well, they are Welsh plays and they are concerned with identity but not in the usual Welsh theatrical manner. The cultural identity of *Safar* is somewhere between Pakistani and British Asian, the identity discussed in *Gulp* is sexual, and *Happiness* deals in social and existential self rather than national. Three Welsh plays in one volume not about definitions of Welshness, good grief! (Teare, 1998: 12)

Teare continually snipes at what he sees as the narrowness and parochialism of the theatre establishment in Wales, particularly with regard to questions of ethnic and sexual identity, and here we have a very interesting set of postcolonial tensions. A director from the London fringe, Teare arrived in Wales seeking to drag what he saw as the fundamentally homogeneous nature of Welsh 'performed' identity kicking and screaming on to stages in Wales and beyond. Predictably the results met with very mixed reactions, and many questioned the theatrical as well as intellectual sophistication of much of the work. Arguably the most positive dimension was that, at times, the company could claim to have reached out to new audiences who saw something for the first time in a Welsh play that was part of their experience of living here. Typical of this was *Gulp* by a young Cardiff writer, Roger Williams: 'It was generally considered to be Cardiff's first professionally produced young, out gay play, referred to by the press as a "cultural milestone". The audience at Chapter was predominantly under 35 with many first-time theatre attenders' (Teare, 1998: 11).

Here the linked concepts of hybridity and mimicry come into play. Made in Wales's critics would argue that it largely produced work that did simply 'mimic' that being produced anywhere in the UK, whilst the more radical formal possibilities that had been so prevalent in Wales during the 1980s and early 1990s were declining. On the other hand, by implicitly linking the subordinate nature of black and gay communities within Wales to the subordinate nature of Wales to England, the company could be said to have been very much part of a postcolonial spirit to redefine and reinvent.

The successor company to Made in Wales and its Welsh-language counterpart, Dalier Slyw – Sgript Cymru, has to some extent extended this tradition, though arguably its output has been less self-consciously concerned with 'minority' representation. Like Made in Wales it has seemed to prioritize the production of new Welsh writing outside Wales and has had high-profile success, particularly with two plays that had extended London fringe runs and consequent press attention. Both were by young writers relatively new to theatre and neither was overtly concerned with Welshness at all, though they clearly contain identifiable Welsh characters and references. *Crazy Gary's Mobile Disco* by Gary Owen and *Art and Guff* by Catherine Tregenna were, to some extent, presented as a kind of 'package' which helped to maximize publicity and create a minor stir around Welsh playwriting getting in on the 'Cool Cymru' act. What seemed to unite them was not so much their concern for Wales as much as the (by now) well-trodden ground of masculinity.

There have, however, been theatrical 'events' in the post-devolutionary period that have sought a much more direct engagement with Welsh identity. For example, both Patrick Jones's *Everything Must Go* and Helen Griffin's *Flesh and Blood* were frequently seen as theatrically crude and naïve by the Welsh theatre establishment, but were also seized upon for their value in contributing to the image of an emerging Wales in London and the rest of the UK. Jones's close relationship with the Manic Street Preachers through his brother, Nicky Wire, obviously contributed to this, and sections of the London press were quick to link the play to the Manics' very direct political agenda.

Theatre in the Welsh language has perhaps suffered most from a crisis of confidence in the post-devolutionary period, though now it seems that the proposal to create a strong national company is nearing some kind of reality. What many fear is that it will come close simply to mirroring Clwyd Theatr Cymru's adoption of a traditional English repertory theatre with a mix of classical translations, the Welsh-language theatre 'canon', and the occasional nod to new writing. Currently a provisional budget has been announced and a steering group established and some considerable debate is now likely over its eventual identity.

Interestingly, it was the Welsh-language company Dalier Slyw that was selected by the Arts Council to form the basis of the funded new-writing company for Wales (now Sgript Cymru), not its English-language counterpart, Made in Wales. There was little or no celebration of this, however, rather a concentration on the fact that now only one new-writing company was being funded, and at a level lower than the combined funding for the previous two. Out of this highly charged set of circumstances it is perhaps not surprising that the new company's most high-profile work to date has been in English, though its current development plans include work in Welsh by one of the most consistent writers for small-scale theatre in Wales in the 1990s, Sera Moore-Williams. There is also an active and innovative community writers' scheme that operates across Wales and in both languages. This in turn leads to regional events showcasing new work in development, again in both languages.

If Sgript Cymru is to help increase the significance of Welsh-language theatre within the whole context of Wales's postcolonial identity, it needs to work on developing its presence outside its current heartland in the north-west. Here Arad Goch, Theatre Bara Caws and others continue to produce a significant body of work that is often rooted in their close relationship with their communities, but in the rest of the country, and therefore for the majority of the population, Welsh-language theatre is largely invisible. It will be a vital task for both Sgript Cymru and the new national company to support the existing small-scale companies to seek to change this, if Welsh-language theatre is to have a clear role in the project of national redefinition.

FILM AND TELEVISION DRAMA

In terms of institutions and public policy, neither film nor television in Wales is postcolonial to even the same limited degree as theatre might be said to be. Broadcasting in Wales remains under the direct control of the Westminster Department of Culture, Media and Sport. There has been talk of an Assembly-controlled film fund for Wales, but for the time being policy-making remains in London.

Clearly, though, this only tells part of the story. S4C has, in one sense, been part of a kind of postcolonial vanguard for two decades; the BBC has long devolved (limited) power to Cardiff and there remains a system of public-service regional broadcasting in the UK with an ITV2 'region' covering Wales (in a very limited way). In film there is a funded agency, Sgrîn, with responsibility for the promotion of moving-image production, distribution and exhibition as well as for media education. However, with the economics of the moving-image industries very little affected by devolution, can there be said to be such a thing as a discernible 'postcolonial response' on the part of film makers?

To take film first, in the absence of any comparable debate about Wales it is interesting to look for a moment at arguments that have been conducted about the much more buoyant Scottish film sector. Colin McArthur and others have strongly criticized the funding agencies in Scotland for tacitly encouraging Scottish film makers to adopt commercially driven strategies at the expense of the establishment of a distinct Scottish film identity:

The emphasis is placed on the creation of a cinema rooted in narra-
tive-based storytelling derived from Hollywood film practice, coupled
with an emphasis on market driven production strategies. This not
only drives up the costs, but also fails to address the more pressing
cultural and social questions to which an indigenous Scottish cinema
ought to be committed. (Petrie, 2000: 163)

Petrie sums up McArthur's prescription for a more culturally
responsible cinema a little further on:

McArthur has elaborated the case for the necessity of a 'low budget,
aesthetically austere, indigenously-orientated' cinema under the label
(somewhat unfortunate for a rallying cry) 'Poor Scottish Cinema'.
Using the subsidised workshop sector as facilitator, and restricting
budgets to a maximum of £300,000, McArthur proposes funding
conditions which would inspire film makers to look to alternative
aesthetic strategies and production methods – touchstones include
individual auteurs like Bill Douglas, Chris Marker, Robert Bresson,
Dusan Makavejev and Derek Jarman. (Petrie, 2000: 163)

As Petrie goes on to say, McArthur's arguments raise key questions 'about the relationship between culture and economics in
the process of the development of cinema in a small country'.
McArthur's ideal is a very 'pure' one in a sense and clearly relates
to the postcolonial identity of film in Wales. Welsh cinema has, for
the most part, had little choice but to be a 'poor cinema', relying
on short film schemes imaginatively stitched together by
producers from scraps from the broadcasters, the lottery and
British-wide funding bodies. It has also, and contentiously, lost
out on Channel 4 funding throughout a period (the 1980s and
1990s) when it was propping up the wider UK industry. However,
this has not stopped feature films being made that are Welsh in
ways that I would argue are relevant to debates about postcolonial identity, and I would now like to move on to examine some
examples that seem to me to illustrate the key issues.

The first of these is *Human Traffic* directed by Justin Kerrigan
and first shown in June 1999. Excitingly for Kerrigan and all
involved with the picture, Philip French in *The Observer* hailed
Human Traffic as a genuine pointer to the future of Welsh cinema:

Just as *Trainspotting* makes a clean break with the traditional
Scotland of tartanry and kailyard, of Scott and Barrie, so *Human
Traffic* turns its back on the Wales of male voice choirs and the whim-
sical humour of *The Englishman Who Went Up a Hill But Came
Down a Mountain* . . . it seems more like an American picture than a

British one; the influences working on it are Quentin Tarantino, Woody Allen, Bob Rafelson's *Head* and early Scorsese. (French, 1999)

So what is the value to a postcolonial Welsh identity of the emergence of a young director who, if French is right, has most in common with American independent cinema (and perhaps with some of their models in Europe)? If the film is so unrecognizably 'Welsh', what can it mean for an emergent culture?

Well, to begin with the film is not so much unrecognizably Welsh as Welsh with a style and wit that it wears very lightly. Set in Cardiff, it justifiably makes its five central characters a diverse bunch, on all levels lacking allegiance to any traditional idea of identity. In terms of form this is no British realist film either. The scenes involving the Cardiff clubs are the closest the film comes to embracing that aesthetic whilst the rest involves a hectic mix of pieces to camera, pure fantasy and mock documentary. It is essentially a playful film, entirely in tune with its subject matter, and it looks exactly as though it comes from the kind of Wales that Ed Thomas described in our opening quotation.

Apart from Kerrigan's début perhaps the next highest-profile film career in the post-devolutionary period has belonged to Sara Sugarman. It is fair to say that Sugarman has tended to foreground the Welsh identity of a number of her films to a greater extent than Kerrigan. However, this foregrounding is not straightforward and can be linked to the hybridity of her own north Welsh/Jewish identity. It is perhaps this 'insider/outsider' tendency that has led to the affectionate, comic, almost surreal take on Valleys life typified by her most recent film, *Very Annie Mary*, a confident film that is unafraid of the traps involved in dealing with the stereotypes that it very consciously trades in.

If Kerrigan and Sugarman represent the possibility of young Welsh film makers both reaching wider audiences and being free to experiment, there have also been high-profile releases in the last three years that are closer to being conventional, and yet also have a degree of importance in the current context. These would include the Oscar-nominated *Solomon and Gaenor*, which very productively uses three languages, Welsh, English and Yiddish, in ways that employ history to comment obliquely not just on contemporary Wales, but also on the lingering xenophobia that surfaces in debates about asylum seekers and the rise of a new European right.

The most commercially ambitious film to emerge from Wales in recent years was *Rancid Aluminium*, the feature début (as director) of Ed Thomas. Sadly, the film was almost universally disliked by reviewers across the spectrum and particularly casti-gated for its perceived attempt to cash in on the success of the British gangster film, *Lock, Stock and Two Smoking Barrels*. As we have already discussed, what Colin McArthur and others would argue is that it is a waste of time trying to get into this level of commercial film making from within Wales. Instead a post-devolutionary Wales should concentrate on a 'poor cinema' that allows the development of voices and images independent of the forms of either Britain or the USA. What this argument ignores, however, are questions of confidence and audience expectation, and in Scotland *Shallow Grave* and *Trainspotting* have arguably allowed a strong low-budget culture to emerge alongside them.

In Wales there have been a number of films working innova-tively on low budgets that perhaps have been representative of the power of 'poor cinema' at its best. For example, *Diwrnod Hollol Mindblowing* ('A Totally Mindblowing Day') directed in 1999 by Euros Lyn, with a finance package that included HTV and lottery money, is powerfully influenced by the Danish Dogma group. It contains elements of the road movie and is an interesting, unsys-tematic exploration of competing north/south, urban/rural identities within contemporary Wales. It is witty and lyrical and turns the imperatives of small budgets and resultant hand-held improvisation to good effect. The commercial result? A complete disappearance and the hardest film to obtain information about of any that I have written about.

A similar fate, though it got a more prominent small-screen airing on S4C, has befallen *Beautiful Mistake* made jointly by Chris Forster and Marc Evans. This is another highly original piece of work based around the idea of bringing John Cale back to Wales and getting him to play with a number of younger Welsh musicians. Cale almost becomes a living embodiment of the hybridity and freewheeling nature of a possible new Welsh iden-tity. Look, the film says, one of the Velvet Underground was a Welshman and here he returns to play alongside James Dean Bradfield and Cerys Matthews. Surely only a lack of marketing imagination could have failed to get this some kind of better distribution deal. Most recently another high-profile casualty of exhibition difficulties has been *Happy Now*, the feature début of

Philippa Collie-Cousins. The film has Ioan Gruffudd in the lead, so has no shortage of marketing potential, and it is in English. But it has failed to secure any kind of distribution deal after reasonable reviews at festivals in Edinburgh, London and Cardiff.

If the mainstream British film industry is obsessed with being acceptable to American markets (with honourable exceptions) and Wales continues to turn out films that are difficult to fit into these categories, then clearly there is a need to look again at strategies needed to secure exhibition. This means on the one hand working with exhibitors to build a modest circuit within Wales itself, and on the other to look beyond England to European markets where the addition of subtitles is not seen as the kiss of death it appears to be in England.

The sorriest tale though is that of TV drama, though it must be said immediately that of the main providers there is a widespread view that S4C's output has shown some signs of development. None the less Dave Berry's pessimistic opinion expressed in 2000 still by and large holds good: 'The disparity between television opportunities in Welsh and English language drama, with the balance firmly in favour of generally seriously underfunded Welsh language work, continues to retard English language writing – and crucially affect confidence and self-esteem in Wales' (Berry, 2000: 128).

As we have already stated, in practical terms broadcasting is outside the Assembly's remit and unaffected by devolution. In postcolonial terms, however, there is little sense of a growing confidence or assertiveness on the part of the broadcasters. As Alan Clayton, himself an ex-HTV drama head, put it,

> For years, there has been a marked lack of self-belief in Welsh writing and directing talent both in Wales and London. There is a perception within Wales that works deriving from Wales won't be sexy enough in London. This feeling has led to compromise and apathy. (quoted in Berry, 2000: 137)

Meic Povey turns the same point into a specific issue of a lingering colonial mentality: 'there's far too much looking over one's shoulder towards London seeking approval . . . We would be much better off now bringing on talent, developing skills for domestic consumption in the first place' (quoted in Berry, 2000: 128).

In limited pockets there have been attempts to realize Meic Povey's vision. HTV Wales's *Nuts and Bolts* combined the production of the Merthyr-based drama series with the setting-up of The Nuts and Bolts Experience, a series of drama workshops aimed at local people with the intention of developing local talent that would eventually feed into the casting, writing and directing of the programme itself. Predictably enough, the programme has become another casualty of the severe cutbacks in all regional programming in the era of ever more concentrated independent television ownership. The BBC in turn has produced two respectable drama series, principally for Wales-only consumption, *Belonging* and *The Bench*, and one high-profile single drama, *Care*, an undeniably powerful piece with its roots in the north Wales child-abuse scandal. The latter followed a familiar pattern by bringing in high-profile acting and directing talent from outside Wales. There is little sense of anything, which on the one hand takes risks, or on the other has the necessary generic clout to be shown on the network and raise industry confidence.

Curiously, considering its early reputation, it is to S4C that we have to look for any signs of something new beginning to emerge. Most commentators suggest that the appointment of Angharad Jones as S4C's drama commissioner has been absolutely key in seeing the channel move towards a consistent output of distinctive work. Previously there had been a strong body of critical opinion within Wales typified by Katie Gramich's view that

> It is by no means unusual to find on a particular evening, while Channel 4 is screening, for example, *Out*, a gay and lesbian magazine programme, that S4C is showing *Rasus*, 'a series about trotting', that is horse races, presented by farmer Dai Jones . . . The Welsh language programming on S4C tends to target a middle-aged audience with distinctly low-brow tastes . . . politically incorrect and culturally undiscriminating. (Gramich, 1997: 106)

Perhaps the work that best typifies the beginnings of something new at S4C is the drama series *Fondue, Rhyw a Deinosors* ('Fondue, Sex and Dinosaurs'), also directed by Tim Lyn, who has been one of the channel's strongest critics. One reviewer called it 'undoubtedly one of the channel's finest achievements' whilst others have made comparisons with ground-breaking work such as *Twin Peaks*, especially in terms of the programme's playful approach to form and genre restrictions:

> The dysfunctionality behind middle-class normality and respectability is dissected in scenes that are by turns farcical, surreal, stylised, naturalistic, deeply touching, excruciatingly painful, and downright

hilarious. The list gives a sense of the sheer vitality of *Fondue* as it plays with these modes and moods. (Walford Davies, 2001: 118)

Whether *Fondue* is as strong and original as the reviewer claims is irrelevant: what is significant is the confidence with which it deals with both contemporary subjects and with form. The number of UK TV dramas that now have the courage to even nudge at the boundaries of generic formulae is tiny; the fact that one comes from the much-criticized S4C is at least encouraging and reflective of a confidence to look beyond the hegemony of the UK network. Potentially S4C is a unique postcolonial space, ideal for the making of genuinely hybrid forms that use language in general, and bilingualism in particular, as distinctive and therefore powerful tools in the making of contemporary drama from Wales.

With regard to gender balance in contemporary Wales, it is tempting to make much of the fact that *Fondue*'s writer is a woman, Delyth Jones, and that Angharad Jones has also helped to nurture the careers of a number of other women who write for television, notably Catrin Clarke. The results are a long way yet from transforming the overall traditionalist image of S4C, but offer at least a glimmer of hope. If we take the success of TV writers and producers together with the emergence of a number of Welsh women feature-film directors (Sugarman, Collie-Cousins and others), as well as women working in animation such as Joanna Quinn and Tracy Spottiswode, we may indeed be witnessing something of a revolution. Whether or not it is possible to link this to any sense of a postcolonial condition is questionable, though at the very least there is a case for saying that the sense of a 'new' space within which to work (a post-devolution Wales) has created an environment with a greater sense of cultural diversity which a number of women artists have seized upon.

CONCLUSION

As we have seen, there is huge variation in the 'postcolonial' material conditions within which each of the art forms considered operates in Wales. For theatre, there is much potential for change. The National Assembly's relationship with the Arts Council of Wales has already fundamentally altered some actual decisions with regard to theatre and there promises to be more of the same. The investment is also likely to be greater. On the other hand, what some would call a colonial mentality prevails with the

apparent desire to have a pale version of the Royal National
Theatre in Clwyd and a Welsh-language parallel in Gwynedd.
This is, of course, far too simple and the National Assembly's
Creative Futures document also pays a great deal of attention to
communities and wider active participation. At the present time,
though, an emerging Welsh theatre looks like being some way
from Roger Owen's vision when he looks to Augusto Boal and
says:

> I would suggest . . . that this model of a theatre which prizes interven-
> tion, argument, negotiation and which has a firm sense of its
> oppressor, is precisely that which is required, not only from a cultural,
> but also from a political point of view, in contemporary Wales.
> (Owen, 2001: 108)

For film, there is a kind of halfway house. The relationship
between the lottery and the Arts Council of Wales means that
there is some post-devolutionary change, and the Assembly
provides funding for Sgrîn, the media agency for Wales, and has
talked about a film fund specifically for Wales. On the other hand,
larger-scale film funding still comes from the UK Film Council or
broadcasters, and policy-making resides in London. Beyond this it
is clearly arguable that the film industry's particular brand of
globalization makes all this peripheral at best. To set against this
we have to look at the cultural advantages enjoyed by Scotland or
Denmark, through producing a significant body of work in film
within similar constraints.

As to the films themselves, it would be hard to argue that a
wholly distinctive postcolonial culture has emerged. However,
there is a strong case for saying that many of the feature films
emerging from Wales do share an interest in playing with stable
realities within recognizable narrative frameworks. They are
frequently about operating in what look like comfortably recognizable worlds, only for these to be subverted by images and ideas
that have been variously characterized as magic realism or sur-
realism. What is currently lacking is a distribution and exhibition
strategy that can offer a realistic chance of the films being seen.

Television is the medium least directly affected by devolution in
any formal sense. In fact, with the recent takeovers affecting the
ownership of ITV, it would be possible to argue that 'Welsh' TV,
with the exception of S4C, is more colonized now than it has ever
been. Sadly, with few exceptions, this is reflected in the kind of TV

drama that has emerged from Wales in recent years. The timidity of the central controllers at both the BBC and the ITV network centre have produced a situation where less and less genuinely Welsh-originated drama is made at all, and still less has any kind of network presence which would give it a chance of a substantial audience, either inside or outside Wales. At S4C, however, there has been a detectable shift towards not only a younger target audience but also the beginnings of a climate more accepting of change and invention.

In terms of dramatic fictions the real prison of a colonial, or quasi-colonial, situation is the sheer narrowness of the range of definitions of 'being Welsh' that have been made available. I started with a quotation from Edward Thomas and, despite a feeling in some quarters that he is 'at best a committed but hopelessly romantic rent-a-gob' (Adams, 1998: 195), I want to close with him as well. For me he still best personifies both the desire for new fictions that reimagine Wales and a practical example of someone working across media, collaborating freely with rock musicians, novelists and opera directors in order to find ways of being free of both a colonized mentality and the most obvious crass responses to that imprisonment:

> I want a Wales at ease with itself and rejoicing in its natural eclecticism. I don't want to see Wales locked in a debate about Welsh and English. I want a multicultural Wales with a myriad sustainable myths . . . The new Wales has to be fast, maverick and imaginative, and innovative and inventive in its aim to be a small, interesting country within a European context, a country where the albatross of Britain has finally fallen from its neck. It certainly has fallen from my neck. I like England, but not Britain. (quoted in Walford Davies, 1998: 117)

For Welsh drama fully to play an emergent role in making such a Wales a reality requires the Assembly's interest in culture to be maintained and strengthened, so that an infrastructure is developed that can genuinely support a film industry, a theatre that has the freedom to work outside conventional forms, and an English-language TV station for Wales that parallels S4C, and can free writers from the dead hand of UK network requirements.

REFERENCES

Adams, D. (1996). *Stage Welsh*, Llandysul: Gomer.

Adams, D. (1998). 'Edward Thomas: negotiating a way through culture', in H. Walford Davies (ed.), *State of Play: Four Playwrights of Wales*, Llandysul: Gomer.

Berry, D. (2000). 'Unearthing the present: television drama in Wales', in S. Blandford (ed.), *Wales on Screen*, Bridgend: Seren.

French, P. (1999). 'Something for the weekend', *The Observer*, 6 June.

Gramich, K. (1997). 'Cymru or Wales? Explorations in a divided sensibility', in S. Basnett (ed.), *Studying British Cultures*, London: Routledge.

Owen, R. (2001). 'The play of history: the performance of identity in Welsh historiography and theatre', in *North American Journal of Welsh Studies*, 1, 2.

Petrie, D. (2000). 'The new Scottish cinema', in M. Hjort and Scott Mackenzie (eds), *Cinema and Nation*, London: Routledge.

Roms, H. (1998). 'Edward Thomas: a profile', in H. Walford Davies (ed.), *State of Play: Four Playwrights of Wales*, Llandysul: Gomer.

Saville, C. (1997). 'Brith Gof', in A.-M. Taylor (ed.), *Staging Wales: Welsh Theatre 1979–1997*, Cardiff: University of Wales Press.

Teare, J. (ed.) (1998). *New Welsh Drama*, Cardiff: Parthian.

Walford Davies, D. (2001). Review of the S4C drama series *Fondue, Sex and Dinosaurs*, *Planet* 147.

Walford Davies, H. (1998). 'Not much of a dream then is it', in H. Walford Davies (ed.), *State of Play: Four Playwrights of Wales*, Llandysul: Gomer.

11

What's in the 'Post'? Mass Media as a 'Site of Struggle'

DAVID M. BARLOW

In considering how to approach an essay on the media in Wales from a postcolonial perspective, I found myself reflecting more on a recent period in Australia than earlier years in England. By way of explanation, Australia has been suggested as 'coloniser, colonised and post-colonial – sometimes all at once' (Ahmad, 1995, cited in Childs and Williams, 1997: 2). Although unable to claim the more engaging 'New South Wales to south Wales' connection, as I lived and worked in Victoria, mention of the latter does nevertheless resonate strongly, as it conjures recollections of Queen Victoria, empire and colonies.

While the use of Australian experience clearly has limited relevance when thinking about Wales, there is some commonality in the sense that both countries have struggled to fashion a media ecology that reflects the social, political and cultural diversity of their respective nations.[1] Furthermore, the indigenous populations in each country have struggled to ensure the survival of their language and culture in the face of 'imposed' and pervasive Anglocentric media. Both nations have also been forced to consider the implications of in-migration, welcomed or otherwise. In particular, this has necessitated consideration of the information, communication and cultural needs of arrivals variously 'labelled' as settlers, incomers, immigrants or asylum seekers, depending on the particular geographic context and the political and other exigencies of the time. With Wales – like Australia – now claiming the mantle of multiculturalism, the adequacy or otherwise of its media must now be judged on the extent to which it reflects the nation's cultural diversity. However, unlike

Australia, which as a sovereign nation is empowered to determine its own media ecology, decisions relating to Wales continue to be made by the British state. This accounts, at least in part, for Wales's idiosyncratic broadcasting history and some contemporary peculiarities.

For newly arrived visitors to Wales who turn to the mass media as a way of acquainting themselves with the local culture, the experience is likely to be one of bemusement. They are likely to be puzzled about the limited amount of locally produced material broadcast by ITV1 Wales (previously HTV) and BBC Wales, and how little the programming schedules of these two services differ from the UK-wide ITV and BBC networks. On the other hand, they may be pleasantly surprised at the range and quality of local programming offered in Welsh on S4C.[2] If resident in hotel or bed and breakfast accommodation in south-east, mid- or north-east Wales, visitors may find that their television news originates from Bristol, Birmingham or Manchester. Initial confusion may turn to frustration once it is realized that these news broadcasts seldom include any reference to Wales. When this occurs in Cardiff – the nation's capital city – such an occurrence might, understandably, be experienced as bizarre.

Radio also has its peculiarities. Visitors who tune to radio when driving around Wales will quickly become accustomed to selected stations 'dropping out'. Furthermore, in some areas, BBC Radio's 1, 2, 3, 4 and 5 (from London) will be easier to access than Radio Wales and Radio Cymru, the two national services for Wales. There will also be surprises for those hoping to sample the nation's cultural diversity by tuning to local commercial radio. For instance, the A55 in north Wales passes through the reception areas of three such stations: Champion FM at Caernarfon, Coast FM at Colwyn Bay, and MFM 103.5 at Wrexham. However, with all three services networked as a result of the same ownership, at certain times listeners will hear the same – predominantly music-based – programmes on each station. The origins of Champion FM are also of interest. From the outset, the station's commercial backers sought to 'target' a working-class and largely Welsh-speaking audience, ignored – or not adequately catered for – by Radio Cymru. The ramifications of this development for the BBC are gradually becoming apparent, with recent surveys indicating that Champion FM now has a greater audience share in this part of Wales than Radio Cymru.

While visitors will hear at least some programming on Champion FM in Welsh, unlike a number of other commercial stations in Wales, they are unlikely to be aware of the ongoing and vigorous debate about the use and 'quality' of the Welsh language being broadcast. Essentially, arguments centre on whether the battle for 'radio ratings' has contributed to a 'dumbing-down' of spoken Welsh on BBC and commercial radio. Such peculiarities, however, are not restricted to radio and television. The nation has no genuinely national newspaper and the biggest-selling daily paper in Wales is the English-produced *Sun*. Visitors may also be surprised to find the editor of a local newspaper in mid-Wales, the *County Times and Express*, describing it as an 'English paper', and the column detailing upcoming cultural events, albeit in Welsh, entitled – when translated literally – 'For the Welsh'.

While it might be expected that the people of Wales are acquainted with the idiosyncratic nature of its mass media, this may not be the case. John Osmond (1992: 5) laments how little people seem to know of their own country, suggesting, by way of example, that residents of the Valleys in south Wales are more likely to have visited Marbella than Machynlleth. Anecdotal evidence also suggests that many people in north Wales are likely to be better acquainted with north-west England than they are with south and south-west Wales. While earlier religious, political, and regional tensions may have contributed to a limited national familiarity, poor communications infrastructure has certainly been a factor. The nation's mass media are also implicated, shaped as they have been by the all-powerful economic and political centre of the UK, London. Most apposite, then, is Raymond Williams's (1989: 8) observation that the visual and aural similarities of 'HQ' and 'UK' are powerfully suggestive.

This chapter draws on ideas from postcolonial theory to suggest the media in Wales as a 'site of struggle'. Primarily it focuses on the press, television and radio, collectively referred to as mass media and still acknowledged – even in a multichannel age – as being instrumental in generating, reflecting and constructing public opinion.

CONTEXTUALIZING THE POSTCOLONIAL

Anyone delving into the literature on postcolonial theory quickly realizes that this area of study is complex and contested, and uses concepts which are highly charged. However, as the brief here is to utilize – rather than evaluate – this body of theory, the chapter will draw on ideas that are thought to be both appropriate and helpful. With this in mind, the suggestion that 'postcolonial' can be understood as an 'anticipatory discourse' is particularly insightful. This position is argued by Childs and Williams (1997: 7), who claim that it is perverse to use 'post' to denote 'a state which is not fully present, and then link it to something [the "colonial"] which has not fully disappeared'. It is, therefore, a sense of 'in-betweenness' that might best characterize the post-colonial era (Childs and Williams, 1997: 7).

Mohammadi (1995: 366) also hints at 'in-betweenness' when assessing the impact of colonialism in the 'developing' world. He asks what the colonial powers leave behind when they begin to pack their bags in preparation for leaving. The evidence suggests all, or some, of the following: a language; an education system; certain values and attitudes; religious practices; ways of organizing public life; and, systems of mass communication. Even if the 'bag-packing' analogy is inappropriate when thinking about Wales – or maybe just premature, it does draw attention to a number of important issues, one of which is infrastructure. Here, it is helpful to draw on the work of Michael Hechter (1975, 1986), who analysed the historical relationship between the core of the British state and its Celtic periphery between 1536 and 1966. While his views are seen by some as controversial, Hechter argues that British capitalist development resulted in the creation of 'internal colonies' in its Celtic fringe.[3]

Hechter (1986: 217–18) offers some pertinent observations on the development of infrastructure in colonial territories. He asserts that such developments are determined by the needs of the metropolitan centre rather those of the peripheral colony. Hence, the routing and sophistication of transportation systems, the distribution and function of cities, and the location and 'reach' of communications infrastructure will, in this view, be organized to complement the 'centre'. Clearly, the outcome of such skewed planning is that the colony experiences significant underdevelopment. While caution must be exercised if seeking to extrapolate from this analysis, a glance at Wales's transportation and other communications infrastructure does prompt questions about whose needs have been prioritized. As regular travellers will know, journeys between Cardiff and Bangor by rail or road are likely to take longer, cost more and be experienced as more difficult than trips between London and these two centres in south and north Wales.

History suggests that the decline of the nation's indigenous press was due, at least in part, to the availability of direct rail services from England (Jones, 2000: 314). Once in place, railways helped create new markets as daily newspapers from London were delivered into and around Wales quickly and efficiently (Hume, 1986: 328). These developments were aided by an accompanying growth in newspaper agents and station-based retailers such as W. H. Smith. As Tunstall (1983: 229) notes, compared with Scotland, Wales's relatively close proximity to London made it extremely difficult to sustain a discrete indigenous newspaper market. The provision of appropriate infrastructure was also an issue in terms of radio and television developments in Wales. Not only was the British government reluctant to support broadcasting services for the people of Wales; it was slow to provide the necessary infrastructure to ensure good reception throughout the country. In response to campaigns aimed at establishing a BBC radio Welsh Region and (later) S4C, voices from London argued that it was technically impossible to provide such services.[4] Even when these claims proved to be baseless, there were significant delays before both services became fully operational.

Setting aside Hechter's views for one moment, how reasonable is it to conceive of the relationship between Wales and England (or the British state) as colonial or post-colonial? If it were possible to put this question to those who have written about Wales and its media, the response would be in the affirmative. At the very least, there would be a strong articulation of powerlessness. Even before the end of the Second World War, Gwynfor Evans (1944: 4) railed against the negative influence of British (and American) media, claiming that 'it will kill our nation', and argued for local control over broadcasting in Wales. Similar sentiments have been expressed repeatedly. The literature on the media in Wales is littered with references to infiltration, exploitation, overwhelmed, hegemony, stereotyping, imposition, conquered, centralism, stranglehold, contempt, and domination. All are directed towards, or respond to, the perceived power of British – essentially English – media institutions. More recently, in a television documentary examining the relationship between England and Wales, the narrator is even more explicit, referring to 'a once

global superpower and its first tiny neglected colony'
(Hargreaves, 2001).

In this regard, the BBC attracts particular attention, as evident
in the following examples, of which there are many. One
employee, a senior producer, describes the BBC's promotion of
'Britishness' – but 'Englishness' in particular – as 'undermin[ing]
our consciousness as Welsh people' (Bevan, 1984: 109). Berry
(2000: 138) cites a similarly placed source, who claims that BBC
Wales is treated by London as if it were a 'colonial outpost'.
Geraint Talfan Davies, a previous controller of BBC Wales, also
acknowledges that the 'obstacles of metropolitanism' have
impacted negatively on local operations (1992: 25). In a similar
vein, Osmond (1993) focuses on matters of accountability and
transparency in respect of the Broadcasting Council for Wales,
entitling his article, 'The last outpost of imperialism'.

Not surprisingly, mention of the media in Wales is likely to
trigger accusations of misrepresentation. K. Williams (1997a: 61)
captures this well when he writes, '[b]eing locked inside someone
else's misrepresentation of your life or community can be a wither-
ing experience.' Likewise, McArthur (1985: 66), referring to
Scotland in this instance, notes how the daily 'living and thinking'
experience of oppressed peoples is shaped by categories proposed
by their oppressors, and that identities are similarly assumed. One
outcome is a 'lack of cultural confidence', which Osmond (1995:
118) observes in Wales. To effect some sense of 'release' or 'liberation', a process of 'mental decolonization' is suggested, and this
can only be achieved by disengaging with those characteristics
that have been assumed, or imposed, as a result of the oppressive
'other' (Childs and Williams, 1997: 69).

Recently, in the wake of a rapidly globalizing economy, the
emphasis has shifted towards a form of cultural imperialism practised by transnational corporations rather than nation-states. This
has been defined by Schiller (1991: 15) as 'transnational corporate cultural domination'. However, despite what appears to be a
'country-neutral' discourse, the USA retains a significant role and
presence in such arrangements (Schiller, 1998: 17). In this regard,
television is often cited. Such concerns are captured by Osmond
(1992: 26), who argues that Wales is subject to a 'surging mass of
English/American culture channelled overwhelmingly through
centralized London-based television'.

IMPLICATING MASS MEDIA

It is generally accepted that the mass media and other organizations involved in the production, distribution and transmission of 'cultural goods' are part of the 'cultural industries'.[5] Increasingly acknowledged as a vital sector of the economy, the cultural industries are both similar to and different from other industries (Golding and Murdock, 2000: 70): similar, because they produce and make available for sale a range of goods and services like other industrial sectors; different, because the goods and services being produced, whether in the form of newspapers, advertisements, radio and television programmes, films, websites or computer games, provide the images and discourses which influence how we understand, interpret and, ultimately, 'act upon' our world (Hesmondhalgh, 2002: 3; Golding and Murdock, 2000: 70).

Dreaming up the Nation

The cultural industries, and particularly the mass media, have long been implicated in the process of helping create the idea of a nation and assisting in its realization. No surprise, then, to find reference to the idea of mass media 'dreaming up the nation' (Jakubowicz, 1995: 182). Anderson (1983: 24–5) provides an example, reminding us how the 'imaginings' enabled by 'new' technical media such as novels and newspapers in the eighteenth century helped re-present 'the *kind* of imagined community that is the nation'. Since that time, this role has been assumed by radio, television and film (amongst other media), all of which stimulate and sustain ideas about the 'imagined community' that 'underlies the cultural dimension of the contemporary nation' (Jakubowicz, 1995: 166).

That such ideas continue to retain currency is evident in the recent proposal for a BBC-type organization to be introduced in Afghanistan in order to assist with the rebuilding of that country. In earlier years and closer to home, it should be remembered that the BBC was employed to project the unity of the British nation. In doing so, it helped construct the so-called 'national regions' of Wales, Scotland and Northern Ireland (Scannell and Cardiff, 1991: 13; Mackay and Powell, 1997: 26). In recalling its formative years, Price (1995: 9) describes the BBC as an 'instrument of elocution enhancement', and refers to the language used on radio and television as 'the language of empire', which in the Celtic lands was English.

In Wales there is ample evidence of the media being instrumental in the process of developing a sense of nation, nationhood and national identity. Aled Jones (2000: 310–11), for instance, argues that the indigenous press in Wales helped establish new forms of national identity by 'underpinning an emerging public sphere, by providing tangible evidence of Wales's relative cultural autonomy, and by mapping its territory in new ways'. Another example – albeit contentious – is provided by John Davies (1994) in his account of the origins of BBC radio in Wales, where it is asserted that 'contemporary Wales could be defined as an artefact produced by broadcasting'.[6] Similarly, Mackay and Powell (1997: 8) refer to radio and, later, television assuming 'the role of standard-bearer of Welsh identity' from the press, and Allan and O'Malley (1999: 128) highlight the role of the media in 'the construction of Welsh identity'.

In Wales, then, it is generally accepted that the media – and particularly BBC radio and television, ITV1 Wales and S4C – have a 'cultural mission' (Mungham and Williams, 1998: 121; K. Williams, 1994: 253). This involves not just the provision of information, education and entertainment, but a role in assisting in the development of Welsh identity – however defined (Griffiths, 1993: 9; Mackay and Powell, 1997: 8; Talfan Davies, 1992; K. Williams, 1998: 121). The rationale for such a mission and the problems associated with it are brought further into light by looking 'across the bridge', in other words, towards England.

Denying the Nation
There is a tendency for accounts dealing with the history and development of the mass media in Britain to commence in England before moving ever outwards to incorporate the peripheral regions and nations of the UK. Some of these accounts also ascribe to Wales (and Scotland) the status of region – rather than nation – or assume or allude to such a position, and fail to address the significance of such matters and the underlying assumptions.[7] Even in relatively recent accounts of the media in Britain, minimal attention is paid to the regions and nations (see, for example, Stokes and Reading, 1999).

Not surprisingly, accounts of British media developments from a Welsh perspective are more likely to approach the task with the mindset of Wales as a nation. In doing so, the view from Wales portrays an omnipresent England, with London looming large. By way of example, Aled Jones refers to the 'media powerhouse of Fleet Street' being viewed with 'awe, anxiety and suspicion' (Jones, 2000: 313), and John Davies recalls the 'struggle between Cardiff and Head Office' from the beginning of BBC radio in Wales (cited in Morris, 1995: 6). Recognition of this uneasy relationship with London draws attention to another long-standing and related matter, that of Wales's status.

Wales has been variously understood as a 'region', 'principality', 'western extension of England', and 'national region' – which until recently was the term used by the BBC (Jones, 2000: 313; Talfan Davies, 1992: 20). It also remains entwined with England for cricket and other purposes through the legislative hybrid, 'England and Wales' (Foulkes, Jones, and Wilford, 1986: 273). Whether past or present, Wales has never been a completely separate entity, nor has it been fully integrated – prompting recall of the postcolonial 'in-betweenness' referred to earlier. Confusion, or denial, about its status has had obvious and far-reaching ramifications.

In the process of organizing the provision of radio services throughout the UK, Wales was linked to the south-west of England in 1927 to form the BBC radio 'West Region' (Davies, 1994: 39). The same ties were imposed in 1958 when Television Wales and the West (TWW) was established to provide the first commercial television service for Wales (Mackay and Powell, 1997: 9; Medhurst, 1998: 336). The unfortunate irony, in both instances, was that the radio and television programmes being broadcast could not be received throughout all of Wales. It is also evident, in both cases, that the links were not based on cultural grounds.

In the case of radio, the regional arrangements took no account of cultural or geographic identity (Crisell, 1997: 25; K. Williams, 1998: 108). In terms of television, links with the west of England were encouraged because it was believed that Wales alone was not sufficiently affluent to sustain a commercial service (Curran and Seaton, 1997: 184; Medhurst, 1998: 336). The ties between Wales and the west of England were maintained in 1968 when HTV was awarded the commercial television franchise (Coe, 1982: 54; K. Williams, 1997b: 11). Essentially, then, the primary criterion to be satisfied in determining the regulatory arrangements for commercial television in Wales (and elsewhere) was 'the convenience of the market' (Curran and Seaton, 1997: 184). With the merger in 2003 of the two remaining commercial television companies, Carlton and Granada, it is interesting to note that the original rationale for the UK's regional ITV structure was to counter the predominantly centralist operation of the BBC (Curran and Seaton, 1997: 184; Talfan Davies, 1992: 20).

Even today it could be argued that some current concerns have their genesis in the earlier ambivalence over Wales's status and the consequent decisions regarding communications infrastructure. Although the figures are disputed and the explanations varied, there are claims that only 13 per cent of the population read daily newspapers produced in Wales, and 14 per cent choose not to watch Welsh television (Welsh Affairs Committee, 1999: para. 46). While this 'leakage' of readers and viewers may have financial repercussions for the relevant media organizations, it also highlights matters of a democratic nature, particularly if 'leakage' is reframed as 'information deficit'. One analysis of voting patterns in the 1997 referendum suggests a tendency to vote 'No' in areas where Welsh television viewing and newspaper readership are least evident, namely Cardiff and surrounds, and the border areas with England (Talfan Davies, 1999: 7; K. Williams, 2000: 96). The nation's communications infrastructure is currently in the spotlight again due to plans by the British government to replace the current analogue television network with a digital system. In its response to the Draft Communications Bill, the National Assembly argues that changes to transmission facilities prior to the introduction of digital television will be essential if Welsh channels are to be accessible throughout the country (National Assembly for Wales, 2002a: para. 3.5).[8]

REHEARSING THE STRUGGLE(S)

It is difficult to see how any account of the history and development of the media in Wales can be given without recourse to the idea of struggle. The veracity of this observation is evident in the widely supported, lengthy and sometimes vitriolic campaigns to establish the BBC radio Welsh Region and S4C. These and other matters prompted John Davies (1994: 38) to describe broadcasting in Wales as 'one of the most contentious of all issues'. In terms of the press, Aled Jones (1993, 1998, 2000) provides a comprehensive analysis of the struggle during the nineteenth and twentieth centuries to maintain a vibrant Welsh press in both languages. In recent years, television has been the site of disquiet owing to the apparent inability, or unwillingness, of BBC Wales and ITV1 Wales to produce an adequate supply of quality local drama.

Since its emergence, the National Assembly has also engaged in a struggle to ensure that Welsh voices would not only be heard in debates about the future of communications policy in the UK, but would also be adequately represented on regulatory bodies (National Assembly for Wales, 2002b). To date, this has met with limited success. Following passage of the Communications Act 2003, the Office of Communications (OfCom) was established as the centrepiece of a new regulatory structure. There is no place for a representative from Wales (or other nations and regions) on the Board of OfCom, which is appointed by the British government. Wales does, though, have representation on a Content Board – which is appointed by OfCom – and an additional channel of communication by way of an OfCom External Relations Team and an Advisory Committee for Wales (OfCom, 2003).

Using 'struggle' as a way of conceptualizing the role of the media is both helpful and legitimate according to Schlesinger (1991) and Ashcroft (2001). The former suggests media as 'battle-fields' or 'spaces in which contests for various forms of dominance takes place' (Schlesinger, 1991: 299). The latter (Ashcroft, 2001: 4) encourages the idea of media as 'sites of struggle', because radio, television, film and to a lesser extent the press, can be considered the key 'means of representation' in contemporary society. In this context, 'representation' is envisaged both as 'the site of identity formation and the site of struggle over identity formation' (Ashcroft, 2001: 4). If both these ideas – media as battlefields, or as sites of struggle – are progressed, it follows that change can only eventuate by gaining some form of control over the means of representation; the aim being to transform existing mass media into 'culturally appropriate vehicles' (Ashcroft, 2001: 5). Such an analysis prompts interesting questions about Wales and its media. In particular, these include issues of control and accountability and whether existing structures are inimical to the notion of culturally appropriate mass media in Wales.

Obviously there are varying ways of tackling these questions. One approach, adopted here, assumes that the financing, organization and regulation of media institutions impacts on both the range of discourses and representations in the public domain, and on audiences' access to them.[9] Hence, the analysis begins by focusing on the patterns of ownership and its consequences, and the relationship between state regulation and media institutions. Such an approach is highly appropriate when examining media in multicultural nations such as Wales. This is because it attends not only to ownership, the organization of production and the texts – or products – that emerge from this process, but the extent to which this output is representative of minorities and intergroup relations (Jakubowicz, 1995: 170).

Contours of Control

In turning to issues of ownership and regulation, it soon becomes apparent that our gaze must shift beyond the borders of Wales. This is the case whether considering the press, television or radio. In terms of the press, it is the Press Complaints Commission (PCC) that operates as the principal regulatory body throughout the UK. It relies on a self-regulatory regime, the effectiveness of which continues to be much debated. The PCC includes no specific representative from Wales (Allan and O'Malley, 1999: 132). Most of the press in Wales is owned outside the country, the concentration of ownership is considerable, and it is the newspapers produced in England that garner significant market share.[10]

Seen as both a boon and a threat to Wales over the years, BBC Wales remains firmly anchored to London. The BBC's broad policy guidelines are decided centrally by the Board of Governors, of which the National Governor for Wales is a member. The British government makes these appointments. The National Governor for Wales chairs the Broadcasting Council for Wales, which advises on programmes and oversees Welsh interests. The Board of Governors appoints members to this body after local advice. It is to both structures and processes that the critics direct attention. In particular, concerns have been raised about the lack of transparency over appointments, the preference for selection over election, and doubts about the 'representativeness' of appointees (Williams, 1997a: 62). More specifically, it is alleged that the independence of the Broadcasting Council for Wales is compromised. This is because the dual roles of management and scrutiny expected of the chair – the National Governor for Wales – are seen as incompatible (Welsh Affairs Committee, 1999: para. 22).

Concerns of a similar nature have been expressed about S4C (Coe, 1982: 61; Ryan, 1986: 188). S4C is accountable to the

S4C Authority, whose members are appointed by the British government. The authority is a self-regulating body that monitors management and programme policy. Specific questions about S4C's accountability centre on three areas. It is under no obligation to consult on changes to its services, neither is it required to undergo a ten-yearly review as with the BBC charter, nor does it have a local advisory body similar to the Broadcasting Council for Wales (Welsh Affairs Committee, 1999: para. 20). However, in 2003, S4C initiated an internal review of its performance and role (S4C, 2004). This was timed to feed into a process which included OfCom's first review of public-service broadcasting in the UK and the Department of Culture, Media and Sport's review of the BBC charter, due for renewal in 2006.

In recent years, the ownership of HTV passed from United News and Media to Carlton Communications. Following the Granada/Carlton digital television fiasco in 2002, it was 're-branded'. This involved removal of the 'HTV' identity logo from all but local programmes and replacing it with 'ITV 1 Wales'. With Carlton and Granada now operating as a single company and the rules on ownership further relaxed as a result of the Communications Act 2003, some sources believe that ITV will become a takeover target for a US media and communications conglomerate in the near future (Campaign for Press and Broadcasting Freedom, 2002). ITV1 Wales, in common with all other commercial television services in the UK, is now regulated by OfCom.

Turning to commercial radio, OfCom oversees the regulation and licensing of all non-BBC radio stations in the UK. Unlike the current OfCom board, the board of the former regulator, the Radio Authority, did include a member for Wales. However, this appointment was made by the British government and only came about once the National Assembly had been established. As a result, during the 'radio boom' of the 1990s when most of Wales's Independent Local Radio (ILR) licences were issued, the Board of the Radio Authority did not include a representative from Wales. Most ILR stations in Wales are now owned by large radio or multimedia conglomerates based outside its borders.

Skewed Representations
In what ways do these regulatory arrangements and patterns of ownership shape the production process and determine – at least

to some extent – the subsequent output of the media in Wales? This is clearly a complex question that can only be partially addressed in the context of this chapter. However, even by way of a few examples, it is possible to illustrate how economic, political and institutional factors exercise constraints on the content and form of what is produced by the broadcast and print media in Wales, and why the issue of representation – or re-presentation – generates such concern. Clearly, the starting-point must be the Welsh language. Its place and prominence remain pivotal in any historical or contemporary analysis of Wales and its media.

From the earliest days of BBC radio in Wales, there was a struggle to achieve an appropriately balanced range of programming in both Welsh and English (Lucas, 1981: 26). The controlling influence of London was eased somewhat in 1937, when the BBC Welsh Region became operational (Davies, 1994: 43; Lucas, 1981: 83). But it was the decision in 1977 to split the previously single radio service and create Radio Wales (in English) and Radio Cymru (in Welsh) that helped cater more effectively for both language groups. These changes did, however, create a significant and ongoing challenge for Radio Cymru. While those who prefer BBC radio services in English are well catered for by Radio Wales and other BBC radio services from England, Welsh-speakers are reliant on one service, Radio Cymru. Faced with the almost impossible task of satisfying everyone all of the time, Radio Cymru's attempts to vary the content and style of its programmes in order to meet the diverse tastes of listeners have proved problematic (Ellis, 2000).

Whilst the emergence of S4C in 1982 improved the television context for both language groups, there is still frustration about the lack of Welsh-produced English-language material being broadcast by BBC Wales and ITV1 Wales. Both organizations have long attracted criticism over the paucity of their locally produced material, owing, at least in part, to a lack of funding from their respective London centres (Ryan, 1986: 189; K. Williams, 1989b: 16, 1995: 7). More recently, ITV1 Wales is alleged to have 'abrogated their responsibilities towards drama in Wales' (Berry, 2000: 139). Even on the rare occasions that local drama productions have achieved a slot on the BBC and ITV UK-wide networks, critics argue that the content has had tenuous links with Wales (Berry, 2000: 131–4; K. Williams, 1997b: 23). Golding and Murdock's (2000: 85) notion of 'televisual tourism' is useful here.

They believe that when the production of television drama is dependent on achieving sales in global markets and thereby subject to international co-production agreements, there will inevitably be constraints on subject matter and narrative styles.

Independent Local Radio (ILR) services are often overlooked in debates about media representations, even though they command a significant audience share in Wales. Reliant for survival on advertising and sponsorship revenue, ILR's sought-after audience tends to be between twenty and fifty years of age, although this varies from station to station. This means that certain segments of the population are unlikely to find their interests represented by this sector of radio. Furthermore, with schedules dominated by a limited range of popular music dictated by carefully crafted 'playlists', the full cultural diversity of the local areas served by such stations is unlikely to be apparent on the airwaves. Not surprisingly, questions have been raised about both the 'localness' and quality of local radio (Barlow, 2003: 80–1; Talfan Davies, 1999: 46). Furthermore, recent changes to legislation will enable a greater concentration of ownership and cross-ownership in local radio, and the probability of ownership beyond Europe.

Finally, turning to the press, in the mid-1980s Ian Hume (1986: 340) argued that the language and styles of presentation used by the English press in Wales was little different from that of their colleagues in Bristol, Birmingham and Manchester. More recently, the indigenous press in Wales has been described as an 'extension of English and international media empires' (Jones, 1993: 202). For instance, the same English-based company owns the *Western Mail*, *Daily Post*, *Wales on Sunday* and *Welsh Daily Mirror*, as it was 'badged' until recently. Critics argue that such concentrated and 'distant' ownership leads to a diminishing plurality of expression, which not only exacerbates Wales's 'information deficit', but undermines local democracy (Hannan, 1998: 9–10; Talfan Davies, 1999: 17).

Furthermore, while the *Western Mail* is promoted as 'The national newspaper of Wales' and the *Daily Post* as 'The paper for Wales', such claims appear fanciful given that newsagents in north Wales are unlikely to stock the former and the latter is rarely on sale in south and south-west Wales. As a result, there are concerns that the news content of these 'national' newspapers favours local and regional issues rather than Wales-wide agendas (K. Williams, 2000: 119). In contrast, Clifford (1999: 25) describes the local press throughout Wales as 'highly developed'. In this category might be included *papurau bro*, the monthly Welsh-language community newspapers which began circulating in the 1970s and continue to thrive (Huws, 1990; K. Williams, 1997b: 19).

CONCLUSION

That the vast majority of the media in Wales – press, television and radio – is owned, controlled and accountable to bodies beyond its borders is indisputable. As a result of such arrangements, it is not surprising to find doubts being raised about the media's ability to represent and fully reflect the nation's cultural diversity. This is thought to have implications for democracy, national identity and cultural development.

Wales's ability to impact on these networks of power and control is also limited. Under the devolution settlement, the Department of Culture, Media and Sport is obliged merely to consult the National Assembly on matters relating to broadcasting in Wales (Department of Culture, Media and Sport, 2000). This includes appointments such as the BBC National Governor for Wales, Wales's representative on the OfCom Content Board and members of the S4C Authority. Furthermore, the emergence of an all-embracing 'one-stop shop' regulator without a formal representative from Wales on its key decision-making body, the OfCom Board, points to a diminished Welsh presence in this new regulatory arena.[11]

The Communications Act 2003 presages an era in which regulation will be further rolled back. A relaxation of ownership rules not only provides the opportunity for non-European companies to acquire media in Wales and the UK, but also gives the green light for greater cross-media ownership (see, for example, Freshfields Bruckhaus Deringer, 2003). This will have implications for local production quotas. Public-service broadcasters will also be under pressure at a time when the 'market' – rather than public service – is seen as the preferred mode of delivery. In such an environment, it is 'ratings' that shape production priorities and scheduling. For the BBC, justifying the licence fee in a multi-channel age will become increasingly problematic, and campaigns to undermine this levy in the lead-up to the renewal of the Royal Charter in 2006 began some time ago (Barnett, 2002: 8). Similar pressures will be experienced by S4C, at one point tagged Britain's most heavily subsidized public-service broadcaster (Tunstall, 1983: 231).

It is at this point that the contradictions of devolution and the resonance of colonialism become apparent. This is evident in two concurrent processes. The first sees the National Assembly embarking on the task of creating a 'new' Wales in which communities will be regenerated, civil society reinvigorated, active citizenship encouraged and young people more engaged in the political process (National Assembly for Wales, 2000). The second sees the British government introducing new communications legislation and a new regulatory structure which marginalizes the role of the National Assembly – the voice of Wales – in decisions about its own 'communicative space', and further distances the nation's media from the public they allegedly serve. It is difficult to see how the latter will assist in the achievement of the former.

These developments raise interesting questions about what we understand by 'postcolonial' and 'post-devolution'. The presence of a National Assembly with limited powers does lend weight to the idea of postcolonial as a period of 'in-betweenness', as suggested earlier. While this may be interpreted in positive terms, when the spotlight is turned on the media in Wales there are grounds for a more sceptical reading of 'postcolonial'. Essentially, whether attention is directed to devolution or colonialism, the critical issue centres on what *is* in the 'post'? In terms of Wales and its media, the struggle(s) looks set to continue.

NOTES

[1] Media ecology, in this context, refers to the various forms and mix of communications media, such as press, radio and television, the regulatory framework in which they operate, and their sources of funding, whether public, private, or a combination of both. The term aims to convey complex communications systems as environments, drawing attention to notions of interdependency, balance and 'health'. Its usage varies, but two recent examples are offered. Prebble (2002) refers to the BBC's increasing commercial strategy impacting negatively on the 'delicate ecology of UK broadcasting', while the National Assembly (2002a: 2) refers to Wales having a 'unique broadcasting ecology' because of its two languages and two publicly funded broadcasters, BBC Wales and S4C.

[2] Sianel Pedwar Cymru or S4C, as it is known, is the Welsh Fourth Channel Authority.

[3] Both Day (1979) and Nairn (1986) take issue with Hechter's analysis.

[4] A number of authors draw attention to these matters (see, for example, Evans, 1944: 7; Medhurst, 1998: 334; Tomos, 1982: 39).

[5] Hesmondhalgh (2002: 3) and McGuigan (1996: 74) discuss the emergence, extent and range of the 'cultural industries'. That the cultural industries are big business is evident in the business pages of the daily press, where details of takeovers, mergers and profit forecasts appear regularly.

[6] Talfan Davies (1999: 10) suggests that Davies's argument is 'over-egged'.

[7] For instance, one might include Crisell (1997), Curran and Seaton (1997) and Negrine (1989).

[8] Reconfiguring the transmission facilities is also seen as a way of ending the 'leakage' of viewers to England. However, the digital facility and the range of programming likely to be made available will enable even more (non-Welsh) television options for viewers.

[9] A political economy approach to the study of communications is outlined by Mosco (1996). See also Boyd-Barrett (1995) and Golding and Murdoch (2000).

[10] A number of authors address these and other contemporary matters related to the press in Wales (see, for example, Allan and O'Malley, 1999; Mackay and Powell, 1997; Mungham and Williams, 1998; Talfan Davies, 1999; K. Williams, 1997b, 2000).

[11] Jenny Randerson, the (then) Assembly minister for culture, sport and the Welsh language, argued similarly in evidence to the Richard Commission (see Randerson, 2002).

REFERENCES

Ahmad, A. (1995) 'The politics of literary postcoloniality', *Race and Class*, 36, 3.

Allan, S. and O'Malley, T. (1999). 'The media in Wales', in D. Dunkerley and A. Thompson (eds), *Wales Today*, Cardiff: University of Wales Press.

Anderson, B. (1983). *Imagined Communities: Reflections on the Origin and Spread of Nationalism*, London: Verso.

Ashcroft, B. (2001). *Post-colonial Transformation*, London: Routledge.

Barlow, D. M. (2003). 'Who controls local radio?', *Planet*, 158, 79–84.

Barnett, S. (2002). 'Lies, damned lies and licence fee opinion polls', *The Observer*, 17 November, 8.

Berry, D. (2000). 'Unearthing the present: television drama in Wales', in S. Blandford (ed.), *Wales on Screen*, Bridgend: Seren.

Bevan, D. (1984). 'The mobilisation of cultural minorities: the case of Sianel Pedwar Cymru', *Media, Culture and Society*, 6, 103–17.

Boyd-Barrett, O. (1995). 'The political economy approach', in O. Boyd-Barrett and C. Newbold (eds), *Approaches to Media*, London: Arnold.

Campaign for Press and Broadcasting Freedom (CPBF) (2002). *The Communications Bill: Some Key Areas of Concern and Suggested Amendments*, London: CPBF (*www.cpbf.org.uk*).

Childs, P. and Williams, P. (1997). *An Introduction to Post-colonial Theory*, London: Prentice Hall.

Clifford, D. (1999). 'The National Assembly and the media', *Planet*, 135, 24–7.

Coe, J. (1982). 'Sianel Pedwar Cymru: fighting for a future', in S. Blanchard and D. Morley (eds), *What's This Channel Fo(u)r?* London: Comedia.

Crisell, A. (1997). *An Introductory History of British Broadcasting*, London: Routledge.

Curran, J. and Seaton, J. (1997). *Power without Responsibility*, fifth edn, London: Routledge.

Davies, J. (1994). *Broadcasting and the BBC in Wales*, Cardiff: University of Wales Press.

Day, G. (1979). 'The sociology of Wales: issues and prospects', *Sociology Review*, 27, 3, 447–74.

Department of Culture, Media and Sport (2000). *Concordat Between the Department for Culture, Media and Sport and the Cabinet of the National Assembly for Wales*, London: Department of Culture, Media and Sport.

Ellis, G. (2000). 'Stereophonic nation: the bi-lingual sounds of Cool Cymru FM', *International Journal of Cultural Studies*, 3, 2, 188–98.

Evans, G. (1944). *The Radio in Wales*, Aberystwyth: The New Wales Union.

Freshfields Bruckhaus Deringer (2003). *Communications Act*, *www.freshfields.com*, accessed 17 February 2004.

Foulkes, D., Jones, J. B. and Wilford, R. A. (1986). 'Wales: a separate administrative unit', in I. Hume and W. T. R. Pryce (eds), *The Welsh and Their Country*, Llandysul: Gomer Press.

Golding, P. and Murdock, G. (2000). 'Culture, communications and political economy', in J. Curran and M. Gurevitch (eds), *Mass Media in Society*, third edn, London: Arnold.

Griffiths, A. (1993). 'The construction of national and cultural identity in a Welsh soap opera', in P. Drummond, R. Paterson and J. Willis (eds), *National Identity and Europe: The Television Revolution*, London: BFI.

Hannan, P. (1998). 'Who's asking the questions?', *Planet*, 126, 7–12.

Hargreaves, I. (2001). 'Enter the Dragon', S4C (broadcast on 2 February 2001).

Hechter, M. (1975). *Internal Colonialism: The Celtic Fringe in British National Development 1536–1966*, London: Routledge and Kegan Paul.

Hechter, M. (1986). 'Towards a theory of ethnic change', in I. Hume and W. T. R. Pryce (eds), *The Welsh and their Country*, Llandysul: Gomer Press.

Hesmondhalgh, D. (2002). *The Cultural Industries*, London: Sage.

Hume, I. (1986). 'Mass media and society in the 1980s', in I. Hume and W. T. R. Pryce (eds), *The Welsh and their Country*, Llandysul: Gomer Press.

Huws, G. (1990). 'Papurau bro', *Planet*, 83, 55–61.

Jakubowicz, A. (1995). 'Media in multicultural nations', in J. Downing, A. Mohammadi and A. Sreberny-Mohammadi (eds), *Questioning the Media: A Critical Introduction*, London: Sage.

Jones, A. (1993). *Press, Politics and Society: A History of Journalism in Wales*, Cardiff: University of Wales Press.

Jones, A. (1998). 'The newspaper press in Wales 1804–1945', in P. H. Jones (ed.), *A Nation and its Books*, Aberystwyth: National Library of Wales.

Jones, A. (2000). 'The nineteenth-century media and Welsh history', in L. Brake, B. Bell and D. Finkelstein (eds), *Nineteenth-Century Media and the Construction of Identities*, Basingstoke: Palgrave.

Lucas, R. (1981). *The Voice of a Nation? A Concise Account of the BBC in Wales*, Llandysul: Gomer.

Mackay, H. and Powell, A. (1997). 'Wales and its media: production, consumption and regulation', in G. Day and D. Thomas (eds), *Contemporary Wales*, 9, 8–39.

McArthur, C. (1985). 'Scotland's story', *Framework*, 26–7, 65–74.

McGuigan, J. (1996). *Culture and the Public Sphere*, London: Routledge.

Medhurst, J. (1998). 'Mass media in 20th century Wales', in P. H. Jones (ed.), *A Nation and its Books*, Aberystwyth: National Library of Wales.

Mohammadi, A. (1995). 'Cultural imperialism and cultural identity', in J. Downing, A. Mohammadi and A. Sreberny-Mohammadi (eds), *Questioning the Media: A Critical Introduction*, London: Sage

Morris, N. (1995). 'Film and broadcasting in Wales', *Books in Wales*, 1, 95, pp. 5–8.

Mosco, V. (1996). *The Political Economy of Communication*, London: Sage.

Mungham, G. and Williams, K. (1998). 'The press and media', in J. Osmond (ed.), *The National Assembly Agenda*, Cardiff: Institute of Welsh Affairs.

Nairn, T. (1986). 'Culture and politics in Wales', in I. Hume and W. T. R. Pryce (eds), *The Welsh and Their Country*, Llandysul: Gomer Press.

National Assembly for Wales (2000). *www.betterwales.com*, Cardiff: National Assembly for Wales.

National Assembly for Wales (2002a). *Welsh Assembly Government Response to the Draft Communications Bill*, Cardiff: National Assembly for Wales (*www.wales.gov.uk*).

National Assembly for Wales (2002b). 'Call for a strong Welsh voice in communications', press release, 9 February 2002 (*www.wales. gov.uk*).

Negrine, R. (1989). *Politics and the Mass Media in Great Britain*, second edn, London: Routledge.

OfCom (2003). *Advisory Committees for the Nations*, press release, 12 September 2003, London: OfCom.

Osmond, J. (1992). *The Democratic Challenge*, Llandysul: Gomer Press.

Osmond, J. (1993). 'The last outpost of imperialism', *Planet*, 99, 40–3.

Osmond, J. (1995). *Welsh Europeans*, Bridgend: Seren.

Prebble, S. (2002). 'Minutes of evidence – Question 97', Select Committee on Culture, Media and Sport (*www.parliament.the-stationery-office.co. uk/pa/cm 200102/ cmselect/cmc.../2012904. htm*).

Price, M. (1995). *Television, the Public Sphere, and National Identity*, Oxford: Clarendon Press.

Randerson, J. (2002). 'Written evidence to the Richard Commission', Cardiff: National Assembly for Wales.

Ryan, M. (1986). 'Blocking the channels: TV and film in Wales', in T. Curtis (ed.), *Wales: The Imagined Nation*, Bridgend: Poetry Press.

S4C (2004). *S4C Review: A Welsh Language Television Service Fit for the 21st Century?*, Cardiff: S4C.

Scannell, P. and Cardiff, D. (1991). *A Social History of British Broadcasting: Volume I, 1922–1939, Serving the Nation*, Oxford: Blackwell.

Schiller, H. (1991). 'Not yet the post-imperialist era', *Critical Studies in Mass Communication*, 8, 13–28.

Schiller, H. (1998). 'Striving for communication dominance: a half-century review', in D. K. Thusso (ed.), *Electronic Empires*, London: Arnold.

Schlesinger, P. (1991). 'Media, the political order and national identity', *Media, Culture and Society*, 13, 297–308.

Stokes, J. and Reading, A. (1999). *The Media in Britain: Current Debates and Developments*, London: Macmillan.

Talfan Davies, G. (1992). 'Broadcasting and the nation', *Planet*, 92, 16–25.

Talfan Davies, G. (1999). *Not By Bread Alone: Information, Media and the National Assembly*, Cardiff: Wales Media Forum.

Tomos, A. (1982). 'Realising a dream', in S. Blanchard and D. Morley (eds), *What's This Channel Fo(u)r?*, London: Comedia.

Tunstall, J. (1983). *The Media in Britain*, London: Constable.

Welsh Affairs Committee (1999). *Broadcasting in Wales and the National Assembly*, London: House of Commons.

Williams, K. (1989). 'Peripheral vision: cultural identity and the deregulation of broadcasting', *Radical Wales*, 23, 15–16.

Williams, K. (1994). 'Are we being served?', in J. Osmond (ed.), *A Parliament for Wales*, Llandysul: Gomer Press.

Williams, K. (1995). 'Crisis? What crisis?', *Planet*, 111, 6–10.

Williams, K. (1997a). 'Dear Ron', *Planet*, 123, 61–4.

Williams, K. (1997b). *Shadows and Substance: The Development of a Media Policy for Wales*, Llandysul: Gomer Press.

Williams, K. (1998). *Get Me a Murder a Day! A History of Mass Communication in Britain*, London: Arnold.

Williams, K. (2000). 'No dreads, only some doubts: the press and the referendum campaign', in J. Barry Jones and D. Balsom (eds), *The Road to the National Assembly for Wales*, Cardiff: University of Wales Press.

Williams, R. (1989). 'Are we becoming more divided?', *Radical Wales*, 23, 8–9.

12

Postcolonial Music in Contemporary Wales: Hybrids and Weird Geographies

DAI GRIFFITHS AND SARAH HILL

> Forget the centre: the margins are where the signals are coming from. Everything is velocity and disappearance and mutation. [Tricky's] *Maxinquaye* is a work of theory. There is nothing that theory can say that isn't already embedded in this wily, uncanny text.
>
> (Penman, 1998: 362)

> Instead of having two guitars, bass, drums, vocal, we destroyed that. It was anything goes – synth, tabla, drum machine, no vocals, instrumentals, gospel singers, sitars. The whole range of anything-goes noises. And suddenly the band were freed. It was a much looser approach to making music.
>
> (Bobby Gillespie of Primal Scream, quoted in Cavanagh, 2000: 464–5)

Before talking about music and postcolonial Wales, we ought first to ask the question: what might a postcolonial music sound like? At the time of writing, *The Karma Collection 2003* (issued by the Ministry of Sound) is a compilation whose tracks take as their starting-point the electronic dance music which has become the lingua franca of mall, bar and taxi, but also incorporate samples and words which 'sound Asian', in a determinedly and sustainedly, if imprecise, way. Are world music compilations that include the music of a country which has emerged from a postcolonial past de facto postcolonial music? So, the *Rough Guide to Banghra* is postcolonial, but not a *Rough Guide to the Music of France*? A *Rough Guide to the Music of Kenya more* postcolonial than the *Rough Guide to the Music of Canada*? Are *any* and *all* of the rough guides to the music of America, be it blues, bluegrass or gospel, in some fundamental and embracing sense postcolonial? And what about the *Rough Guide to the Music of Wales*, a rough musical guide to a postcolonial nation? These ideas of postcolonial music are going to be difficult to describe because the originating term, 'colony', is difficult to pin down.[1] Nevertheless, 'hybrid music' is one of the key indicators of postcolonial music; this chapter aims to provide a suitable soundtrack to issues discussed elsewhere in this collection.

Perhaps postcolonial music is more a matter of *weird geographies*. The party in Cardiff which has a Led Zeppelin album as background music is nothing singular, but when the host, Bethan, who works for Radio Cymru, and likes Thai cuisine, puts on the *Rough Guide to Bollywood*, now isn't that closer to the moment we're looking for? Oh, and she's hoping to impress Ian, who's doing a Ph.D. on Conrad and Said at Pontypridd and once got a poem in *Planet*. That's it, there we are: Bethan, Ian and an earful of noisy Bombay film music. That very moment, that decentring, that dislocation, that acknowledgement. And that scepticism: the sense that we may be dealing here with a conceptual framework which makes sense only in a certain academic context, and makes it on to the streets (of Canton rather than Bombay) only through a select few mediations – *The Guardian, New Left Review, Third Text*. In Portadown, Northern Ireland, a bunch of musicians want to carry a sound down the Garvarghy Road, but is prevented from doing so. A postcolonial, musical moment, or the promise of a postcolonial, musical future? And that's a real old sound, the oldest, one imagines: drums and pipes. The negotiation around that sound, between religions and politics and communities, around a colonizing moment: the negotiation is postcolonialism itself? Daniel Barenboim plays Beethoven in Palestine – postcolonial, or something different again – the imagination of a postcolonial freedom? And, at the time of writing, let's imagine something else: Christina Aguilera (herself a kind of newly bold assertion of Latino identity) used as the front of Coke's marketing strategy in a post-war Iraq – postcolonial, post-postcolonial, or just new-colonial?[2] These geographies surely get us closer to a postcolonial music, though we shouldn't overlook the hybridities. So this chapter provides further musical ideas of a postcolonial Wales as well.

History matters greatly in this context, especially in its shifting and movement. To return to the Asian references of *Karma*

Collection 2003: the idea of Asian music, mediated through a British pop context, shifts historically. It turns on a sequence of dates, notably 1947 and the moment of Indian independence. The track 'Goodness gracious me', a hit for Peter Sellers and Sophia Loren in 1960, is surely still a properly colonial music: Sellers is wearing boot polish, and imitating Indian voices from a position that surely allowed no real possibility of comeback or dialogue. Enter George Harrison, and surely there's a change, a change even from 'Love You To' to 'Within You Without You' to 'My Sweet Lord': they meet the Maharishi, he studies with Ravi Shankar, he immerses himself in the culture – everything the Beatles did was on the Beatles' terms, but there's something going on there – the beginning of respect, as well as an early hybridity (see Spencer, 2002: 76–81). By the 1990s a band like Asian Dub Foundation is conducting this negotiation on a totally different premise: the track 'Free Saptal Ram' does the same trick – Asian-sounding sample, words – but now entirely on the band's own terms, as well as seeking to rectify a real injustice. Time has changed: Asian Dub Foundation is British, a long distance from India but nevertheless sure of the necessity of that reference (see Hesmondhalgh, 2000; Sharma et al., 1996).[3] Postcolonial music? surely, and not only in an academic setting: postcolonialism really might be the most appropriate language of discussion for this, the most expressive British pop – its refusal in the scepticism referred to earlier only evidence of a *block* on thinking characteristic of a capital-dictated media.

Of course there are inevitable problems with the idea of postcolonial music. If the musics mentioned above are postcolonial primarily because of their home cultures' former political associations with Great Britain (the British Empire), can it be possible to imagine a postcolonial Welsh music? Given Wales's continued political associations with Great Britain (the United Kingdom), on what grounds would a Welsh music be considered postcolonial? And what kind of Welsh music are we talking about here?

There are certainly recent examples of Welsh music in the classical and 'folk' idioms which have approached the kind of hybridity we just mentioned. These hybridities are accessible to both 'native' Welsh people and more recent arrivals; any references embedded in the music could be understandable to anyone conversant with the culture. The question is whether or not that is enough to qualify the music as Welsh, let alone postcolonial.

There needs to be something else. Musical sounds are borrowed across cultures to such an extent that one person's postcolonial might just be another person's postmodern. Whatever the musical signifier of 'Welsh' might be – the harp, the male voice choir, Tom Jones's unmistakable howl – the one cultural referent unique to Wales is, like it or not, the Welsh language. In more ways than one, it is easier to gauge the post- in Welsh-language music than it is in Anglophone Welsh music. This is not to discount the importance of Welsh musics in English; just that for the purposes of this chapter, the most fertile musical ground is to be found somewhere *between* the Welsh and English languages. In popular music – in the post-war, 'pop' music sense of the term – this linguistic relationship has fostered some interesting and problematic fodder for extended academic exercises, concerned with Welsh-language and Anglophone cultures alike (see Griffiths, 2000; Hill, 2000, 2002).

The problem – and the potential – for Welsh popular music is its anonymity in the world market. Go into any record store overseas and look in the 'World music' section. You may find 'Celtic music', which would be full of Irish 'folk' (fiddles and pipes) and Scottish 'folk' (ditto); there would be a separate section for English 'folk' (with the obligatory Morris dancers on the album covers); but Welsh music, if it is there at all, would probably be filed under 'miscellaneous'. More to the point, 'Welsh music' over there in the 'World' section would probably lean more towards old recordings of Morriston Orpheus and Ar Log than anything more cutting-edge. The more 'popular', all-embracing Welsh pop – Manic Street Preachers, Stereophonics – would get filed alongside their Irish (U2, Sinead O'Connor) and Scottish (Belle and Sebastian, Arab Strap) cousins in the main Anglo-American 'pop' section; even bilingual recordings by Gorky's Zygotic Mynci and Super Furry Animals are filed along with 'mainstream' pop music in some larger American record stores. But go into Spillers Records in Cardiff and recordings 'of Welsh interest' are kept quietly off to the side, in a 'World' of their own. So if integration is one of the deciding factors in a music's ability to convey a sense of its home country's political and social life to an outside audience, Welsh music is at a peculiar disadvantage. Its 'unique' musical heritage is marginalized and largely unknown abroad, while its 'borrowed' popular culture is fractionalized at home. Who is the audience?

Well, there is always the home radio audience, and Radio Wales and Radio Cymru present two very interesting takes on the idea of 'Welsh music'. For Radio Wales, 'Welsh' is almost exclusively Anglophone; for Radio Cymru, 'Welsh' used to be a purely linguistic qualifier, but has recently become much more inclusive. Radio Cymru, the radio *of Wales*, once the safe home of Dafydd Iwan, Geraint Jarman and Ceffyl Pren, is now just as happy to promote the Anglophone music *of Wales* during peak listening times. Twenty years ago, that would have been both scandalous and embarrassing. Welsh popular music existed in part to engage the younger audience with the language movement; to play it alongside its Anglo-American contemporaries would diminish the power of an all-Welsh-language service, while highlighting the relative weakness of the musical product. When Radio 1 DJ John Peel began to develop an interest in Welsh-language pop in the late 1970s and early 1980s, he (perhaps unknowingly) instilled in the Welsh pop community a kind of confidence that Welsh pop – both monolingual Welsh (Datblygu) and bilingual (Gorky's Zygotic Mynci) – was good enough to warrant a larger, 'British' audience. It is tempting to argue that this was one of the original postcolonial moments in the history of Welsh pop. But there were surely others, roughly one every decade: Dafydd Iwan singing 'Carlo' on *Y Dydd* in 1969; the 1989 Live Aid-inspired concert at St David's Hall in Cardiff, when Wales Was the World, raising its *own* money for Ethiopian famine relief; the 1999 Stereophonics concert at Morfa Stadium and the Manic Street Preachers' Millennium Eve concert at Cardiff's Millennium Stadium. These all represented some articulation of Welshness, asserting an individual identity within Britain, if not the wider world; some event that allowed, however fleetingly, a fragile community to form and feel stronger in the face of a larger, more powerful, social or political system – a fine metaphor, in fact, for the common experience of the pop band seeking critical recognition and popular stardom in an often cruel industry.

It really should not come as much of a surprise to learn that the 'political liberation' of Wales coincided with a certain liberation of Welsh-language popular music. Much has been said of the resurgence of British popular music in the early 1990s, and the suggestion that Britpop was effectively killed the moment Noel Gallagher and Meg Matthews stepped into 10 Downing Street (see Harris, 2003);[4] what needs to be made now is the connection between the emergence on to the 'mainstream' UK scene of Anglo-Welsh bands like Super Furry Animals, Catatonia, Stereophonics, Manic Street Preachers and Gorky's Zygotic Mynci around the time that Blair was pushing for devolution. Further, it needs to be said now that all of this happened around the time that hip hop finally hit the shores of Cardigan Bay.

Welsh-language popular music, throughout its relatively short history, has been notoriously slow to catch up with contemporary Anglo-American pop. There were certain points in early Welsh pop history when the Welsh-language Top 10, 'Deg Ucha'r Cymro', charted the popularity of music which might have been popular elsewhere, in English, twenty-five years previously. Of course this was a necessary matter of natural musical evolution – after all, there could be no Beck today without Glen Campbell in the 1970s; but it is still difficult to imagine a Led Zeppelin fan in 1974 switching tapes in the eight-track to get a taste of the new Edward H. Dafis.

This all changed in the 1980s, with the emergence of the 'independent' record labels in Wales. The importance – and enormous significance – of Ankst, for example, is that it allowed a new generation of Welsh musicians, from 1988 onwards, to become contemporaneous with Anglo-American pop, and to contribute to the growth of a relevant Welsh popular culture. That much of this music, from the sublime Datblygu onward, commented on a decidedly *colonial* Wales is the important point of rupture. The political and the musical had rejoined; the linguistic medium was the message, and the message was pretty bleak.[5] For Welsh popular music to reach the postcolonial stage, the political system had to change (which it did); the musical climate in Wales had to change (which it did); and the sense of cultural self-confidence had to emerge (which it did).

As mentioned earlier, bands on the Ankst roster were often noticed by Radio 1 DJ John Peel, which led to a growing cultural self-confidence. This self-confidence manifested itself in, amongst other things, a gradual contemporaneity with Anglo-American trends and, given the state of popular music in the late 1980s and early 1990s, it was only a matter of time before the Welsh musical community adopted rap as a form of expression. There had been 'rap' in Welsh before – recordings by Llwybr Llaethog, Tŷ Gwydr, Diffiniad and Hanner Pei had all hinted at it – but it wasn't until Y Tystion formed in Aberystwyth that the idea of a Welsh hip hop collective was considered a possibility. Still, the idea of Welsh rap is problematic for a number of reasons. First of all, Welsh pop was, for the first fifty years of its modern incarnation, a rural music. This is not to suggest a backwater community culture; merely that the idea of the 'city', of urban life, was rarely addressed in Welsh popular music in the post-war years. In other words, if the hybridity at issue in this discussion of 1990s Welsh 'pop' is a linguistic one, the hybridity of Welsh rap is a contextual one. Rap emerged in New York in the late 1970s in a particular urban environment, under particular social circumstances. It has since been incorporated into innumerable vernacular cultures and resonates with the particular political and societal needs of those cultures (see Mitchell, 2001). Y Tystion were politicized in the tradition of much of their Welsh pop forebears; but their particular kind of hybrid rural rap could only have been possible in a devolution-era Wales. Whether the Welsh rap voice is therefore a postcolonial voice is left to the listener's inference; but the Welshness being explored in Y Tystion and, more recently, Pep Le Pew, is at once reverential and ironic, a combination never truly realized in the earlier days of Welsh pop.

There is one song, 'Dysgwch am y Doethion', on Pep Le Pew's début album, *Y Da, Y Drwg ac Yr Hyll* (Ankst, 2001), which is a good example of the postcolonial in Welsh pop. The rhythmic delivery of the words rests somewhere between sung and spoken poetic Welsh, and the supporting musical structure is punctuated with the sound of the harp, itself a signifier of Welsh identity. This juxtaposition of the arcadian (harp), the urban (hip hop) and the rural (Pep le Pew recorded the album in the Garndolbenmaen 'hood') represents a distillation of the process of Welsh popular music from the 1960s to the present day. More importantly, it defines the kind of cultural self-confidence only attempted in earlier moments of Welsh pop. The physicality of the music, the insistent presence of the Welsh language, and the contemporaneity of the medium and the message, are the most recent result of a fifty-year cultural process. Is this a political music? Yes and no. Yes, because it uses an international musical language to infuse life into a minority-language music, and cites Welsh figures alongside Anglo-American figures as founders of contemporary culture; no, because it remains on the 'outside' of mainstream culture. Is this a postcolonial music? No and yes, for the same reasons.

During the 1990s Welsh pop musicians were involved in nego-
tiations of power and control which can be read as evoking
postcolonial themes – local and global, mainstream and independent, essentialist and hybrid – all gathered broadly under the
heading of geographical dislocation. Some terms, such as 'independent' and 'authenticity', work hard in both popular music and
postcolonial discourse. The points which follow do not necessarily concern language or the nature of the musical material as
such: they are concerned more with the way social and political
context, position, place, began to shift during the period,
producing moments of interest, sparking debates. Three such
dislocations are interpreted: the records of Gorky's Zygotic
Mynci; the Stereophonics and concert performance; and some
points about markers of place.

Gorky's Zygotic Mynci were tremendously productive
following their appearance in 1993, with eight studio albums
produced in an eight-year period, as well as a number of extended
singles with additional B-side material, a total of around 130
recorded tracks.[6] Their first three albums, and several singles,
were issued on Welsh independent label Ankst (see figure 6), the
next two on major label Fontana, and the last three on independent label Mantra.[7] The contrast between Ankst and Fontana
is expressive enough: Ankst was a small, localized, Welsh, independent label, while Fontana was a division of Mercury, which
was in turn owned by Seagram, which also owned Universal
Studios and Absolut Vodka. The move from independent to major
label is a familiar event in pop music, with a now predictable
sense of 'selling out': however, for many Welsh bands, Gorky's
included, this was conjoined with issues around geography and
language. The more distinctive 1990s twist was the subsequent
'downsizing' by Fontana which saw Gorky's effectively dropped,[8]
lending these eight years in the music industry the distinct air of
the portfolio career. This is all very little to do with Wales, since a
similar fate befell many bands at the time, and what was Welsh
about Gorky's best resides in the tracks themselves. However, we
wish to interpret the way that these shifts were reflected, to an
extent, in the visual appearance of Gorky's. The records on Ankst
are characterized by a unified visual presentation, with the
covers designed by Gorwel Owen, and evoking a distinctive and
energetic style, which seemed at the time like a Welsh reference via
the eye of the cartoonist Steve Bell. With the crossover to Fontana

a blander visual style is presented, one which loses its Welsh evocation. With the move to Mantra a third style became used, evoking a slicker, and possibly Americanized pop art. Interestingly, the reissue programme has seen the return of Gorwel Owen artwork. The early Ankst records presented a balance of visual projection and musical content, distinctively and independently Welsh. Time moved on and the band doubtless wished to escape a position in danger of reduction and repetition: 'post-colonially', however, one might suggest that the original position was limited but apposite. The lovely, later song 'Spanish Dance Troupe' seemed to offer a comment: 'Woke up on Monday and got ready for school. Put on my uniform it was three sizes too small. I said, "dear, dear, dear teacher, I've been six years away, and ain't finished my essay, coz rock 'n' roll rules ok." My conclusion this summer was there was too much rain. So I ran off on Thursday with a dance troupe from Spain.'[9] Our paraphrase: major record labels mess people around and eventually one returns to something as localized as school, before heading to Spain imagining new cross-artform possibilities.

The problems of balancing locality and global industry in a Welsh context are interestingly presented in a debate which followed a concert at Morfa Stadium by the Stereophonics. The Stereophonics were by this point (31 July 1999) enjoying great popularity, in Wales and beyond. Their records preserved a careful balance between markers of Wales, notably the voice of Kelly Jones and their evocation of south Wales Valley life. However, Kelly Jones managed to be quite specific in terms of place while never actually mentioning anywhere, like Springsteen at his best in a song like 'Tougher than the rest'.[10] The idea of something quite specific evoking at the same time a 'universal human condition' is something which postcolonial theory is necessarily attentive towards, because what is taken to be universality is in all likelihood the product of specific conditions made into a second nature, made into 'common sense' (see Ashcroft et al., 1988: 235–7). Postcolonial theory thus asks the observer to hone in on moments of border-crossing, when general and specific are blurred, even when those are the tiny moments of marginal presence. This the Stereophonics certainly did, subtly and minutely, in a way which had to do with almost everything about the Morfa gig, with being there, with singing along, with the songs, with their stage presence . . .

Less subtly, they also showed some videos. Sports videos. Videos of rugby triumphs: Wales beating England at Wembley in 1999, and two famous moments of the 1970s – a try by Gareth Edwards against Scotland in 1972, and one by the same player for the Barbarians against New Zealand in 1973. From here on, the discussion concerns what it was to be in the audience of the concert itself, and the focus is a debate conducted in some detail in the pages of the *NME*. The gig was reviewed by Stuart Baillie in the issue dated 14 August 1999. The controversy began with some non-Welsh fans writing in to the paper to complain about the videos (21 August) under the editorial banner, 'Is Wales the new Germany?' The debate quite quickly became concerned specifically with *England*: Boris of Telford suggested that 'you only have to wave a St George's flag to show some pride in your country and you get branded a Nazi'. James Oldham for the *NME* linked the 'thin line between patriotism and nationalism' to the fact that 'race related attacks in South Wales are dramatically on the rise'. The debate disappeared for two weeks in the *NME*, while evidently appearing elsewhere in the UK national media. However, it returned to the *NME* of 11 September with a summary article and many more letters.[11] Ramona Sprague of Gwent and E. Edwards of north Wales put a case against England, again specifically, with Cyril of Swansea going on the attack with 'You can stick your Chariots of Fire up your arse', and Kerr Dorman of Hankswell coming on strong with 'sheep-shagging language' and asking that the Stereophonics 'sing their songs in the same fucking jibberish. We'll see how many records they sell then.' Polarizing of opinion and the selection of invective are of course established editorial tricks. The debate was nearly over, although the 18 September issue reminded readers that 'it's the Welsh issue that continues to cripple the mail man'. Ian Titherington of Plaid Cymru on 25 September pointed out that 'there is a cultural renaissance going on in Wales as we approach the millennium', and there was a coda of sorts on 2 October with Caroline Connor of Coleraine in Northern Ireland explaining that, 'coming from Northern Ireland, I suffer the consequences of arguing between rival groups' and asking, 'do you really want to turn out like us?' That was about it and, interestingly, the Stereophonics' gig at Cardiff that December was reviewed (18 December) with no letter response at all. Stephen Dalton, reviewing the latter concert, said that there was no 'chest-beating nationalism onstage tonight' and that 'only a paranoid English tourist' could interpret the crowd's cries of 'Wales, Wales' as 'hostility. This isn't Kosovo, for Christ's sake.'

So it goes. A simple switch of a video player, in a particular context, sets off the discursive chain, one which would speak to a nationalist context, to prejudice and stereotyping, but also to the sensitivities of a postcolonial world. We would suggest that, while music and sport have enormous amounts in common, there is a basic difficulty in reconciling that aspect of rock festivals which is, however insincerely, concerned with losing one's self in community with the them-and-us world of the rugby game, organized by place as sport invariably is. During the 1990s, it was at rock concerts that Welsh flags flew like question marks, possibly more so than in sport, where the *English* flag, the flag of St George, became more prominently and questioningly present at soccer matches (Griffiths, 2001: 215). In the case of the Stereophonics concert, evidence of the moment itself is hard to come by, and it has become a moment of erasure: the commercial video of the concert shows the offending videos, but not particularly clearly, and carefully blurs the sound of the crowd. In addition, even though the video contains several band interviews, true to pop escapism, the controversy is never raised. Furthermore, Kelly Jones's performance of the little song 'As long as we beat the English' is not included.[12]

It is one thing for the songs to adopt a placeless realism, another simply to name Wales, and it was interesting that 1990s Welsh pop tended not to do the latter. The Stereophonics were one of the English-language Welsh bands who rose to prominence in the 1990s: like the 60ft Dolls or the Manic Street Preachers they were from the English-speaking south, while many of the other bands, Super Furry Animals, Gorky's Zygotic Mynci and Catatonia, all crossed over from earlier Welsh-language bands. In all of these bands, taken together, there are to be found relatively few cases of John Davies's tip to Anglo-Welsh poets: 'spray place names around' (Davies, 1984: 316–17). Examples of the deliberate naming of Welsh places in songs can be found in earlier Anglo-Welsh pop music: John Cale, Man, The Men They Couldn't Hang, The Alarm.[13] Also, of course, at the same time as Welsh pop music's ascendancy in the 1990s, 'Britpop' itself drew attention to specific English places, notably Blur's London and Pulp's Sheffield. Gorky's mention two places, Llanfwrog and Broadhaven; Catatonia mention Rhyl and Connah's Quay; the Manics eventually mentioned Wattsville,[14] the Stereophonics nowhere in Wales. Something small seemed to have changed. While it is probably the case that a Manics track entitled 'I Have a Cousin, Eira, and She Lives in Craig-y-Nos' wouldn't get too far with the management at Sony, the absence of place names may nevertheless suggest an expressive space which tells us something about the 'world-view' which these bands were portraying. Against this – and pop songs are of course not only about their words – is the markedness of voice at this time. As comparison one might set Mike Peters singing 'Absolute Reality' in 1985 with The Alarm, next to the voice of Kelly Jones. Peters is seemingly trying very hard to sound like a London punk, the voice elsewhere, like that of Mick Hucknall, Bono or Jim Kerr at the time; with Kelly Jones, the songs may be metonymic, realist and applicable to small-town life well beyond their immediate locality, but the voice is full of bodily presence. And then try 'The Heart of Kentucky' by Gorky's Zygotic Mynci, mentioning Kentucky and pretending to be a country and western band; but where the juxtaposition with their Harvest-label, psychedelic noise means that the style is put firmly in quotation marks.[15]

Feeling out of place in Morfa, the offended non-Welsh Stereophonics fans need not have worried too much. The concert held to mark devolution in Cardiff Bay in 1998, and filmed by the BBC as *Starry Starry Night*, made something much lighter of Welsh pride and patriotism, while carefully avoiding most of the music we discuss here in favour of a time capsule whose centre of gravity lay somewhere around 1981. Shirley Bassey's version of *La Cage aux folles* diva classic (probably via Gloria Gaynor in 1984) 'I Am What I Am', Max Boyce's witty update of 1973's 'Hymns and Arias', Bonnie Tyler's 1983 smash, 'Total eclipse of the heart', Iris Williams's version of the 'Cavatina' which had spread like cover-version chickenpox around 1979, Charlotte Church's impressively close-to-the-note rendition of 'Pie Jesu', Lloyd Webber Hell *c*.1985, Mike Peters's 'A New South Wales', dated 1989 but surely intended as a tribute to Mott the Hoople around 1974: all of these seemed to evoke an earlier 'classic' Welsh popular music. If anything, and the association of Bonnie Tyler's record with producer Jim Steinman and John Cale's brooding presence both reinforced this impression, the concert was 'always already' less postcolonial and more the old favourite of the American Wales (Smith, 1993). Tom Jones went with 'Green, green grass of home', complete with that 'sad old padre' which suggests that the song is country-and-western through and through, and that what made sense for Porter Wagoner's American listeners in 1965 did so too for Tom's south Wales a year later. Michael Ball offered a bizarre arrangement of Joseph Parry's 'Cwm Rhondda' as a sort of 'Iko-Iko' New Orleans gumbo. But it was left to the conclusion to sum it up, as the luminaries of daytime airplay on Radio Wales gathered to listen to two singers negotiate the Welsh-language verses to Catatonia's 'International velvet', joining in a chorus rousing, if knocking on, and evocative of a Wales gone but still powerfully present. The strange, sampled rhythm which underpins 'International Velvet' served as reminder to this time-specific presentation that its world was now subtly different and that the finale's steely, stellar line was based upon a degree of denial, not least that much of English-speaking Wales again dependably voted 'No' to devolution itself.[16] Whatever a postcolonial Wales might possibly mean, for pop music, this concert seemed to suggest, it could not come quickly enough.

A more contemporary contribution might have been sought from the Super Furry Animals. Revelling in its place on the margins of both mainstream Anglophone and Welsh popular cultures, this band has managed to dabble on both sides of the post/colonial divide, shifting effortlessly from one linguistic medium to the other, maintaining 'indie' roots in Wales and the UK while moving from one label to another, and infusing both their Welsh and English songs with references cribbed equally from the pop standards and obscurities of both repertories.

Their initial shift from Welsh to bilingual pop coincided with their shift from Ankst to Creation, and introduced their Welsh and English audiences to some rather unique and innovative marketing strategies. First, their appearances at the 1996 Llandeilo Eisteddfod, accompanied by a bright blue customized (decommissioned) tank, emblazoned with the band's name and the inscription 'A oes heddwch?' (fitting for the Eisteddfod, perhaps, but what did the crowd at the Reading Rock Festival that year think of it?). Then there was the band's wholly inspired sponsorship of the Cardiff football team, garnering a nice spot on the evening news for singer Gruff Rhys (really a Bangor supporter) and a couple of bemused players, holding up the team's jerseys emblazoned with the band's Pete Fowler-designed logo across the front. One can imagine very few bands who get a free plug on the sports report, local or national.[17] Then there was the international release of *Rings Around the World* (Sony, 2001), accompanied by the first-ever DVD video album, featuring not the band themselves, but a series of commissioned 'interpretations' of the different songs. Going into Amoeba Records in Berkeley, California, the diehard Anglophone fan of Welsh popular music would be delighted to find the *Rings Around the World* DVD on sale in the same bin as the *Supernatural* concert by Santana, the Bay Area's version of the postcolonial local hero becoming the global megastar. All of these strategies suggest a relaxed kind of independent–mainstream negotiation, and illuminate the significance of the 2000 release of the Furries' *Mwng*, the supreme postcolonial Welsh pop moment.[18]

There are many points to be made about *Mwng*, most of which can be distilled to a few salient words: independence, freedom, linguistic signification. The Super Furries had long established their cultural (linguistic) credentials 'at home' and their indie (musical) credentials in Britain and beyond; the release of *Mwng* was therefore greeted by the Welsh press with almost unprecedented ecstasy, and by the British press as a welcome addition to the band's refreshingly unpredictable recorded output. The fact that the British press paid any notice whatsoever to a Welsh-language release was itself an enormous milestone;[19] the fact that the band provided song lyrics and translations only on their website suggested either a pared-down packaging budget or an unapologetic assumption that fans of the album would not find Welsh an insurmountable obstacle to the enjoyment of the music. And why should they? Since at least 1986 music fans have embraced musics of cultures generally considered 'foreign'.[20] Why should Welsh pop not be accepted outside Wales as part of the 'World' of music? This boils down to the cultural self-confidence mentioned earlier, but more pointedly to that issue of (post-)colonial power.

And here's where the Super Furry Animals turn the argument on its head. There are two songs on *Mwng* which need to be singled out in this context. 'Y Teimlad' (The feeling) was written by David R. Edwards and released by Datblygu in 1985.[21] In its original version it is a paean to mid-1980s synth-pop, sounding something like a cross between Joy Division and Kate Bush; in Super Furry Animals' version, it becomes a timeless and painful epic of longing. Nostalgia – *hiraeth* – has been the central *idée fixe* of Welsh expressive culture since time immemorial. It has sold thousands of books of poetry, thousands of novels, and perhaps tens of copies of the Morriston Orpheus in larger overseas record shops. People understand *hiraeth; hiraeth* sells. It just never sounded quite like the Super Furry Animals. It has never been a respectful reiteration of an indigenous, yet marginalized, *popular* cultural utterance. What Super Furry Animals did with 'Y Teimlad' was to install Datblygu in the consciousness of a wider public – to suggest, in effect, the equally weighted importance of local culture and internationally shared popular culture.[22] In so doing, they shifted the balance of cultural power just a little bit from the centre to the periphery.

'Ymaelodi â'r Ymylon' ('Joining the Periphery') goes one step further:

> Maen nhw'n dweud
> Bo' ni ar yr ymylon
> Yn weision bach ffyddlon
> Yn arw ac estron
> Ac mae hi'n llugoer yn llygad y ffynnon
> Ond ar yr ymylon
> Mae'r danadl poethion.
>
> (Well, they say we're peripheral people
> Spineless and feeble
> Roughneck and evil
> And it's so cool in the eye of the fountain
> But the peripheries sustain
> The hottest nettle.)[23]

The periphery at issue here is double-sided: the periphery of Anglo-American popular culture, and the periphery of Welsh musical culture. Super Furry Animals inhabit both at the same time, neither exclusively Welsh nor exclusively 'British' (and certainly never 'English'), what Homi Bhabha calls 'the in-between space':

> we should remember that it is the 'inter' – the cutting edge of translation and negotiation, the *in-between* space – that carries the burden of the meaning of culture. It makes it possible to begin envisaging national, anti-nationalist histories of the 'people'. And by exploring this Third Space, we may elude the politics of polarity and emerge as the others of our selves. (Bhabha, 1994: 38–9)

Whether postcolonial theory offers suitable clues for the pop music of this period is debatable. Welsh pop music was by this point a complex thing, and the reader may well feel that not enough time has elapsed, for instance in clarifying the story itself, before bringing interpretive theory to bear on the material. When something as canon-reflecting as the *New Grove Dictionary of Music and Musicians* appeared in a revised edition in 2001 with its entry for Wales still divided into art and folk music, with no room for pop music in either Welsh or English languages, then clearly there is still work to be done.[24] But for music the leap from a conception of music as still essentially that of 'classical' music, with folk music as something more overtly national, to a conception which seeks to be all-embracing, is not entirely removed from the moment of the questions raised by postcolonialism itself. If anything, theoretically, one ought at least to acknowledge the possibility of two other 'posts-': the postmodern, which would also embrace some of the features to which we have referred, and, for the pop music of this period, a phrase such as 'post-industrial'. The bands we refer to above were often determinedly *bands* – singer, bass player, drummer, guitarist, piling into a Ford Transit to head down the M4 to London or, God help them, the A470 from south to north Wales. Their dreams and strategies revolved around *record labels*, knowing full well that a Welsh-language label was the nearest to absolute independence that could be imagined. At this time, however, both these foundations came under question: music technology had made aspects of the band redundant, while the internet threw the industry into great and possibly fatal confusion. Here we can observe a continuum. At one end the Stereophonics, seemingly defending the unity of rock authenticity: a central singer-songwriter; the stripped, power-trio tradition of Cream, Jam and Nirvana; tightly controlled product and marketing on Branson's V2 label; the careful scheduling of albums and live gigs for consumption by loyal fans. On the other end the Super Furry Animals: all band members throwing in ideas; experimenting with dance-music practice; blurring record label distinctions; mixed-media presentation; fans ready to be stretched and challenged. If the idea of postcolonialism is brought to the distinction, and it's a fair-sized 'if', it would seem to us that the latter is where the theory makes more sense.

NOTES

1 All compilations referred to are issued by the World Music Network, based in London. Visit their site at: *www.worldmusic.net*
2 A parallel to these multiples might be found in Paul Gilroy's term 'anti-anti-essentialism' (Gilroy, 1993: 102).
3 On Asian Dub Foundation, see Stubbs, 2003: 27–31. 'Free Saptal Ram' is found on *Rafi's Revenge* (Nation, 1998).
4 See, for example, the documentary film *Live Forever* (John Dower, 2002).
5 Examples of 'bleak' Welsh pop can be found in much of Datblygu's back catalogue. Interested parties should invest in the reissues, *Wyau and Pyst* (Ankst, 1995) and *Datblygu 1985–1995* (Ankst, 1999) for a comprehensive understanding of the nature of Welsh pop during the Thatcher years.
6 We are extremely grateful to Jeni Williams for detailed responses to this section of the chapter.
7 On Ankst: *Patio* (1993), *Tatay* (1994) *Bwyd Time* (1995); on Fontana: *Barafundle* (1997), *Five* (1998); on Mantra: *Spanish Dance Troupe* (1999), *The Blue Trees* (2000), *How I Long to Feel That Summer in My Heart* (2001). At the time of writing, Castle/Sanctuary are in the process of reissuing the Ankst output.
8 See the *NME* for 3 October 1988 and *Music Week* journal at the time for how Gorky's change of label was perceived.
9 'Spanish Dance Troupe' is the title track of the Gorky's 1999 album on Mantra.
10 'Tougher than the rest' is on *Tunnel of Love* (Columbia, 1987).
11 The article itself, titled 'Welsh pride or fascism?', without named author, is highly recommended as the best snapshot of the dispute.
12 It can be heard on a bootleg of the concert, *Morfa Yer Money*, and doubtless on the internet.
13 For examples, see John Cale, 'Ship of fools', *Fear* (Island, 1974), The Men They Couldn't Hang, 'The rabid underdog', *How Green is the Valley* (MCA, 1986), and The Alarm, 'A New South Wales' (1989), *Standards* (IRS, 1990). A vinyl original of Man's *Be Good to Yourself at Least Once a Day* (United Artists, 1972) is well worth tracking down, its gatefold sleeve opening into a pop-up map of Wales, with England firmly separated by water, while *Back into the Future* (United Artists, 1973) includes a lengthy attempt to get an audience at London's Roundhouse to join in 'Sospan Fach' in Welsh.
14 The Manic Street Preachers are characteristically complicated in this respect, since they do evoke many place names in a way whose purpose would seem to be to place themselves in a wider historical setting reminiscent perhaps of an earlier, international left. This culminates in their being actually in Havana shaking hands with Castro himself. 'Wattsville blues', a track on *Know Your Enemy* (Epic, 2001), refers to Wattsville, a village in the Sirhowy valley, but still sounds American, much as the area in Swansea called Jersey Marine sounds like it might have been invented by Bruce Springsteen. Gorky's place names are found on the *Llanfwrog* EP (Ankst, 1995) and on *Five* (Fontana, 1998); Catatonia's on *International Velvet* and *Paper Scissors Stone* (Blanco y Negro, 1998 and 2001).
15 'Absolute reality' (1985) is found on *Standards*; 'The heart of Kentucky' on the *Amber Gambler* EP (Ankst, 1996). For Kelly Jones, start with 'A thousand trees' on *Word Gets Around* (V2, 1997).
16 See *Golwg*, 10/4, 25 September 1997.
17 The obvious exception here is the Grateful Dead, whose 1992 sponsorship of

the Lithuanian Olympic basketball team earned a bit of press coverage, if not for the band's continued charitable donations via its Rex Foundation offshoot, then for the specially designed tie-dyed uniforms the team proudly modelled as they accepted their bronze medals.

[18] Creation Records, home to Super Furry Animals from *Fuzzy Logic* (1996) to *Guerrilla* (1999), was dissolved in 2000. The band had a backlog of Welsh-language songs that they wanted to record, so they recorded them in a relatively brief period of time and released *Mwng* on their own Placid Casual label in 2000.

[19] *The Sunday Times* even went so far as to review *Mwng* as the 'album of the week', ending their review by saying:

> the language issue isn't really a hindrance; in fact, on tracks such as Gwreiddiau Dwfn (Deep Roots) the inability to follow the lyrics leaves you more time to ponder the fact that the Super Furrys are rapidly approaching the melodic sophistication of old-school songwriters such as Burt Bacharach. Career-wise, who knows what this will do to the band; but musically, they've made exactly the right move. This is a delicate, organic, melancholic, utterly charming record. (14 May, 2000)

[20] It is in 1987 that 'world music' became an industry term for the otherwise uncategorizable 'other' musics slowly gaining in popularity as a result, perhaps, of the more notable introduction of African musicians on albums such as Paul Simon's *Graceland* (Warner, 1986). On the invention of 'world music' (in July 1987 in a London pub), see Frith, 2000: 305–22. Reference to world music predates that time, in examples such as Joni Mitchell's *The Hissing of Summer Lawns* (Asylum, 1975), Peter Gabriel, *Peter Gabriel* (Charisma, 1980), and Brian Eno and David Byrne's *My Life in the Bush of Ghosts* (Polydor, 1981).

'Foreign' is a difficult term to justify. The us/them, inside/outside, centre/periphery oppositions are implicit in it, and many examples could be made of the imposition of that kind of baggage on musicians from marginal-ized communities even *within* Anglo-American popular culture. Why, for example, in de facto bilingual areas of the world such as California, did the mid-1980s popularity of 'La bamba' and the subsequent wider acknowledge-ment of Los Lobos as *Hispanic rock 'n' roll* artists raise more than a few eyebrows?

[21] 'Y Teimlad' is available on *Datblygu 1985–1995* (Ankst, 1999).

[22] In a conversation with Sarah Hill, David R. Edwards said that he was unaware of the Furries' intention to record 'Y Teimlad' until he heard Gruff Rhys singing it on Radio 2. When asked how that made him feel, he said, 'it was like getting the most wonderful love letter'.

[23] Lyrics by Super Furry Animals; translation from *www.mwng.co.uk*

[24] The same applied to Scotland and Ireland. Stephen Banfield's entry for 'England' managed to set a quite fresh agenda and was, ironically enough, the only one of the entries for the home countries to mention devolution. See Sadie, 2001.

REFERENCES

Ashcroft, B., Griffiths, G. and Tiffin, H. (1988). *Key Concepts in Post-Colonial Studies*, London: Routledge.

Bhabha, H. (1994). *The Location of Culture*, London: Routledge.

Cavanagh, D. (2000). *The Creation Records Story: My Magpie Eyes are Hungry for the Prize*, London: Virgin.

Davies, J. (1984). 'How to write Anglo-Welsh poetry', in Raymond Garlick and Roland Mathias (eds), *Anglo-Welsh Poetry 1480–1980*, Bridgend: Poetry Wales Press.

Frith, S. (2000). 'The discourse of world music', in G. Born and D. Hesmondhalgh (eds), *Western Music and Its Others*, Berkeley: University of California Press, pp. 305–22.

Gilroy, P. (1993). *The Black Atlantic: Modernity and Double Consciousness*, London: Verso.

Griffiths, D. (2000). 'Home is living like a man on the run: John Cale's Welsh Atlantic', *Welsh Music History*, 4, Cardiff: University of Wales Press, pp. 159–85; reprinted in Martin Stokes and Philip V. Bohlman, *Celtic Modern: Music at the Global Fringe* (Lanham and Oxford: Scarecrow Press, 2003), pp. 171–99.

Griffiths, D. (2001). 'Kelly, Cerys, and James Dean Bradfield', in Trevor Herbert and Peter Stead (eds), *Hymns and Arias: Great Welsh Voices*, Cardiff: University of Wales Press.

Harris, J. (2003). *The Last Party: Britpop, Blair and the Demise of English Rock*, London: HarperCollins.

Hesmondhalgh, D. (2000). 'International times: fusions, exoticism and antiracism in electronic dance music', in Georgina Born and David Hesmondhalgh (eds), *Western Music and Its Others*, Berkeley: University of California Press, pp. 280–304.

Hill, S. (2000). 'Families of Resemblance: Welsh popular music and other marginalia', *Welsh Music History*, 4, Cardiff: University of Wales Press, pp. 138–47.

Hill, S. (2002). '"Blerwytirhwng?" Welsh popular music, language and the politics of identity', Ph.D. thesis, Cardiff University.

Mitchell, T. (ed.) (2001).*Global Noise: Rap and Hip Hop Outside the USA*, Middletown: Wesleyan University Press.

Penman, I. (1998). *Vital Signs: Music, Movies and Other Manias*, London: Serpent's Tail.

Sadie, S. (ed.) (2001). *New Grove Dictionary of Music and Musicians*, 2nd edn, London: Macmillan.

Sharma, S., Hutnyk, J. and Sharma, A. (1996). *Dis-Orienting Rhythms: The Politics of the New Asian Dance Music*, London: Zed Books.

Smith, D. (1993). *Aneurin Bevan and the World of South Wales*, Cardiff: University of Wales Press.

Spencer, I. (2002). 'Eastern rising', *The Psychedelic Beatles*, *Mojo Special Limited Edition,* Emap, 76–81.

Stubbs, D. (1998). 'Fences and windows', *The Wire*, 227 (2003), 27–31.

13

Horizon Wales: Visual Art and the Postcolonial

IWAN BALA

Culture is not made through consensus or imposition. It is made through ideas that are strongly felt, undeniable feelings where one acknowledges the course of history in relation to the present.

(Morgan, 1998: 193)

1

Is Wales postcolonial? Is any place? Transnational corporations have become the new exponents of colonialism, and have spread the idea of a global visual culture, expounded by large power-house art galleries, and the exhibitions and festivals that spring up in every corner of the developed world. Where, in all this, is Wales? Some have argued that historically Wales has been a province, not a colony. Is that why our art is assumed to be provincial? Perhaps the question we need to ask is, can we become 'post-provincial'?

Whatever the argument, it is difficult to deny a sense in Wales of ongoing cultural colonialism, and this leads me to the belief that postcolonialism with us needs to be a state of mind as much, if not more than, a political position. Wales may not have seen armies of occupation for some time, but it has felt the economic and cultural consequence of imperialism, and it has suffered its paralysing side-effect, the colonized mentality. Visual art in Wales has inevitably reflected this psychological inheritance. Welsh art depicts an enforced duality, revealing, on the one hand, a 'culture shame' that induces an eagerness to please, to adopt the rhetoric of British patriotism and to assimilate; on the other hand, it can also show a stubborn avowal of difference and an insistence upon cultural Otherness. Both its acquiescence and its resistance are traits of the colonized.

The term 'Wales art' is now often substituted for 'Welsh art'; 'Wales art' suggests a freedom from ethnic overtones and is perhaps a more realistic label with which to describe the art scene as it is, but, in going for a 'made in Wales' uniformity, the term does imply an avoidance of the issue of being 'Welsh'. Even if the backgrounds of individual practitioners within what could be called the 'Wales art world' are multivarious, I would argue that the institutions, the collective behaviour, the pathology, that animates this world still reflects vestiges of its unreconstructed 'Welsh' make-up – its colonized traits. Its duality is revealed, on one hand, by an overcompensating boastfulness, and on the other, by an adolescent dependence. Value is still accorded in Wales to those who 'escape' the country's boundaries and succeed else-where, and this, though it might be only an economic necessity for the artist to begin with, becomes very much a part of the Welsh condition. As in other Welsh cultural fields, a lack of entrepre-neurial vision and of self-belief stunt the support systems that in other parts of the world promote artists' careers. Grand gestures are often followed by dithering and collapse, as in the case of Cardiff's Centre for Visual Art, or the National Botanic Gardens, or Zaha Hadid's cancelled Opera House design. In short, vision and confident support on a financial, political and ideological level is needed.

Are we by now starting to rid ourselves of colonized traits? Is the apparatus of postcolonialism in place in Wales? If we invoke Frantz Fanon's analysis in his famous text of anti-colonialism, *The Wretched of the Earth*, then it would appear that it is not, for the Welsh have not undergone a process of decolonization, a process which Fanon believes 'is always a violent phenomenon' (1961: 35). Nationalist violence is a rare thing in Wales, a fact which could be said to reflect the partly consensual nature of our colonization. However, we can detect occurrences of a deferred and vicarious violence in the visual arts of the last thirty years, and a romanticization of figures that came close to embodying violence. Ivor Davies, a leading painter of politicized narratives, portrays Mudiad Amddiffyn Cymru leader, John Jenkins, as a revolutionary hero in his *Tryweryn a John Jenkins* (1993); Jenkins served a jail sentence in the 1960s for setting explosives in the

Tryweryn Valley, flooded against the wishes of its inhabitants and of the Welsh people as a whole to provide water for Liverpool (for further information on Jenkins and Tryweryn, see Clewes, 1980). Other, more pacifist yet still inflammatory heroes, such as Saunders Lewis, D. J. Williams and Lewis Valentine, who burned an RAF bombing school in the Llŷn peninsula in 1936, are celebrated in his *Delw Danbaid* (2002) (for further information on the resultant court case, see Lewis, 1983). In an assemblage work, *The Writing on the Wall* (2001; see figure 7) Davies depicts a Welsh family bible and two other Methodist books ripped in half by an ancient rifle: William Williams, Pantycelyn, eighteenth-century hymn-writer and Welsh cultural leader, is seen in reproduction on one of the pages. In other works, Davies has turned the red earth of Epynt, Brecknockshire, into pigment for paintings that comment on the seizure of that land for the British army's firing range. This art, if not postcolonial, is certainly anti-colonial; further, in its insistence on partisan representation, it demonstrates the fact that it is not simply 'identity' that is the key issue for marginalized groups but 'representation'. Who represents who, and can marginal groups regain control of their own representation?

In this contemporary Wales, postcolonial discourse can provide a useful tool, a 'discursive terminology' that may help us to understand a complex pathology, and explore art production in its light. Using the terminology can also provide a link between Welsh culture and interesting and dynamic art produced in other cultures that can more unequivocally be termed postcolonial, and involve us in critical dissemination. Such associations open up new possibilities and new references for our visual artists, as they do, of course, for all producers of culture. The space of one essay does not allow for detailed analysis of all these new or potential influences, or of the work of individual artists, but it may serve to raise possible subjects and scenarios for a discussion that is long overdue in the context of visual art in Wales. Postcolonial issues are of relevance, for example, in any discussions on the establishing of a National Gallery of Welsh art: what form would it take, which artists would be shown and which would remain in storage? Despite the fact that postcolonial studies concentrate primarily on countries in the so-called Third World it is clear that the long-term effects of postcolonialism function also within areas of the First World. T. Minh-Ha Trinh, a Vietnamese film maker now working in the USA, has said of her own situation and that of many others who have migrated to the West, 'There is a Third World in every First World, and vice versa' (Trinh, 1987). A legacy of colonialism is a new 'nomadism'; artists increasingly cross cultural and political borders forming a 'transnational' exchange of ideas and conditions.

2

Artists, by and large, perform to suit the conditions of the time they live in, and desire to express their individual and collective identity. The fulfilment of that desire in Wales has been on view in the Arts and Crafts pavilions of each National Eisteddfod since 1990. Yet artists in Wales, both Welsh and non-Welsh, rarely contemplate or engage with the notion of Wales as a colony, post- or otherwise, unless it directly impacts on their 'professional development'. This may be due to the fact that the colonized state of mind is so deep-rooted and seemingly so well disguised. In postcolonial terminology, it is a case of 'subaltern mentality'. Artists who are Welsh-speakers tend to be more conscious of the condition, perhaps because they retain a certain sense of 'differ- ence'. Historically, the industrial working classes of Wales (primarily though not exclusively non-Welsh speaking in the twentieth century) have seen their subaltern situation as a 'class' rather than a 'culture' issue, and many artists in Wales come from that cultural formation.

Artists face the problems associated with being 'peripheral' to the centres of art production and marketing, and on the whole they prefer to avoid being labelled in any way that would deny them the widest field of play. We might compare this instinct to the resistance of black British artists to being ghettoized into 'special' exhibitions, rather than being viewed as part of main- stream British art, to which (all being equal) we all contribute. There has accordingly been a tendency for artists to believe that success can only be measured on the 'macro' scale, British rather than Welsh, a tendency emphasized by the attitudes of the London press towards the 'periphery'. There are signs that this tendency is entrenched and endemic. The selectors of Wales's first Venice Biennale exhibition, *Further*, in 2003, were criticized in Wales for ignoring the internal community of artists. The two Welsh (indeed Welsh-speaking) artists selected, Cerith Wyn Evans and Bethan

Huws, both created their careers outside Wales. Wales's presence
at the Biennale warrants celebration: it is a statement that identifies Wales as an independent entity. At the same time the selectors
for Wales seemed too eager to appear 'internationalist' at the
expense of recognizing and promoting Wales's own 'underpriv-
ileged' artists. The Welsh representation seemed marked by
ambivalence – partly resistant, partly acquiescent – and serves to
some degree as an indicator of a lack of confidence rather than of
the much-vaunted 'new confidence' of a nation redefining itself.
Such conflict reflects the duality at the heart of postmodernism,
between cultural identity based on 'roots' in one corner and a
transnational, non-specific and non-attached identity in the other.
Wyn Evans's piece at Venice, *Cleave 03* (see figure 8) utilized a
World War II searchlight beam shot skywards, relaying in Morse
code words from Ellis Wynne's canonical Welsh text of 1703,
Gweledigaethau y Bardd Cwsc (Visions of the sleeping bard).
Gweledigaethau y Bardd Cwsc is a translation of a translation:
the work quoted is itself based on a 1627 Spanish text, *Suenos y
Discursos* by Fransisco de Quevedo, encountered by Ellis Wynne
in an English translation. The intermittent beam signalled Wales's
arrival in Venice as much as it signalled the diffusion of one
language translated into another, of text into art and, poignantly
it seemed to me, of y *Gymraeg* into thin air.

At the same time, we in Wales do have our alternative artists,
involved in practice outside the mainstream (in terms of content if
not form), and intent upon producing what I have elsewhere
described in my book *Certain Welsh Artists* as a 'custodial
aesthetics' (Bala, 1999). As its title suggests, this book was not a
survey of art in Wales; rather, it took particular case histories, and,
using the artists' own words, argued that their art was driven by
their 'custodial responsibility' to the specifics of place, culture and
memory, and that they therefore operated outside the dominant
market or fashion-led art world. Raymond Williams's theory of
'formation and alignment' is invoked by several of these artists,
who refer to the model he proposed that divides human culture
into dominant, residual and emergent domains. According to
Williams, the dominant maintains its hegemony by the use of a
'selective tradition':

> In any society, in any particular period, there is a central system of
> practices, meanings and values, which we can properly call dominant
> and effective. This implies no presumption about its value. It is this

central system that formulates the selective tradition; that which, within the terms of an effective dominant culture, is always passed off as '*the* tradition', 'the significant past'. (Williams, 1980: 38–9)

In opposition to this 'selective tradition' there exists a 'residual culture', which is reactionary, and an 'emergent culture', which is revolutionary. In this context that which is avant-garde in art is an 'emergent' and culturally revolutionary force of revitalization, which offers an alternative 'tradition' to that of moribund and lethargic monumental systems. The production of art that questions the hegemony of the state or the market, or dismantles prejudices, racism and imperialism, can also be seen as the act of 'compensating the canon', that is, of offering alternative variants to the accepted and 'selective tradition'. Wales has artists who are doing that now, joining a growing movement of artists who seek to examine issues of their particular identity, its political and gender borders, and the nature of the global market. World-wide, the threat of homogenization and the loss of cultural independence have been and are being resisted in art: an indigenous 'alternative modernism' was practised throughout the last century in Latin America. In Europe, Basque culture has produced art 'authentic' to its own cultural experience, evidenced in the work of Ibarolla, Chillida and Jorge de Oteiza, which is none the less international in its scope. It should be stressed, then, that art that challenges the 'selective tradition' as it exists in Wales, is not bound by the situation in Wales only, but reflects artistic concerns of many artists in many places.

3

It is hard to imagine another medium that has undergone such radical shifts in terms of what it can be made of, or be about, as we have seen in visual art over the last forty years. Postcolonialism and its ally, postmodernist art, has encouraged hybridity and syncretism or, to give it a popular name, 'Fusion'. Artists are able to absorb from their indigenous culture (often many-layered and depending on multiple understandings of the 'indigenous'), from colonialist culture, and from global culture generally, giving rise to a new and vibrant art language that speaks of the complex here and now: in Havana, in Harare, in Dublin, in Cardiff. Postcolonial confidence gives free rein to the appropriative appetites of such artists, unburdened by guilt, either of their own history and identity or of that imposed upon them by the colonizer. Issues of identity, it is argued, can be both sources of inspiration and inhibitors: once identity is established or re-affirmed we are then free of it, or so we may hope. The concept of postcolonial 'hybridity' proposes a new form of identity. According to the Cuban writer Gerardo Mosquera,

> The 'liberation' of identity allows us to understand it in a more flex-ible manner, erasing the essentialisms that forever limited its theory and practice. This is particularly useful for postcolonial cultures, frequently caught between the 'authenticity' of their 'roots' and the 'colonialism' of contemporary life. Complexes and incomprehensions disappear in the creation of new culture, inventing identity according to the syncretism characteristic of current processes. (Mosquera, 1994)

We might interpret such initiatives as the g39 exhibition space in Cardiff, or the (brief) appearance of 'Welsh' artists alongside international 'names' at the ill-fated Centre for Visual Art, as instances of postcolonial 'mixedness'. We might look at the phenomenon of the 'intimate outsider' – the artists who choose to make Wales their home and source of inspiration – as a reflection of a new 'mixedness', rather than as merely the continuation of a very old practice. Or we may have to look deeper to find in Wales an authentic 'new culture', as Mosquera calls it.

Issues seen from the perspective of 'Otherness' or 'difference' are themselves being fetishized by the market-place. Jean Fisher argues that 'cultural marginality is no longer a problem of invisi-bility but one of excess visibility in terms of a reading of cultural difference that is too easily marketable' (Fisher, 1996). In a sense, art produced to question and challenge the Eurocentric hierarchy of the West can too easily become 'collectable'. At the same time, attempts to liberate art from market forces through process-based art forms, installations, and revivals of the Fluxus 'happenings' flourish, all of which are relatively resistant to commodification. But, of course, for those who understood culture as the authorita-tive, autonomous and privileged object of formalist modernism, these happenings were *not* 'art'. In Wales, an instance of the non-commodified 'event' was introduced by the Artists' Project, established in the early 1990s with close links to the Artists' Museum in Lodz, Poland, which was set up to support Solidarnosc. The Artists' Project heralded a movement towards large site-specific events, with artists travelling from all over the world to create work on the spot, collaborating and living together for a week or two, then dispersing. By heading an initiative to create a European network of like-minded, artist-led bodies, it proved that Wales can lead the way in Europe. The Artists' Project hosted a major event on New York's Staten Island in June 2002, and another event is planned back in Wales for 2005. Locws International has held its second site-specific event in Swansea, in a similar venture. Other instances of art making inroads into communities, outside galleries, might include the Harlech Biennale or Cywaith Cymru's residencies. These events bring together local artists and invited artists from beyond Wales's borders.

Events, unlike monuments, are of their nature ephemeral and need recording; contemporary art needs contextualizing; and both these functions are usually the preserve of the critic. Artists need writers of calibre, like Mosquera in Cuba, not only to write their history, but also to write them into history. To do that, we need publications and books that encourage writing on the visual arts specifically. In the Winter 2000/1 issue of *Agenda*, the journal of the Institute of Welsh Affairs, Shelagh Hourahane, herself an incisive writer on visual art, argues that 'there is a need for a serious vehicle for dissemination and discussion of ideas' in Wales because the complex, multifaceted art world of today relies more and more on such a dissemination of information. Existing art magazines in the UK are focused parochially on central London; though new developments in Glasgow or Newcastle are beginning to make inroads, the comedy cliché of 'province' Wales still has currency in such periodicals. This was noticeable even when as accomplished an artist as Shani Rhys James was reviewed on winning the Jerwood Prize in London in 2003. Born in Australia, James has chosen to settle in her father's homeland. Her abandonment of London for rural mid-Wales obviously does not contribute to her acceptance by the metropolitan critics, despite the fact that her choice of 'otherness' is a crucial aspect of her work, which very much reflects on her own situation: an existential outsider stares out of her canvases, defiant and accusing (see figure 9). Her face, her demeanour, her physical stature, seem to encapsulate certain traits attributed to the Welsh by the metropolitan English, a stubborn, unyielding 'otherness' that is hard for them to accept.

In the same article Hourahane quotes the historian and writer Peter Stead as having recently 'proposed that the road to a healthy future for Wales might lie primarily with cultural activity, rather than through political solutions', and adds that, in justifying this statement, Stead 'also expressed the opinion that it is the visual arts, which are presently the most dynamic of the art forms in Wales' (Hourahane, 2001: 57). If this is indeed the case, then it must be said that from the point of view of the practitioner, Wales is not currently providing much in terms of a quid pro quo for the dynamic leadership it expects from its visual artists. Very few artists in Wales today can hope to make a living from the sale of art work alone: the market for Welsh art, though growing, is still small and, on the whole, conservative.

4

The art historian Peter Lord has made an invaluable contribution to the process of Welsh decolonization, laying claim to representation by writing from within the culture rather than pronouncing from the outside, and placing art firmly into a social context. His history nevertheless terminates in 1960 on the basis that

> The rapid expansion of government funding of higher education changed the nature of art colleges by drawing in large numbers of young teachers, mostly from outside Wales, at a time when ideas about art as an international language were already marginalizing those for whom cultural individuation was the central concern. (Lord, 2000: 9)

This argument suggests that it is no longer possible for the college-trained artists to 'visualize the nation' of Wales in the way that they might have done before 1960. Yet it is hard to imagine a time when Welsh artists have been free from the influence of art produced outside Wales, but for all that they still, if they chose to, made art that was relevant to their own specific experience, and they continue to do so today. The remarkable survival of Wales's sense of identity, in the face of extreme external pressure to erase it, is due to each generation's discovery of a voice of protest. Young artists reinvent the meaning of partisanship according to an international climate, whether that climate be classicism, romanticism, modernism or, as now, postmodernism. Whilst it is true that art colleges in the 1960s and 1970s tended to be influenced by North American art, there was also a rapid politicization of students that made artists of my own generation (I went to Cardiff Art College in 1976) aware through Vietnam to Nicaragua of American imperialism, of feminism, of 'anarchy in the UK', the tyranny of capitalism and the erosion of the environment. Despite the influence of formalism, politics was creeping into art. A small number of art students in the 1970s were also aware of Welsh political issues, though it was not deemed a subject fit for serious exploration: a great many more students are finding that it can be explored today. Yet for students from Bangor, Carmarthen or Bala at Cardiff, the decline of the Welsh language and culture, and issues of nationalism, republicanism or socialism, were as important (if not more so) than lithography, Jackson Pollock or the Tate bricks. Thus I would argue that, despite the influence of a selective tradition both taught and consumed via art magazines and books, the work and teaching of Paul Davies, Ivor Davies, Peter Prendergast and Mary Lloyd Jones from the 1970s onwards and, more recently, of Lois Williams, Tim Davies, David Garner, Peter Finnemore and Carwyn Evans, are as much an influence and as authentic a visualization of Wales at this particular time as were Christopher Williams's or Hugh Hughes's at theirs, and more democratically diverse, as befits the modern era.

Landscape painting has been pre-eminently the art form most associated with 'visualizing' Wales; for the world outside, if not for the inmates, the romantic beauty of its terrain and the interest of its industrial panorama constituted its main claim to attention. Since the Welsh-born Richard Wilson 'invented' it, landscape painting, both poetic and prosaic, has been central to the visual production of Wales. Landscape, as the writer Emyr Humphreys says,

> immortalizes experience, so as the stream of life flows on, and we are carried with it, the residue that it leaves in landscape is myth. This is what human beings of the past left behind them; and what they left behind them is now part of our present. So it's a deposit, a vital deposit, a raw material in the literal sense. Just as you dig down for gold, or coal, you dig down for myth as well. It is a raw material vital for your well-being. (quoted in Thomas, 2002: 11)

However, until recently, the Welsh landscape was mainly a romanticized ideal, painted for tourists by touring artists like Turner, Sisley, Sutherland, John Piper and Paul Nash, and

honoured though we may feel by their attentions, their work
participated in a colonization of Welsh landscape through art.
They came, they painted, and they tamed Wales, at a time when
much of it was owned by the English or Anglicized landed gentry.
In an interview with Emyr Humphreys, the critic M. Wynn
Thomas says of the English Romantic poets in Wales that they
'perfectly exemplify the colonial mentality. They come to a place
and fail to see the culture because they see the landscape only as
a natural resource of which they're free to make whatever they
like.' The same was certainly true of the Romantic landscape
artist; further, twentieth-century landscape painting in Wales can
be said to be not only a continuation of such 'tourism', but also a
result of the realization in the 1930s that the British Empire was
in sharp decline. Artists increasingly began to look inwards, to the
'home islands', in direct proportion to the decreasing opportunity
to exercise the outward gaze of imperialism. But Wynn Thomas
suggests that Humphreys, in his poetry collection *Landscapes*,
sought to reclaim the land for its people; the volume was
'intended for, or addressed to, a colonized people who have been
deprived of the ability to see how the record of their pre-colonial
history lies all around them in the now mute language of the landscape' (Thomas, 2002: 8). In what can be seen as a parallel
activity, a homology, visual artists have also been slowly
reclaiming that landscape and with it proclaiming a liberated
identity.

In the 1970s, the Beca group of artists, which included brothers
Peter and Paul Davies and Ivor Davies, set out to make political
Welsh art. Radical in format, they drew on the influence of Fluxus
and the Paris underground of the 1960s; political on specific
Welsh issues, they operated very like much contemporary Latin
American art. Their works can be interpreted as traditional 'landscape' only in the loosest sense, but they are also real and truthful
in their descriptions of the wider landscape of Wales, in its meta-
physical as well as physical terrain. Similarly, Mary Lloyd Jones's
work, which more closely resembles the tradition of watercolour
and oil 'studies' of the landscape, nevertheless also shows a
radical departure in terms of the context in which she develops
her representation. She has dug down to expose the palimpsest
history located in the 'deep time' of her home environment by
severely abstracting nature, creating map-like patterns and forms
that operate similarly to the 'songline' paintings of Australian

Aboriginal art. In her work Iron Age sites and traces of poetry become visible once more, reminding us, in a tribal way, of ancestors and a sense of rootedness. A similar aim underlies the paintings of Geoffrey Olsen, though his work is as much about the layering processes of painting itself, as equivalent, rather than illustration, of the layers of history superimposed on to the land by historic time. He is an artist who has taken this palimpsest background that being Welsh accredits us with, and, moving out into the world teaching and exhibiting, takes it with him.

Protest as a vehicle for decolonization is visible, not without some symbolic violence, in the work that Beca produced; Ivor Davies was once, after all, a maker of exploding artworks. Similarly, a displaced violence of action and process is evident in David Garner's work and in Tim Davies's repeated use of burning. Responses to Tryweryn and the drowning of the village of Capel Celyn, that catalyst that woke us from our colonized slumber, have been numerous and varied (see Bala, 2002). Tim Davies is an artist of the social landscape and politics of Wales, who deals with the post-industrial and post-devolution, and with cultural change in a particular as well as a universal sense. He is not confined to 'painting' or 'sculpture' and in that sense is a 'conceptual artist', whose aesthetics have been influenced by minimalism and formalism, but who again reveals a dense layering of 'meaning' that is rare in mainstream European art. His process-based installation methods replicate the rediscovery of hidden meanings and hidden history implicit in the process of decolonization also; thus, in a sense, he goes beyond the mere illustration of this concept, as his work becomes embodied with the same energy. Recent work, for example, involves the excising of the traditionally dressed Welsh lady from old postcards, presenting the cards with a neatly delineated outline silhouette, an empty space in the surrounding landscape of hills and castles and cottages (see figure 10). By choosing to make issue-based work, when this is seen from some quarters as unfashionable, and then succeeding in proving its resonance and relevance, and winning critical appreciation beyond Wales, Tim Davies exemplifies a true confidence in the ability of art to operate with a social function, and to combat the colonized mentality.

5

Other nations in the fraternity of the postcolonial have come to regard Wales as a fellow-traveller and not as a wet western province of England. Hence Welsh exhibitions are organized abroad under the premise that we are an autonomous entity – not always, of course, a premise shared back home. An exhibition of Welsh art funded by the British Council and creatively curated by Alex Farquharson was seen in Zagreb in 2002, and an exhibition of 'new generation' artists from Wales was held in Milan in 2000. It would appear that there is an attempt on some levels in the British establishment to appear benevolently multicultural and show Britain in all its multifarious constituent parts, rather than be merely London-centric; on the other hand this development may rather mark a reactionary attempt at a Union of Diversity, a late redefinition of 'Britishness' as a more inclusive identity. A more recent development in Wales is the establishment of the Artes Mundi prize, at £40,000 amongst the world's largest, brought about through the endeavours of artist and enabler, William Wilkins. Through the generosity of the Derek Williams Trust, another £30,000 has been made available for purchases to the National Museum. Added to the Venice Biennale venture, this award gives Wales a platform to proclaim a new dedication to visual arts, certainly a new concept for many. The shortlist of ten artists for the first award holds a particular relevance to the view of Wales that I have outlined above. Of the ten, only the Welshman Tim Davies is European by birth; several are from Asia, one from South Africa. All are committed to making work that furthers our understanding of the human condition in this complex age of global cross-fertilization. The award went to Chinese artist Xu Bing.

By bringing shortlisted artists previously unseen in Britain to work and exhibit in Wales from areas hitherto peripheral to the traditional centres, the aim of the prize is two-handed. It shows the world that we in Wales love and respect contemporary art whilst also showing 'us in Wales' why we should love and respect contemporary art. The art celebrated, as selector Declan McGonagle has said, is 'in the world, but rooted to a particular place', and importantly is about real issues. McGonagle's ambitious vision of a 'new modernism' underpins the initiative and implies a shift in perspective, so that there is a more equitable and 'negotiated space' replacing the notion of centre and periphery.

The National Museum and Gallery of Wales, which will host these artists, placed as it is in the complex of institutions in Cathays Park that include the Law Courts, City Hall, Welsh Office and Temple of Peace, is ostensibly a statement of Cardiff's status in the world, displaying the visionary optimism of its Edwardian industrialist city fathers. Alternatively it could itself be seen as an instance of colonial symbolism. There are those who argue that it still is a colonial institution that has made little attempt in the past to be truly national in the Welsh sense, but currently it seems to be making attempts to convince us otherwise, and to metamorphose into an institution worthy of a postcolonial Wales. Yet though the current debate concerning the extending of the NMGW, literally and metaphorically, into a National Gallery to house a permanent collection is worthy, it is decades late. We must also deal with the lack of any large, prestigious art space in the capital city for the display of major touring exhibitions; for it will only be when Wales hosts visiting artists, and Wales's artists gain entry into a wider world, that we can assert a 'visible' presence.

It goes without saying that we need a building that might be called the National Gallery of Modern and Contemporary Welsh Art to cement our relationship with the international community, echoing the optimism and vision of those Cardiff city fathers a century ago. If not like Dublin, Edinburgh or Bilbao, Cardiff in this respect should at the very least be like Salford, Gateshead and Walsall. There has to be a note of caution here, however; culturally and economically we are being colonized by the United States and by multinational corporations and multinational art. No one would deny the importance of showing international art in Wales: it is essential in order to draw audiences (which the Artes Mundi experience proves can be done) and garner the much-needed press and critical interest. However, the 'international art' should be of relevance to Wales's particular position, and not just a roll-call of those reified artists that we see in every major gallery in every major city in the world. It seems that the Artes Mundi prize may help achieve this aim. Of course many artists of international stature have passed through Wales before now. Turner prize nominees Mona Hatoum and Cornelia Parker both benefited from a fellowship at Cardiff's College of Art that allowed them time and funding to develop their now high-profile careers, but both seem reluctant to acknowledge the time spent in Wales, which has yet to attain the 'kudos' required to be impressive on an artist's CV. Others, however, have found Wales conducive to their practice. Andre Stitt was drawn to Wales by its reputation for physical performance theatre, exemplified by companies like Brith Gof and Moving Being, only to be surprised to find how unaware we are of our own distinctive tradition.

6

The title of this chapter comes from a series of drawings and paintings of my own, depicting an island on a distant horizon, its outline based on the map of Wales; sometimes resembling an animal skull, or a ruined castle, its shape shifts to become a heart or a claw grasping for roots (see figure 11). The iconic island is a barren piece of land that needs revitalizing, a large percentage of its mass is submerged, either hidden or drowned. It's an image of duality, a place on to which we can project our hopes and our disappointments. But it is also separated from the viewer by a stretch of water, and suggests an unattainable and 'fantasy island' like 'Gwales' in the Welsh myth cycle the *Mabinogi*, a free Wales, free of care, but also a diverting reverie, a mirage. It marks a stage in the complex and confusing process of decolonization.

In papers given at an early 1990s 'Global Visions' conference, hosted by the Institute of International Visual Arts, Gilane Tawadros, whilst dismantling the construct of cultural homogeneity, concedes that

> the forces of nationalism and internationalism have been powerful catalysts of change and regeneration in our past century, but only when they grow out of present realities and not abstract concepts floating somewhere high up in the stratosphere, far removed from lived experience. (Tawadros, 1994)

The work of artists here today proves that Wales's present realities can be harnessed and used as pointers for change and regeneration, as long as they are truthfully represented. But we have to conclude that truly postcolonial art from Wales has little to do with or about Wales, in terms of its traditional customary representations. Raymond Williams, I am sure, would have much to say at this juncture in Welsh history. In a defining statement that echoes Tawadros, Williams said: 'Anything as deep as a dominant structure of feeling is only changed by active new experience' (in Eagleton, 1989: 108). The dominant structures of feeling in Wales are shifting: on the surface a new experience of feeling and imagination, a new optimism and pride, at least on a cultural level, is blossoming. Nowhere is this more evident than in the field of visual art. The big initiatives are without doubt significant, but also, on the ground, the swelling number of artists and audience and buyers, of public art projects and residencies, is proof that, if not postcolonial, we are in Wales certainly post-provincial. Yet this optimism is a fragile growth that at the moment appears to be grafted on to the surface of Welsh life. It must find deeper roots and become a more substantial reality, so that a new structure of feeling may replace that state of mind that has burdened us for so long, that of the colonized 'ambivalence', or, in more inflammatory parlance, 'culture cringe'. When that process of change has taken place, then we will truly be able to say that we are postcolonial, should that term still be in existence.

REFERENCES

Bala, I. (ed.) (1999). *Certain Welsh Artists*, Bridgend: Seren.

Bala, I. (2002). 'Capel Celyn: a collective trauma visualized', *Planet*, 152, 35–43.

Clewes, R. (1980). *To Dream of Freedom: The Story of MAC and the Free Wales Army*, Talybont: Y Lolfa, second edn, 2001.

Eagleton, T. (ed.) (1989). 'Raymond Williams: a photographic sketch' (compiled by Robin Gable; insert between pages 107 and 108), in *Raymond Williams: Critical Perspectives*, Cambridge: Polity Press.

Fanon, F. (1961). *The Wretched of the Earth* [1961], trans. Constance Farrington, New York: Grove Press, 1963.

Fisher, J. (1996). 'The syncretic turn: cross-cultural practices in the age of multiculturalism', in M. Kalinovska, L. Gangitano and S. Nelson (eds), *New Histories*, Boston: Institute of Contemporary Arts.

Hourahane, S. (2001). 'Impact of the printed word', *Agenda* (Spring), 57–8.

Lewis, S. (1983). 'The Caernarfon court speech', in A. R. Jones and G. Thomas (eds), *Presenting Saunders Lewis*, Cardiff: University of Wales Press, pp. 115–26.

Lord, P. (2000). *Imaging the Nation*, Cardiff: University of Wales Press.

Morgan, R. C. (1998). *The End of the Art World*, New York: Allworth Press.

Mosquera, G. (1994). 'Ernesto Pujol: my homeland', *Third Text* (Autumn/Winter), 28/9, 135–8.

Tawadros, G. (1994). 'The case of the missing body: a cultural mystery in several parts', in *Global Visions: Towards a New Internationalism in Visual Arts*, London: Kala Press.

Thomas, M. W. (ed.) (2002). *Emyr Humphreys: Conversations and Reflections*, Cardiff: University of Wales Press.

Trinh, T. M. (1987). 'Discussions in contemporary culture', in Hal Foster (ed.), *Discussions in Contemporary Culture*, Seattle: Bay Press.

Williams, R. (1980). 'Base and superstructure in Marxist cultural theory', in *Problems in Materialism and Culture: Selected Essays*, London: Verso.

Index

self, concepts of 15, 67
Sellers, Peter 217
Sgrîn 183, 190
Sgript Cymru 181, 182–3
60ft Dolls 225
Slemon, Stephen 12
Smith, Anthony D. 43
Smith, Dai 7, 45
Solomon and Gaenor 185
Spivak, Gayatri 11
Spottiswode, Tracy 189
Spring, Howard 64–5
Squires, Judith 118
Stead, Peter 242
Stereophonics 218, 219, 220,
    223–5, 226, 230
Subaltern Studies 15
subalternity xvi, 15–16, 237
Sugarman, Sara 185
Super Furry Animals 218, 220, 225,
    227–9, 230

Tawadros, Gilane 248
Teare, Jeff 180–1
Thatcher, Margaret 33
Theatr Clwyd 178
Thomas, Alfred 160
Thomas, Dylan 145, 159, 167, 168
Thomas, Ed 177, 178, 180, 186,
    191
Thomas, George 7
Thomas, Gwyn 159, 166–7, 168
Thomas, H. Elwyn 160
Thomas, M. Wynn 244
Thomas, Ned 88
Thomas, R. S. 151, 152, 155, 160
Thomas, William 152–3
Thompson, Andrew *see* Allan,
    Stuart and Andrew Thompson;
    Fevre, Ralph and Andrew
    Thompson
Tomos, Angharad 137
Tonkin, Elizabeth 42
Treason of the Blue Books (1847)
    5–6, 153
Tregenna, Catherine 181–2
Tresize, Rachel 173
Trinh, Thi Minh-Ha 67, 236–7
Tugwell, George 160

Tunstall, Jeremy 197
Turvey, Roger 39
Tyler, Bonnie 226
Tynged yr Iaith ('The Fate of the
    Language') 100, 104
Tystion, Y 220–1

Valentine, Lewis 236
Vaughan, Henry 160
Vaughan, Hilda 162–3
Vaughan, Richard 168
Venice Biennale 237–8, 246
Volpert, Lily 62

Walcott, Derek 153
Wales Congress in Support of
    Mining Communities 116
Washbrook, D. A. 11
Webb, Harri 155
Welsh Army of the Workers'
    Republic 7
Welsh Assembly Government 93–6,
    97
    Iaith Pawb 108–9
Welsh economy 7–9, 30–2
Welsh identity xvi, 13, 14–15, 16
Welsh language, status of 5, 9, 29,
    105–6, 107, 141
Welsh Language Act (1967) 141
Welsh Language Board 107
Welsh Language Society
    (Cymdeithas yr Iaith Gymraeg)
    100, 102, 105
Welsh Office 6, 85, 115
Welsh people, English attitudes
    towards 5
Welsh Sunday Closing Act (1881) 6
Welsh Women's Aid 116, 125
Wesley, John Doe 56–7, 58–9, 60
Whistler, Peggy 163–4
Wilkins, William 246
Williams, Cate *see* Williams, Mallt
    and Cate Williams
Williams, Charlotte 55, 57–8, 65,
    68, 73–5, 77–8, 174
Williams, Chris (historian) 46,
    115–16
Williams, Christopher (artist) 243
Williams, D. J. 169, 236